Eugene C. Barker: *Historian*

EUGENE C. BARKER. "He had about him an unconscious austerity, the sort found in generals and Indian chiefs." The painting by Robert Joy now hanging in the Barker Texas History Center.

EUGENE C. BARKER

Historian

By William C. Pool

TEXAS STATE HISTORICAL ASSOCIATION

AUSTIN

Standard Book Number 87611-025-1
Library of Congress Catalog Card No. 76-627820
Copyright © 1971 William C. Pool
Printed in the United States

To The Barker Grandchildren

PREFACE

My acquaintance with Eugene C. Barker began on a September registration afternoon in 1939. Having decided to be a historian rather late in my undergraduate career, I needed an advanced course (Dr. Barker's History 325) that could be taken concurrently with the last semester of old History 15. Someone at the history table pointed toward a formidable-looking individual and remarked, "You'll have to get his permission." I introduced myself to Professor Barker and explained my need. I shall never forget the twinkle in his eye as he initialed my schedule card and said, "I'll see you in class on Monday." From this date until his death in the autumn of 1956, Eugene C. Barker was my friend and academic advisor on both the undergraduate and graduate levels; his guidance and encouragement were significant factors during my student days.

Since Eugene C. Barker and a score or more other individuals built on foundations inherited from such men as George P. Garrison and Lester G. Bugbee, they must necessarily be placed in the middle generation that contributed to the growth of a University "of the first class." Playing an important role in this growth, Barker was a fine scholar, an excellent classroom teacher, an humble citizen of the University community, and a faculty power who stood for honesty and integrity above all else; he was, by all measures, a great man.

Many people have helped in the compilation of this narrative. In the early stages Miss Winnie Allen, then archivist at the Barker History Center, went far beyond the call of duty in offering aid and assistance. Later, Chester Kielman, her successor, was equally helpful and encouraging. In addition to the two archivists, I remember with gratitude the aid of Mrs. A. C. Arledge of Crockett, Texas; David Barker and his children of Austin, Texas; the late Walter P. Webb and the late Roy Bedichek, two of Barker's closest friends in Austin; and Dr. Llerena Friend, distinguished Texas historian and formerly librarian of the Barker History Center, who also loved "the Chief." And finally, two of my colleagues at Southwest Texas State College—Dr. Ione Young, professor of English, and Dr. Leland Derrick, professor of English and dean of the Graduate School—offered valuable constructive criticism as work on the manuscript progressed. I owe my greatest debt, however, to my wife, Sarah Jeannette Pool, who has been my inspiration and my helper for more than a quarter of a century.

WILLIAM C. POOL
San Marcos, Texas

CONTENTS

ILLUSTRATIONS

Eugene C. Barker: *Historian*

Youth and Education

On a warm spring afternoon in April, 1950, Eugene C. Barker was accorded the greatest honor ever bestowed upon a living faculty member of the University of Texas. The venerable professor of history looked on as the Fifty-Fourth Annual Meeting of the Texas State Historical Association was assembled in the Old Library Building on the campus of the University to dedicate the Eugene C. Barker Texas History Center. In the words of H. Bailey Carroll, the occasion represented "one of the most memorable events in the history of . . . the Association," and later in the day Dr. Herbert Gambrell reported in his dinner address that "Today a precedent is being set. A functional part of the campus is being given the name of a living member of The University of Texas."[1] Never before in the history of the University had such a thing been done and the reasons behind it were without parallel. If memorable in the history of the Texas State Historical Association, the ceremonies of April 27, 1950, certainly marked a memorable day in the life of Eugene C. Barker.

The program that followed during the afternoon and early evening was brief, dignified, and to the point. Eugene C. Barker heard addresses by Dudley K. Woodward, Jr., the chairman of the Board of Regents; Roy L. Ledbetter of Dallas, who presented the Frank Reaugh collection of paintings to the University; Dr. P. I. Nixon of San Antonio; Dr. T. S. Painter, the president of the University

---

[1] H. Bailey Carroll, "The Affairs of the Association," *The Southwestern Historical Quarterly,* LIV (July, 1950), 70; Herbert P. Gambrell, "The Eugene C. Barker Texas History Center," in ibid., 1.

of Texas; and Herbert Gambrell, chairman of the Department of History of Southern Methodist University. It may be assumed that as he listened to the significant events of the day, Eugene C. Barker recalled fleeting impressions of many another occasion in his long career of teaching and scholarship at the University of Texas. No doubt there were memories of his poverty-stricken student days, of early friends in and near the University, of classroom routine and the difficult labor of scholarly research, of fishing trips and afternoons on the golf course, of pleasant evenings at the Town and Gown Club, and of the academic arguments with faculty and administrative colleagues. In all of his activities the motivating factor was his love for the University and his concern for its general welfare. In fact, since September, 1894, his life had been entwined with the history of the Main University. Without design, his career had been one in which his reputation as a scholar was surpassed only by his reputation for character, integrity, and unflinching courage. Now, on the eve of his retirement, and sitting through the last public demonstration to be held in his honor, the old professor could not forget that the road had been long and the journey tedious that led from the Trinity River borderlands of the Big Thicket to the beautifully landscaped campus of the University of Texas as it existed at the mid-point of the twentieth century.

The life of Eugene Campbell Barker began in the small hamlet of Riverside in Walker County, Texas, on November 10, 1874. His parents were Joseph and Fannie Holland Barker, and Eugene was their first child. Riverside had been established in 1872 near where Harmon Creek flows into the Trinity River. The Big Thicket of Texas lay to the east of the river; the pine forests of Walker and neighboring counties could be seen far to the south and east. In between these wooded areas, the small farms of the river valley had their roots in the sandy loam soils of northeast Walker County. The Houston and Great Northern Railroad (later the International and Great Northern), which built south to north across Walker County in 1871, bypassed Huntsville and ran from Phelps to Riverside as it continued through the East Texas woodlands to

Palestine. In fact, the community of Riverside resulted from the construction of the railroad. Joseph and Fannie Holland Barker were among the pioneer settlers of the little town; and since both the Barker and Holland families had long histories in the heart of East Texas, Eugene C. Barker could write with accuracy many years later, "I qualify as an East Texan."[2]

Joseph Barker's father, William Barker, was born in Louisiana in the year 1810. He married Alitia Humble, a resident of Baton Rouge, and migrated to Liberty County, Texas, in January, 1836. According to family tradition, William Barker took part in the battle of San Jacinto, but "the tradition seems to have been erroneous."[3] Sometime during the next decade, William Barker moved his growing family to Walker County, where he settled on a farm southeast of Huntsville. It was here that Joseph Barker was born on April 24, 1850, the seventh of eleven children. The elder Barker died in 1865 and was buried in a rural cemetery about five miles southeast of Huntsville; his widow continued to operate the Barker farm. The United States Census for the year 1870 for Walker County lists the Alitia Barker family post office as Huntsville, places the farm in precinct 3 of Walker County, and lists the children as Joe Barker, 20, farmhand; Cicero Barker, 18, farmhand; Charles Barker, 16, farmhand; Amanda Barker, 14, at home; and Altha Barker, 12, at home. Alitia Humble Barker made an impression on her grandson. Eugene C. Barker could recall: "I remember my grandmother as a great traveler, by train, going from her farm in Walker County near Huntsville, to West Texas, near Mullen, where her son Henry lived. My mother then lived at Palestine and my grandmother usually visited us on these trips."[4]

Eugene Barker's maternal great-grandfather, Spearman Holland, moved to Harrison County, Texas, from Holly Springs, Mississippi, in 1842, evidently "under some financial embarrassment." His father-in-law wrote him on the eve of his departure from

[2] Eugene C. Barker Papers, Speeches, 1941–1950, Archives, University of Texas Library, Austin, Texas (The Eugene C. Barker Papers are hereafter cited as Barker Papers).

[3] Barker Papers, Family Notes.

[4] Ibid.

Holly Springs, "your removal involves no principle of moral turpitude. It is merely a measure of sensible self-protection, and is best for your creditors, provided your debts are paid in the future with interest." The elder man then answered very candidly a request for advice: "Your hobbies—speculation, cotton, and ambition—have all stumbled, and altho' they have not absolutely thrown you, yet they have caused you to hold a tight rein. You requested my advice. I have only to say plant more corn, raise hogs, and have plenty of good milk cows." Holland was also warned that "In Texas you may make more cotton, but will be subject to the same drawbacks if you pursue the same policy. If you wish to be happy, settle permanently on a good body of rich land . . . attend to your business, and never repine at your neighbor's riding a better horse, having more negroes, or a prettier wife than you have." On their arrival in Harrison County, the Holland family settled at Elysian Fields. Devereux Dunlap Holland, Spearman Holland's son, lived for many years in Panola County and it was there that Fannie Holland, who had been born in Holly Springs, Mississippi, on January 12, 1853, spent her childhood.[5] Joseph Barker and Fannie Holland were married in Walker County in 1872; a few months later the young married couple moved to Riverside where Joseph Barker built a general mercantile store. He was to remain a merchant for the rest of his life.

Information concerning Eugene Barker's early years is fragmentary. Speaking of his childhood, Barker could remember many years later that, "In the early eighties, when my memories of East Texas faintly begin, most country homes were log houses of two, three, or four rooms, or two room shacks built of lumber." He remembered Riverside as a town composed of a "railroad station, a water tank, one store, a saloon—called a grocery—and two or three little houses." The first school that he attended was "taught in a one room shack by a young man who had received some training at the 'Huntsville Normal.' " Young Barker walked the railroad ties 2½ miles to the school house in the country. At the time when these recollections of East Texas begin, other im-

[5] Barker Papers, Speeches, 1941–1950.

pressions that had a lasting effect on the young mind of Barker included daily scenes and activities about the home; for example, he remembered,

Furniture was generally home-made or manufactured at the Huntsville penitentiary. Kerosene lamps and pine knots gave the prevailing illumination, but home-moulded candles were not uncommon. Water was carried in wooden buckets from a neighborhood spring or drawn from a well by windlass or pulley. I doubt if there was a bathroom in all rural East Texas. Sulphur matches were used sparingly to kindle fires, but paper spills were less expensive for lighting lamps and candles, and live coals were sometimes carried from house to house to relight a fire carelessly allowed to go out. Railroads connected a few villages, but most people traveled by horseback or wagon. One of my most vivid recollections is of neighborhood families loading all their possessions into covered wagons now and then and moving to West Texas—the West being then for most of us somewhere in the vicinity of Lampasas, Brownwood, and Coleman.[6]

The recollection of his early days, no doubt, represented activities in which Eugene Barker participated around his modest home and his father's store. It can be assumed that the store provided the essentials of life for the Joseph Barker family but that there was no room for luxuries in the meager budget. As the years passed, the family grew. Ivy D. Barker was born on July 12, 1877; Paul Barker, on July 29, 1880; and Nettie Barker, on June 19, 1884. The three boys and a girl comprised a compact and happy family group; but as the 1880's wore on the time for real happiness was running short; sorrow and heartache entered the family circle all too soon. On June 19, 1888, Joseph Barker died at the age of thirty-eight. Eugene was not at home at the time; he was living with an aunt at Dodge, a small community south of Riverside, where "the school was a little better." Nettie Barker remembered that "father died on my 4th birthday."[7] He was buried at Riverside. As soon as Fannie Barker could sell the

[6] Eugene C. Barker, *Speeches, Responses, and Essays, Critical and Historical*, 10 (hereafter cited as Barker, *Essays*).

[7] Mrs. Edgar C. [Nettie Barker] Arledge to William C. Pool, February 23, 1959.

store, she moved to Palestine and bought a home, knowing that the schools would be better and the boys could find work in the new location. It is impossible to know the thoughts that must have passed through the mind of fourteen-year-old Eugene Barker during the weeks immediately following the death of his father. His brief childhood had ended as the responsibilities of an adult descended upon the youth. He had to help the family; his dreams of an education were now secondary.

After the family settled in Palestine, Eugene Barker quit school and went to work. He found a job as a waterboy and helper to the blacksmiths in the International and Great Northern Railroad shops. Within three or four years he became an expert blacksmith, "able to make nearly anything that can be made on a hand forge and anvil."[8] As his skill increased he became a member of the National Railway Master Blacksmith's Association. Despite his success in the railroad shops, he could never forget his ambition to enter the University of Texas. But a high school education was impossible because of his hours of employment. According to the report of Bates H. McFarland, "It was about this time that the remarkable Miss Shirley Green started her evening school; and Eugene became a pupil. He would work in the shops all day, come home and wash up, and put in two or three hours at school, under her inspiration, shaping his course toward the University."[9]

Without a high school education, young Barker could enter the University only through examination. According to the *Catalogue* of the Department of Literature, Science, and Arts, "Candidates for admission to the University on examination will be required to stand entrance examinations in English, History, and Mathematics as laid down in the Catalogue." In addition to the subjects listed above, "candidates for admission to the A.B. course" were required to "stand entrance examinations in Latin and Greek . . . or [they] will take Greek A in case they fail to take the entrance examination in Greek." The details about the entrance

---

[8] Bates H. McFarland to Roy Bedichek, April 21, 1926, in the Barker Papers, Letters, 1899–1956 (unless otherwise noted all correspondence can be found in the Barker Papers, Letters, 1899–1956).

[9] Ibid.

examination in English included information to the effect that "Candidates will be examined upon Grammar and upon Rhetoric and Composition. An opinion of the Character and amount of knowledge expected in the latter subject may be formed from the high-school Rhetoric of Scott and Denny, of A. S. Hill, or of Carpenter. Several themes for composition will be assigned from the books named below, and the candidate is expected to be familiar with all the books named for the year in which he enters." The reading list for 1894–1895 included Macaulay's "Life of Samuel Johnson," Hawthorne's *Twice Told Tales*, Scott's *Marmion*, Shakespeare's *As You Like It*, Goldsmith's *Vicar of Wakefield*, Carlyle's "Essay on Burns," and Hawthorne's *House of Seven Gables*. And finally, the *Catalogue* warned that "no student who fails the examination in English will be admitted."[10]

Eugene C. Barker went to Austin in September, 1894, to take the entrance examinations; he failed in English. Decades later Bates McFarland remembered that Morgan Calloway, Jr., of "the long-tailed comma" fame, "busted him in English."[11] Denied admission as the result of his deficiency in grammar, Barker returned to Palestine, picked up his hammer, and went back to work in the I.&G.N. blacksmith shop. The long winter nights were spent in study under the supervision and inspiration of Shirley Green. Barker knew that in the autumn of 1895 the subjects for the English composition, "correct in spelling, punctuation, capitalization, grammar, sentence-construction, and paragraphing," would be taken from Shakespeare's *Merchant of Venice*, Dickens' *David Copperfield*, and Lowell's *Vision of Sir Launfal*. In preparation for the admission examination in history, he again read P. N. Meyer's *Outlines of General History*. Decades later he remembered, "I should give credit, too, to P. V. N. Meyer's *General History*, which I read for an entrance examination. It was the most fascinating book that I ever read."[12] When the determined youth caught the train for Austin in September, 1895, he was better prepared for the examinations than he had been the previous

10 *Catalogue of the University of Texas*, 1894–1895, p. 16.
11 McFarland to Bedichek, April 21, 1926.
12 Barker to William R. Hogan, September 24, 1945.

year. On this occasion he passed all phases of the test and was admitted to the University as a member of the first year class— the class of 1899. Concerning this significant milestone in Barker's life, Bates McFarland remembered that "He came back in the fall of 1895, and we took the examinations together, and fortunately made the grade."[13]

When Eugene C. Barker enrolled in the University of Texas on September 23, 1895, the small school was only twelve years old. It is significant, however, that the idea of a university for Texas can be traced to Mirabeau B. Lamar, who, on December 20, 1838, reminded the Congress of the Republic of Texas that the "cultivated mind is the guardian genius of democracy. . . . It is the only dictator that freemen acknowledge and the only security that freemen desire." Early in 1839 the Congress of the Republic, in an act locating the permanent capital of Texas, ordered that a site be set apart for a university in the "city of Austin," a town to be located "at some point between the rivers Trinidad and Colorado and above the old San Antonio Road." A few days later, fifty leagues of land were set aside by Congress for the establishment and endowment of two colleges or universities. Such was the origin of a noble dream.[14] Forty-three years later, on November 17, 1882, the cornerstone of the west wing of the Main Building was laid; and in September, 1883, the University was formally opened.

Eugene Barker found that by the fall of the year 1895 the enrollment of the Main University had expanded to 482 students; the teaching staff to 25 professors, instructors, and tutors; and the physical plant to three buildings. The University *Catalogue* included information to the effect that "the buildings in Austin are located on a tract of forty acres bounded by Twenty-first, San

[13] McFarland to Bedichek, April 21, 1926.

[14] H. Y. Benedict (compiler), *A Source Book Relating to the History of the University of Texas: Legislative, Legal, Bibliographical, and Statistical,* University of Texas Bulletin No. 1757 (Austin, 1917), 3, 15–16, 223, 260 ff. (hereafter cited as Benedict, *History of the University*); W. J. Battle, "A Concise History of the University of Texas, 1883–1950," *Southwestern Historical Quarterly,* LIV (April, 1951), 392.

Marcos, Twenty-fourth, and Lampasas streets, about three quarters of a mile north of the State Capitol." The buildings of the University were described as follows:

The Main Building occupies a position at the center of the campus, facing south. It is of light colored brick, with white stone trimming. The west wing, erected in 1883, is three stories in height, with a high basement. Its dimensions, outside measurements, are 78 x 108 feet. The central portion of the building, together with the north wing, was erected in 1889. Exclusive of the assembly hall, it is four stories in height, surmounted by a tower 24 x 24 feet, rising to a height of 160 feet. The assembly hall, in the second story of the north wing of the main building, is of the Gothic style architecture . . . and is finished in pine, with a gallery and a stage. It is furnished with opera chairs, and has a seating capacity of about 1,700 persons. This building is heated by steam.

University Hall, the gift of Mr. George W. Brackenridge of San Antonio, one of the Regents of the University, was completed on December 1, 1890. Its situation is directly east of the main building.

The Chemical Building was erected in 1891. . . . It is a substantial edifice of brick, with white stone and red brick trimmings . . . two stories in height.

The University library now contains 15,676 volumes. . . . The Palm Library, supposed to contain about 25,000 volumes and pamphlets, recently donated to the University by Sir Swante Palm . . . is arranged on the east side of the large room . . . in the Main Building.[15]

The three buildings listed above and the Power Plant comprised the physical plant of the University.

By far most important man on the campus in 1895 was Leslie Waggener, the president *ad interim*. In addition to being professor of literature and history, Dr. Waggener had served as chairman of the faculty from 1884 until 1894 and was acting as president while the Board of Regents searched for a man to fill the job permanently. Waggener was ably assisted by James B. Clark as "Proctor, Librarian, and Secretary to the Faculties of the Main University."[16] The faculty of the Department of Litera-

---

[15] *Catalogue of the University of Texas*, 1896–1897, 94 ff.
[16] *The Cactus*, 1896, pp. 25–26.

ture, Science, and Arts—the Academic Department—included such distinguished teachers and scholars as Thomas U. Taylor in applied mathematics, George Bruce Halstead in pure mathematics, George Pierce Garrison in history, David Franklin Houston in political science, Henry Winston Harper in chemistry, Sidney E. Mezes in philosophy, and Morgan Callaway, Jr., in English. The Law Department was staffed by Robert S. Gould, Robert L. Batts, and Victor Lee Brooks.[17]

Barker enrolled in the Department of Literature, Science, and Arts and elected a program of studies leading to the Bachelor of Arts degree. At this time, the Academic Department offered the degrees of Bachelor of Literature, Bachelor of Sciences, and Bachelor of Arts. Each degree plan required twenty full courses, or units, for graduation. The degree plan leading to the Bachelor of Arts specified these twenty units as a requisite for graduation and stated briefly that three full courses (a course lasting the entire academic year) must be completed in one subject, that none of the courses named in the curricula of the freshman year could be elected in the senior year except biology and chemistry, and that each degree candidate must complete one full course in political science.[18] During his first year at the University, Barker's class schedule included Greek A, French, German, English, and physics. In Greek he met, for the first time, William James Battle. Forty-five years later, Barker remarked,

> To speak of Dr. Battle's meaning to the University of Texas, I must begin with autobiography. My acquaintance with him goes back to the fall of 1895, when, with some dozen other freshmen, I became a member of his class in Greek A. He was one of the two vivid and revered personalities that I met that year. Later I was to meet three or four others. I took three courses in Greek with Dr. Battle, and it is not his fault that my memory of the subject long ago vanished in the process of what Dr. Benedict jestingly called "learning more and more about less and less." He was a stimulating and inspiring teacher—and I doubt not that he is so still. . . .
>
> At the time of which I speak Dr. Battle was twenty-five years old. He

[17] Ibid.
[18] *Catalogue of the University of Texas*, 1895–1896, 46 ff.

had come to the University of Texas two years before with the rank of associate professor. His scholarship was already attested by degrees of A.B. (with honors), A.M., and Ph.D. from the University of North Carolina, and by the Ph.D. from Harvard. His face was a little more round, his forehead was only a little less high, his blushes came a little more easily, and the leash on his patience was a little less secure.[19]

As the young freshman remembered, Battle was one of the two "vivid and revered personalities" whom he met during the first year. The other was Lafayette R. Hamberlin, the professor of English who taught Barker's freshman class in rhetoric and composition. Hamberlin was a native of Mississippi who graduated from Richmond College in 1884. After several years teaching in the public schools of Tennessee and Louisiana, Hamberlin returned to Richmond College as instructor of elocution. He later moved to the University of North Carolina and came to the University of Texas in 1892 as a member of the English faculty. Hamberlin, an excellent classroom teacher, made a significant impression on Eugene Barker, who wavered between English and history as an academic major during most of his undergraduate years. When school closed in the spring of 1896, Barker's grades ranged from satisfactory to excellent in all subjects.

In his sophomore year Barker enrolled for the second-year courses in English, French, German, Latin, and Greek, and rounded out his six-course load with History 1—the history of the "ancient East, Greece, and Rome to 476 A.D." At this time ancient history was taught by Lester Gladstone Bugbee, a young tutor in the School of History who had recently returned from a two-year leave of absence to continue his doctoral studies at Columbia University. In 1896 Bugbee and George P. Garrison comprised the faculty of the School of History. Although the young student from Palestine did not realize it at the time, the remarkable Bugbee was to become the greatest single influence in Barker's decision to become an historian. With an admiration that knew no limitations, Barker later wrote,

[19] Barker, *Essays*, 34. Barker's course of study for the five years he attended the University was furnished by the registrar of the University of Texas.

When I entered the University of Texas in September, 1895, Lester Gladstone Bugbee had just returned, after two years of graduate work at Columbia College, New York, to be a tutor in history. I became a member of his class the next year and was associated with him thereafter until his untimely death in 1902. He was the most effective and inspiring teacher that I met anywhere during my student career; and possessed qualities of mind and industry that—given a normal lifetime for their exercise—would have made him a great American historian.[20]

Lester G. Bugbee, coming from Hill and Johnson counties, Texas, entered the University on January 31, 1887, after preparatory work at old Mansfield College. While a student of the University, he did his major work under Leslie Waggener, the chairman of the faculty and professor of the English language, literature, and history; H. Tallichet, professor of modern languages; and George P. Garrison, instructor in history. Bugbee was an excellent student and was awarded the Master of Arts degree in June, 1893. At Columbia University, where he received a $500 fellowship the following autumn, Bugbee studied with nearly all of the well-known scholars of the Department of Political Science and History—particularly with Herbert E. Osgood, John Bassett Moore, E. R. A. Seligman, and John W. Burgess. In 1895 George P. Garrison was able to bring Bugbee back to the University of Texas as tutor in history at a salary of $600 per year. Concerning Bugbee's classroom technique and mannerisms, Barker wrote,

> I can describe some of the characteristics of Bugbee's teaching, but can convey only a faint idea of the impression that he made on freshman and sophomore classes. In the first place, he was always completely prepared. Before going to a class, he reduced his subject to a very brief outline on a slip of paper about the size of a postal card and used no other notes. He never sat at a desk, never lectured formally, but moved around the room asking questions and discussing the answers. This is a type of instruction that generally consumes much time and leads to muddling, but somehow he avoided confusion and always reached the end of the day's assignment. He frequently sent students

---

[20] Eugene C. Barker, "Lester Gladstone Bugbee, Teacher and Historian," *Southwestern Historical Quarterly*, XLIX (July, 1945), 1; Barker, *Essays*, 42.

to a wall map to locate places and explain the geography of a subject. He required classes to hand in maps, outlines, and summaries, and gave frequent quizzes—some unannounced. He graded all of the papers, and his marginal comments were models of precision and neatness. Aside from the facts of the subject, I think students got from him habits of logical organization, precision of thought and expression, and a feeling for the long-run orderly progression of history. He had one mannerism that all who saw him in class will remember, the habit of playing with his watch chain, winding and unwinding it around the index finger of his right hand. I have seen students gather around his desk and talk for an hour after a recitation. He never seemed in a hurry, never seemed to have anything else to do. I have never understood how he accomplished so much; the only explanation seems to be that he must have worked long hours when other men slept. Even mediocre students respected his quiet dignity and ability, and serious students trusted and admired him. In common with most great teachers, he early discerned qualities of potential scholarship in promising students and encouraged them by understanding appraisal of their work. In his writing, he was a master of conciseness and compression, never over-elaborating details, always relating his investigation to the broader field of history of which it was a part. As Professor Osgood wrote, he had "unusual keenness of insight and power of generalization."[21]

During the first three years of Barker's student career, the young scholar experienced great difficulty scraping together sufficient funds to stay in school. His mother probably sent him a small sum each month, although Barker does not mention the fact. It is also possible that Paul and Ivy Barker, both of whom had gone to work for the railroad, helped their brother stay in school. In any event finances were a pressing problem for Eugene Barker. At one time during his college career, he arranged his courses so that he could take a job as mail clerk on the night run of the Houston and Texas Central Railroad from Austin to Houston. He held this difficult post for a major part of a spring term. An excellent student from the beginning, Barker also earned small sums tutoring students who were in scholastic difficulty. A common characteristic of all of his jobs, however, was the fact that the hours were long and the pay small.

[21] Barker, "Lester Gladstone Bugbee, Teacher and Historian," 15.

Shortly after the beginning of his third year in Austin, on October 16, 1897, Fannie Holland Barker died and Eugene made the sad journey to Palestine to attend the last rites for his mother. It is no wonder that, for a time after his mother's sudden death, Barker was overcome by despair and defeat. Bates McFarland says that Barker lost a part of one year "through the necessity of going to work."[22] Thus, young Eugene Barker had many problems other than those posed by his studies.

As is the case with all working students, his social life was severely limited in scope by the meager condition of his finances. Therefore, concerning Barker's social relationships in the University community, there is not much to record. The University yearbook for the year 1896 reports that it was shortly after the beginning of the fall term "that the '99's plunge into the gay society whirl. Receptions became a passion. And oh what joy it was to ride with a girl in a carriage, which is, it must be confessed, less rasping than the old Studebaker wagons, to which most of us were accustomed down on the farm."[23] But the gay social whirl had little meaning for Eugene Barker, who could afford neither the carriage nor the luxury of a good time. For about five years his roommate was Bates H. McFarland, a second cousin who had his mind set on a legal career. The two young men were inseparable companions. McFarland recalled the following experience with his friend:

When he [Barker] first came down to Austin he was at times painfully embarrassed; and I remember on one occasion he had me go with him to church to meet a young lady from Palestine, about whose charms we . . . had received certain shy confidences. After the service, we intercepted her in the lobby, and Eugene attempting to perform the introduction became as red as a Bolshevik flag and spent some moments making a tremendous effort to swallow. . . . the young lady merrily came to the front by holding out her hand and telling me her name and I did likewise and we were actually engaged in conversation before Eugene could disengage the first word from his larynx. I should have

22 McFarland to Bedichek, April 21, 1926.
23 *The Cactus*, 1896, p. 42.

thought nothing further of it had it not been for the humble, elaborate, and soul-shriving apology that he tendered me that night.[24]

Barker's most significant social activity during his undergraduate years came as the result of his membership in the Texas Beta chapter of the Phi Delta Theta fraternity; he joined Phi Delta Theta early in his freshman year. Since Barker became a severe critic of social fraternities during the late years of his life, his activities in Phi Delta Theta may seem incongruous to many persons. A partial explanation lies in the fact that social fraternities seem to have changed with the passage of time. In the 1890's fraternal organizations appear to have been long on the idea of brotherhood and short on social emphasis. Many young fraternity leaders of Barker's day were working students of meager financial means. In Phi Delta Theta Barker formed lasting friendships with W. P. Baker, S. R. Robertson, Norman Cozier, Leigh Ellis, R. B. Renfro, R. S. Baker, W. P. Donaldson, Edgar E. Witt, Tom E. Connally, Roy Bedichek, John A. Lomax, and others. At Barker's urging, Bates McFarland became a member of the Phi Delta group; David Franklin Houston and Morgan Callaway, Jr., were *fratres in facultate*. Over forty years later the venerable Senator Tom Connally remembered his student days with the following appraisal of Eugene Barker:

> When I first knew Eugene C. Barker, he was not a Ph.D. He was an undergraduate student. We lived at a boarding house on Fourteenth Street near Lavaca. He was a Phi Delta Theta and approached me with a view to my becoming a member of that fraternity. I yielded to his solicitation.
>
> He was then a rugged, hard-working, earnest student. He had come out of the I.&G.N. shops at Palestine to the University to get an education. He brought some of the iron from the shops in his backbone and in his blood. He was inflexibly honest. For most of his time he was serious and grim. However, he relished now and then a joke or an amusing story.[25]

[24] McFarland to Bedichek, April 21, 1926.

[25] Tom Connally, December 20, 1941, in the Barker Papers, "Eugene C. Barker, Portrait of a Historian." This collection consists of typescript memo-

Another interesting account of Barker's student days is the one written by Roy Bedichek:

I have never in forty-five years seen him [Barker] pose for an instant. He is positively the worst actor I ever saw. What a sorry poker-player he would make, even if he had learned to tell one card from another.

I happen to know that this acerbity was early developed by a kind of knock-down-and-drag-out repartee competition which raged at the boarding house between him and Bates McFarland in their student years. The other boarders were amazed after witnessing these savage exchanges across the dinner table to see the two walk off arm in arm apparently the best of friends.[26]

Aside from his interest in his brothers of Phi Delta Theta, Barker was active in the University YMCA during his first year in Austin and, possibly, for longer. In 1896 he was listed as the chairman of the Committee on Bible Study at the University Y. Among the active members of the YMCA for that year were John A. Lomax, W. J. Battle, R. S. Baker, Morgan Callaway, Jr., George P. Garrison, W. H. Matthews, W. T. Miller, J. M. Kuehne, David Franklin Houston, Leslie Waggener, E. W. Winkler, and T. U. Taylor. In the realm of campus politics, Eugene Barker served as president of the sophomore class, 1896–1897. His fellow officers included Belle Chapman, vice-president; T. C. Frost, Jr., secretary; and Frances Waggener, treasurer. The only comment carried by the *Cactus* concerning the activities of the sophomore class was a brief notation to the effect that "in our freshman year we gave one reception, which was a brilliant failure. As sophomores our receptions have not been so numerous."[27] This comment is written in the terse style of the class president.

In his junior year Barker's class schedule included English 3, Greek 2, History 2, Latin 2, and Mathematics 1. In second-year Greek, Barker finished his third course with William James Bat-

———
rial letters, bound and presented to Dr. Barker by the Texas State Historical Association on the occasion of the presentation of the Barker portrait by Artist Robert Joy, April 10, 1942. Subsequent references to this source will be cited as Barker Papers, "Portrait of a Historian."

26 Roy Bedichek, December 15, 1941, in ibid.
27 *The Cactus*, 1897.

tle; in History 2, the history of the middle ages, he had his second and last course with Lester G. Bugbee. At the end of the term and with the aid of Bugbee, Barker was given a job as student assistant in the School of History. The appointment paid about $33 per month and eased Eugene's financial worries considerably. In his fourth and final year of undergraduate work, Barker completed History 3, Latin 3, Mathematics 2, pedagogy, physiology and hygiene, and philosophy. In physiology and hygiene he was introduced to the teaching of Dr. Henry Winston Harper, who impressed Barker because of "his unfailing, unhurried courtesy; his comprehensive grasp of many fields of knowledge; and his unwillingness to sacrifice thoroughness of exposition to the rude exigencies of time."[28] In History 3: the history of modern Europe, he was exposed for the first time to the teaching skill of George P. Garrison, the chairman of the school and another one of the four or five people who had great influence on Barker's early scholarship.

George Pierce Garrison was a native of Georgia and a graduate of the University of Edinburgh. In 1884 he joined the University of Texas faculty as an instructor of literature and history. Garrison took his Ph.D. at the University of Chicago in 1897, and the following year he was promoted to the "full rank of Professor of American History."[29] It seemed to Eugene Barker that Dr. Garrison was a person who "considered it the first duty of a professor in a State University to teach, and he was a remarkably successful teacher."[30] From 1895 until 1910 Garrison annually taught classes of from fifty to one hundred students and served on numerous faculty committees relative to the physical, intellectual, and spiritual welfare of the student body. As a result he was one of the most popular members of the faculty.

A summary reveals that when Eugene C. Barker finished his undergraduate studies in the spring of 1899, he had completed three courses each in history, Latin, Greek, and English, two courses each in French and German; the remainder of the twenty

[28] Barker, *Essays*, 31.
[29] Ibid., 40.
[30] Ibid., 39.

units presented for graduation consisted of courses in mathematics, pedagogy, philosophy, and physiology—a liberal education in the broadest scope of the term. In the June commencement of 1899 he was awarded the Bachelor of Arts degree. By this time his course had been set. He received an appointment as tutor in history—an appointment that Barker credited to Lester G. Bugbee—and he decided to remain at the University of Texas for graduate work. During the following year Barker taught two classes of ancient history, completed five courses of graduate instruction, and wrote a thesis on "The Unification of Public Sentiment for the Texas Revolution." He received the Master of Arts degree in June, 1900, with a major in history and a minor in pedagogy.

During the weeks that followed the commencement exercises of June, 1900, E. C. Barker sat at a desk in the School of History section of the old Main Building and prepared his first articles for publication. The Texas State Historical Association had been founded in 1897 by Bugbee, Garrison, and others, and the _Quarterly_ of the Association gave young Barker an outlet for his work. Then, too, the energetic Bugbee had been instrumental in bringing the Bexar Archives to the library of the University and had also made the initial contact with Guy M. Bryan concerning the use of the Stephen F. Austin papers. As a result the unexplored field of Texas and Southwestern frontier history was open to both Bugbee and Barker. Bugbee was so jubilant at his prospects for the future that a friend could write, "He was literally on top of the world. He felt that professionally his future was assured, and that every ambition and dream of his life were certain of realization."[31] Barker shared the dreams and ambition of Bugbee. During the previous year, J. Franklin Jameson, editor of the _American Historical Review_, had written Bugbee asking for some documentary material from the Bexar Archives. In reply Bugbee sent him, from the Austin Papers, some sample pages from the diary of Moses Austin on his journey from Wythe County, Virginia, to

[31] Ethel Rather Villavaso to E. C. Barker, February 4, 1945.

Missouri in 1796–1797. Jameson accepted the diary with enthusiasm in a letter of February 4, 1899. Bugbee was to send him the remaining pages and presumably was to edit the document for the *Review*. For some reason, however, it was edited by Professor Garrison and appeared in the *Review* of April, 1900. Garrison explained to the readers that "The journal of Moses Austin given below is published through the courtesy of his grandson, Colonel Guy M. Bryan, of Austin."[32] Barker was somewhat provoked because Garrison took credit for Bugbee's contribution.

Barker's article on "The Difficulties of a Mexican Revenue Officer in Texas"—a narrative recording the hardships and activities of Captain Antonio Tenorio and Don José Gonzales as they established the customs houses at Anahuac and Galveston Island in 1835—appeared in *The Quarterly of the Texas State Historical Association* for January, 1901. The article was based primarily on materials gathered from the Bexar Archives and the Austin Papers. In April, 1901, the *Quarterly* carried the results of his research on "The San Jacinto Campaign," and in January, 1903, a brief survey of "The African Slave Trade in Texas" appeared in the same publication. Concerning the problem of the slave trade in Texas, Barker noted that "the African slave trade never reached any considerable proportions in Texas. That it did not was due in part, no doubt, to the law-abiding character of most of the population; but chiefly, perhaps, to the fact that Texas did not begin her great development until after the activity of the United States and England had given the traffic its death blow."[33] In the meanwhile, Barker's articles on "The Organization of the Texas Revolution" and "Documents of the Texas Revolution" were published in the *Publications of the Southern Historical Association* of January and November, 1901. Seeking recognition in his profession, Barker mailed copies of these early publications to James Ford

[32] George P. Garrison, "A Memorandum of M. Austin's Journey from the Lead Mines in the County of Wythe in the State of Virginia to the Lead Mines in the Province of Louisiana West of the Mississippi River," *American Historical Review*, V (April, 1900), 18.

[33] E. C. Barker, "The African Slave Trade in Texas," *The Quarterly of the Texas State Historical Association*, VI (January, 1903), 169 n.

Rhodes, Charles M. Andrews, Edward C. Channing, Albert Bushnell Hart, Charles H. Haskins, Frederick Jackson Turner, and
others.

In 1901 the University's School of History consisted of George
P. Garrison (professor), Lester G. Bugbee (adjunct professor),
and Eugene C. Barker (instructor). E. W. Winkler, another M.A.
in history, was listed as a fellow in the department by the school
Catalogue of 1900. Dr. Garrison, who taught all courses on American history, was "head of the department and never let you forget it."[34] But if Garrison was the strong man of the young School
of History, Lester Gladstone Bugbee was its heart and soul. By
this time Barker admired Bugbee above all other persons and
later remembered: "It seems to me that one received from him an
impression of thoughtful maturity, a feeling that 'here is a man
utterly free of pretense, whose judgment and character can be
trusted.'" Barker also recalled that students flocked about Bugbee's desk after a class recitation, and

in the same way colleagues and associates gathered in his office and
overflowed into the adjacent classroom of the old Main Building, sometimes working, sometimes talking and killing his time. In one of his
letters he remarked: "Intended to move this afternoon, but Barker and
Pessels came in and we spent until 6 o'clock talking; then I played ten-
nis." Another afternoon, more profitable let us hope: "There is a crowd
in the room, Wagner is working at a table on my left, Pessels is reading
a manuscript novel which has been submitted to my critical judgment,
and Barker is clicking away at a typewriter behind me."[35]

Bugbee's traits of character and personality—his social charm,
thoughtful maturity, freedom from pretense and sham, intelligence, and love of learning, and his broad interest in people—
continued to make a profound impression on Eugene Barker.
Later on, Barker's character and personality would conform to
much the same design. The thoughtfulness of Barker is illustrated
by a note written on the occasion of Bugbee's promotion to adjunct professor of history on July 13, 1900; it read, "I didn't get

[34] Walter P. Webb, *An Honest Preface and Other Essays*, 19.
[35] Barker, *Essays*, 66; Barker, "Lester Gladstone Bugbee," 30.

to see you this morning, but I think you will know that I am heartily glad of your promotion and that you have my sincere congratulations."[36] At this time, however, the popular Bugbee had less than two years to live.

E. C. Barker did not remember the origin of his friend's fatal illness. It was later revealed by the Bugbee correspondence that for several years prior to realization of the nature of his illness, Dr. Edward Blount of Nacogdoches, a friend of student days, had been sending Bugbee prescriptions for chronic bronchitis— Bugbee's own diagnosis of his condition. There is little doubt that this was the beginning of tuberculosis. In early February, 1901, Dr. J. M. Steiner of Austin informed Bugbee that he was suffering from the dread disease. Realizing the seriousness of his illness, Bugbee took a month vacation and left Austin on February 18 for Junction, Texas. On reaching his destination, he followed a program of vigorous exercise that was then considered as the standard treatment for tuberculosis. His days were spent in hunting, fishing, horseback riding, and tramping along the Llano River. He returned to Austin worse rather than better for his vacation.

At the close of the spring term, Bugbee took a leave of absence to visit El Paso, the mecca for those suffering from lung disease. He left Austin for the last time on July 27, 1901. From Bugbee's departure until his death on March 27, 1902, Eugene Barker wrote frequent letters to his stricken friend, keeping him abreast of the news of Austin and the University. Barker replaced Bugbee as corresponding secretary of the Texas State Historical Association and as the adjunct member for Texas on the Public Archives Commission of the Austin Historical Association, but Bugbee's absence placed a burden on Barker and Garrison in the classroom and necessitated a search for a replacement. On September 21, 1901, Barker wrote Bugbee:

Garrison told me this morning that the new man has not yet been found, despite a furious correspondence on the part of both himself and

[36] Barker to Bugbee, July 13, 1900, in the Lester Gladstone Bugbee Papers, Archives, University of Texas Library.

the president. As a consequence, he informs me that I must carry temporarily A, 1, and 2 which I can reduce to 21 hours by compressing A into four sections. I hope they'll soon get him. I wonder how much they are offering him? If Garrison were anybody but himself this might work to my advantage next year, but I doubt whether I can get him to recommended me for $1200, though I am determined at least to worry him. I'm afraid that the Regents will forget that I am working for them, now that you are gone—unless I can attract their attention through him. We seem to be on very excellent terms at present.

I see our last year's football coach around today. Only two or three of the old team will be back, and they have hardly begun to practice yet, though a game is arranged with Oklahoma for October 5. Our honorable record seems to me in danger.[37]

On November 4, 1901, Barker wrote Bugbee a longer letter to describe the adjustments made within the staff of the History Department:

I've been intending for a month to write you a summary of the developments within the school of History, but my hands have been so full—and at times my heart, too—that I have never felt that I could spare the time to do the subject justice.

You know of course that the new man is from Wisconsin, with a Ph.D. from Pennsylvania. American history was his major, though, and he was teaching American History at Wisconsin State Normal when we got him. Took his doctoral degree in '99, I think. He is rather good looking, a blond, about six feet tall; and I believe he will prove a pretty good teacher. . . . His rank is Instructor and his salary $1500. And his name, if you don't happen to know, is H. E. Bolton.

When Garrison told me of his election, he gratuitously added the information that his salary at Wisc. was $1450 and that he made about $200 more in the summer school, so I thought it prudent to say a word about our summer school for myself. I told him that in case you did not come back next summer, I expected to apply for your place. He replied that it was his impression that Bolton would want to work in the summer, too, and then I exploded. I'm always reminding myself of that frog who spent all his days in climbing out of a well and all his nights in slipping back. I gained the impression, and have since verified it,

37 Barker to Bugbee, September 21, 1901, Bugbee Papers.

that Bolton came with the full expectation of teaching in the summer as often as he chooses.

Barker concluded his letter to Bugbee with a tinge of bitterness as he remarked: "I imagine it will warm his [Garrison's] heart to have Bolton report regularly for proof-reading, as he has been doing for the past week. The two Fellows, it seems to me, are doing less than usual."[38] Barker's letter reveals an irritation with both Garrison and Bolton; with Garrison, the feeling was to be permanent; with Bolton, Barker's ill will was short-lived and the two young historians were soon steadfast friends. In the words of Barker, Bolton "proved to be a pretty good teacher." He, too, found the door to advancement in American history closed by the Garrison monopoly and turned to the frontier of New Spain to develop the new field of Latin American history.

When the fall term began, Bolton took over the full course on European expansion, described in the *Catalogue* for 1901–1902 as "a study of the social, economic, religious, and political forces that led to the activities of the European nations during the sixteenth, seventeenth, and eighteenth centuries; the methods employed by the important nations; the field occupied by each; and the effects of these expansion activities upon the parent states." Bolton added, "Emphasis will be placed on Spanish colonization." In the year 1903 it was announced that in the following year the course would "be confined to Spanish colonization" and by 1905 the course was "devoted to the colonial activities of Spain."[39]

In the summer of 1901, Barker, having no summer school teaching assignment, journeyed to the University of Chicago to pursue his graduate studies. His experience at Chicago was disappointing and he wrote Bugbee the following complaint:

My work is a bit disappointing here. I have two courses under Thatcher and he is about the poorest you ever saw. He is lazy and verbose as Fitzhugh and not nearly so bright a man. Shevill, however, is very fine. I find, too, that the work I am doing is undergraduate and

[38] Barker to Bugbee, November 4, 1901, ibid.

[39] "Development of Latin American Studies at the University of Texas," *Information Bulletin of the Institute of Latin American Studies, 5.*

can't be counted for a degree, but that was not much of a surprise, for I half way expected it before I came.[40]

When Barker returned to Austin at the end of the summer, he left the University of Chicago never to return as a student.

From 1900 until the fall of 1906 Eugene C. Barker taught History 1, a course described as "the history of Greece, of the Roman Republic, and of the early Roman Empire." His students were freshmen in the University. Barker's classroom mannerisms during this formative period are described by young Charles Wilson Hackett, a freshman student at the University in 1905–1906:

The class in ancient history which Professor Barker taught in my freshman year had about sixty members. It met on the north side of the east wing of the old Main Building, directly across from the offices of the President and Dean of the College, and practically all the seats in that large, gloomy, ground floor room were filled. I distinctly remember some of the members of that class and also the seating arrangement. Directly in front of the rostrum on which Professor Barker seated himself at a table, sat Rawlings Colquitt, whose father at that time was governor. Directly across from Colquitt sat Mike Hogg. At two seats at the immediate right of the rostrum and facing it sat Dolly Belle Rutherford (now Mrs. Hobart Key of Marshall) and Sing Wooldridge (now Mrs. Frank Lanham), daughter of A. P. Wooldridge, banker and sometimes mayor of Austin. Incidentally, these two young women were among the most popular in the entire University. Near the center of the north wall sat Lutcher Stark; across from him I had my seat, and across from me sat Jesse Jenkins . . .

Even in his youthful experience as a tutor, Dr. Barker was subject to "volcanic explosions at the presence of injustice, or laziness, or suspected political folly." For example, one of the students of that class was notoriously lazy and seemed to take pride in it. Dr. Barker found this out, and, before the term had advanced very far he made it a rule at 12:26 p.m. to ask this particular student a question. As quickly as a response could be made, the reply was . . . "I don't know." Dr. Barker always had a caustic response to this regular formula of an answer. Frequently he would turn to one of the non-serious young women in

---

[40] Barker to Bugbee, June 30, 1901, ibid. During the winter of 1901–1902, Bugbee grew weaker. He died at Pleasant Point, Texas, March 27, 1902.

the class and repeat the question. On one occasion after he had asked a certain young lady the same question that he had asked the non-serious young gentleman, he replied rather sarcastically: "Miss ————, if you and Mr. ———— ever learn anything about anything, won't you come up to the rostrum after class and tell me about it so I can give you credit for knowing some one thing about something."[41]

Hackett remembered that "from Dr. Barker, more than any other person I received the inspiration to become a student of history."

On May 6, 1903, Eugene C. Barker married Matilda LeGrand Weeden, whose charm and social grace were to smooth the pathway of her scholarly husband all the days of her life. Several months later Barker admitted to Dr. Alex Dienst of Temple, "I got married last summer, and now am putting in all my spare time sawing wood, planting beans, and such like. But I like it immensely."[42]

As the months of 1904 and 1905 passed, E. C. Barker made plans to complete his graduate study. In the meanwhile, however, his articles concerning the period of the Texas Revolution continued to appear in *The Quarterly of the Texas State Historical Association*, in the *Publications of the Southern Historical Association*, and in the *Political Science Quarterly*.[43] In 1903 and 1904 he collaborated with Herbert Eugene Bolton to compile a reader in Texas history for young students. The collection was published by the American Book Company in 1904 under the title, *With the*

[41] Charles W. Hackett, November 25, 1941, Barker Papers, "Portrait of a Historian."

[42] Barker to Dr. A. A. Dienst, March 3, 1904, in the Claude Elliott Collection, Southwest Texas State College Library, San Marcos, Texas.

[43] Barker's early writings included "The Tampico Expedition," *The Quarterly of the Texas State Historical Association*, VI (January, 1903); "Journal of the Permanent Council (October 11–27, 1835)," ibid., VII (April, 1904); "Journal of Stephen F. Austin on His First Trip to Texas, 1821," ibid.; "Land Speculation as a Cause of the Texas Revolution," ibid., X (July, 1906); "The Texas Revolutionary Army," ibid., IX (April, 1906); "Mirabeau Buonaparte Lamar," *The University of Texas Record*, V (August, 1903); "Documentary Progress of Texas Revolutionary Sentiment as Seen in Columbia," *Publications of the Southern Historical Association*, VII (January–July, 1903); "Pioneer Municipalities in the Texas Revolution," ibid., VIII (January,

Makers of Texas. Barker's thoughts, however, were never far removed from the task of finishing the doctoral degree. In the spring
of 1906 he wrote Dr. Alex Dienst to the effect that Bolton would
look after the details of publishing the Dienst narrative on the
Texas Navy in the *Quarterly* because he, Barker, planned to go
"away next year to do some studying—probably at the University
of Wisconsin."[44] But instead of Wisconsin, Barker chose the University of Pennsylvania. It may be assumed that his choice was
dictated by three considerations: (1) Herbert Eugene Bolton had
been a student of John B. McMaster at Pennsylvania, and Bolton
had a considerable influence over his younger colleague. (2)
Isaac Joslin Cox, another friend of Barker's, entered the University of Pennsylvania in 1902 to complete the work on a doctoral
degree; Cox wrote glowing reports, such as this: "I like the work
pretty well, especially that with Cheyney. Prof. McMaster is very
pleasant in personal conferences . . . but his seminar is not equal
to Cheyney's."[45] And (3) Barker received a $500 Harrison fellow-
ship to study at Pennsylvania. As a result, in the summer of 1906
Eugene and Matilda Barker left Austin for Philadelphia. They
traveled by way of Washington, D.C., and arrived in Philadelphia
in September.

Shortly after arriving on the Pennsylvania campus, Barker
wrote John A. Lomax, who had gone to Harvard to study, to the
effect that "I sure wish I had my $500 fellowship at Harvard and
were with you." Barker went on to explain that he and his young
wife had arrived in Philadelphia during the middle of September,
and, after looking around for several days, located a place to set
up housekeeping. Barker continued,

We are located about half a block from College Hall and a block from
the Library, in two rooms, for which we pay $25.00 a month unfur-

---

1904); "Texas Revolution Documents," ibid. (March, 1904); "Conserva-
tives and Renegades in the Texas Revolution," ibid. (September, 1904);
"The First Clash in the Texas Revolution—the Taking of Anahuac by
Travis," ibid., IX (March–July, 1905); "Finances of the Texas Revolution,"
Political Science Quarterly, XIX (December, 1904).

44 Barker to Alex Dienst, April 1, 1906, in the Elliott Collection.
45 Isaac Joslin Cox to Barker, November 6, 1902.

nished. They are excellent rooms—one of them is 22 feet square, east front—but think of the price! Of course we can't afford much furniture for these magnificent quarters, and they are likely to retain an appearance of camp life during the winter. This large 22 foot apartment is in process of being converted into a kitchen, dining room, study, and parlor by the simple expedient of curtaining off a space about ten by six for a gas range. This space contains also a large closet, with shelves, which we will use for pantry, safe, and kitchen table—second shelf serves as table. There is also a wash stand in the enclosure with hot and cold water—this is for lavatory purposes exclusively and will not be used for a sink, but you can readily see the convenience of having the water so near the kitchen. The remaining 420 square feet in this room will be used as aforesaid for dining room, parlor, and study. I dare say we are not as comfortably fixed as you and Mrs. Lomax, and we are paying a good deal more. But it would be real "elegant" if we had some of our furniture from home.[46]

At Pennsylvania Barker studied under John B. McMaster, E. P. Cheyney, W. E. Lingelbach, and Charles H. Haskins.[47] The Department of History at Pennsylvania was largely the creation of John Bach McMaster, the Brooklyn-born civil engineer and historian who was called to the new chair of American history at Pennsylvania in 1883 following the publication of the first volume of *A History of the People of the United States*. Aside from Barker, McMaster's roll of students over the years included Herbert E. Bolton, E. P. Cheyney, W. E. Lingelbach, A. C. Meyers, E. P. Oberholtzer, F. L. Paxson, W. T. Root, W. R. Shepherd, W. W. Sweet, and Claude H. Van Tyne. When Barker met McMaster in 1906, the older man was at the height of his career. According to William T. Hutchinson, "McMaster was the first historian to appreciate the importance of the history of the West and to give it a significant place in the story of the United States."[48] It is also

[46] Barker to John A. Lomax, September 30, 1906, in the John A. Lomax Papers, Letters from E. C. Barker, Archives, University of Texas Library, Austin, Texas.

[47] Eugene C. Barker's Personnel Folder, Office of the President of the University of Texas.

[48] William T. Hutchinson, "John Bach McMaster," in Hutchinson (ed.),

of significance to note that McMaster had no tendency to glorify the men and events of the late eighteenth century and pointed out that the delegates to the Annapolis and Philadelphia conventions of 1786 and 1787 "were brought together in response to the demands of the businessmen of the country, not to form an ideal plan of government but such a practical plan as would meet the business needs of the people."[49] This statement makes McMaster a pioneer of the economic school of historians. It is noteworthy, however, that he held the framers of the Constitution in high regard and wrote that they were a "most remarkable assemblage of men."[50] Although the social and economic aspects of American life furnished McMaster with the materials for his scholarship, he taught a course in American constitutional history and, with Frederick D. Stone, compiled a work entitled *Pennsylvania and the Federal Constitution.* The philosophy of McMaster concerning the early national period of the history of the United States had considerable influence on the mind of Barker. In later years Professor Barker would have a great deal to say about the period of the Confederation and the Constitution.

Barker spent the academic year of 1907–1908 at Harvard University as an Austin scholar. While at Cambridge he taught history at Radcliffe and broadened his scholarly experiences by working with Albert Bushnell Hart, Edward Channing, Ephrim Emerton, Archibald Carey Coolidge, and Roger Merriman. In the spring of 1908 the University of Pennsylvania awarded Eugene Campbell Barker the Doctor of Philosophy degree. When Barker returned to the School of History at the University of Texas the following fall, he was assigned to teach courses in Modern European history—"Having thus passed a milestone on the road from the field of ancient history to the field of his chosen interest, namely, American history."[51] In the meanwhile Bolton had left

---

The Marcus W. Jernegan Essays in American Historiography (Chicago, 1937), 138.

[49] Ibid., 130, citing McMaster's *History of the People of the United States* (8 vols.; 1883–1913), I, 399, 438, 533.

[50] Ibid.

[51] Charles W. Hackett to Harbert Davenport, November 25, 1941.

the University of Texas for a position on the staff of Leland Stanford University; Bolton, too, was angry with Dr. Garrison. Barker was so irritated because of this latest turn of events that he wrote Herman V. Ames, professor of history and graduate dean at Pennsylvania, to solicit aid in locating another position. Professor Ames, an understanding man, replied,

> In regard to the matter of your future plans at Texas, I was about to write and ask why the work which Bolton has been doing in the American field would not now be opened to you inasmuch as he is to leave at the end of this college year, but your letter seems to indicate that the door is closed. We all recognize the limitations under which you work in the European field away from any considerable collection of material. We feel, however, that it would be decidedly unwise for you to cut loose from your present position until something else opens. . . . It is very unfortunate that Professor Garrison is not willing to welcome others into the same field with him, as it would seem plenty large enough for co-workers.
>
> If you should come North, you would be cut off from the material of the history of the Spanish southwest. If it is still possible for you to continue your research work along the lines of Spanish History without crippling your European History teaching, I should still urge you to do so, as you already have a grasp upon that field and the men who understand it are few and will be, like Bolton, in demand.[52]

Encouraged by the Ames letter, Barker approached Dr. Garrison and requested advanced courses in the general field of the history of the Spanish borderlands and the American southwest. Much to the surprise of the younger man, Dr. Garrison agreed to the Barker suggestions. As a result, Eugene C. Barker found himself preparing to teach the history of Mexico and the Anglo-American southwest; he wrote Herbert E. Bolton to tell the good news; Bolton's reply had the nature of a prophecy:

> It was a good day for Texas when it was decided to put you into the Southwestern field. I have your course all mapped out for you now. You will get into the field that has a local interest, and when Garrison steps aside you will succeed to his position and influence. I don't think

---

[52] Herman V. Ames to Barker, February 2, 1909.

I'd try very hard now to get away if I were you, although offers outside are a good thing to "consider," at least, even if you do not intend to accept them.[53]

It appears that in the spring of 1910 Barker was completely happy for the first time as a member of George P. Garrison's History Department. But Bolton's prediction of the future came true all too quickly. On July 3, 1910, Professor Garrison died at his home in Austin, the victim of a heart attack. Speaking to the Texas Federation of Women's Clubs at San Antonio several months later, Barker recalled that,

A busy session had just closed, the last paper of the final examination had been read and the grades turned in to the office, and he [Garrison] lay down to rest before beginning a term in the Summer School; the proof sheets of a massive volume of the Diplomatic Correspondence of the Republic of Texas, which he was editing, were upon his desk; he edited copy for the July number of *The Quarterly* as he lay in bed; and he had just written an article on the Navy of Texas, which will appear shortly in *Harper's Magazine*. This is as he would have it. The sadness of it is that we are no longer stimulated by his presence, and the capital which he had accumulated for half a dozen other books is lost.[54]

A few days after Garrison's untimely death, President Sidney Edward Mezes appointed Eugene Campbell Barker acting chairman of the School of History. At the next meeting of the Board of Regents of the University, the appointment was confirmed and Barker began his long tenure as department head. Frederic L. Paxson wrote his Texas colleague, "I am glad that the mantle of Garrison has fallen upon you and am confident that the lines of work which he started will be in competent hands."[55] Thus the first period in the career of Eugene C. Barker—an era of diligent study and preparation set against a backdrop of poverty and economic hardship—had come to a close. A great task lay before the young historian.

---

53 Bolton to Barker, April 15, 1910.
54 Barker, *Essays*, 41.
55 Frederic L. Paxson to Barker, October 16, 1910.

Years of Growth

Aside from his teaching and scholarship, Eugene C. Barker's most significant service to the University of Texas was the building of a department of history that came to rank with the finest among the state universities of the nation. This rather difficult task was completed, for the most part, during the first five years of the Barker era. When Professor Barker became chairman of the School of History in 1910 his teaching staff consisted of Charles W. Ramsdell and Frederic Duncalf, two young and unknown newcomers. Bolton had left Texas in 1909 after a quarrel with Garrison concerning the distribution of the courses in American history. Remembering these difficult times, Ramsdell later remarked that "it was a supremely fortunate thing both for the University and for the cause of Texas History that when Professor Garrison dropped his unfinished work in 1910, Barker was at hand to take it up. The Department of History had been shaken and apparently demoralized by the departure of Bolton in 1909 and the death of Garrison."[1]

As the academic year of 1910–1911 approached, Barker realized that the small staff of the history faculty must be expanded to meet the needs of a growing school. By the beginning of the fall term the University enrollment comprised 1,677 students, and the Austin campus furnished the setting for seven buildings. In October of 1911 Barker wrote Frederic L. Paxson that "Duncalf and Krey were beginning the year with about 450 Freshmen in

[1] Charles W. Ramsdell, "Barker as a Historian," in Barker, *Essays*, ix.

Medieval History and seem to enjoy it, despite the mid-summer temperature that continues here."[2] Always small during the Garrison era, the teaching staff of the School of History consisted of professors Garrison, Bolton, and Barker from 1902 until 1906, the year that Barker left for graduate study. During the same time the student assistants included Mattie Austin Hatcher, Ethel Z. Rather, and Charles Ramsdell. During the years 1906, 1907, and 1908, James E. Winston and Fred W. Householder, two graduate students, helped Garrison carry the load while both Bolton and Barker were on leaves of absence. It is apparent that, in the late years of his tenure, Dr. Garrison was having a difficult time locating and retaining outstanding scholars. In 1909 Frederic Duncalf, a young Ph.D. from the University of Wisconsin, was added to the staff as a tutor in history, an appointment so ridiculous from the viewpoint of rank that H. Y. Benedict considered it a joke.[3] But at the time Garrison could offer nothing more. Therefore, one of the initial tasks facing Eugene C. Barker in 1910 was the recruiting of new staff members. Within a few months Thad Weed Riker, Frank Burr Marsh, William R. Manning, and Augustus Charles Krey were added to the faculty of the School of History. Two years later, Milton R. Gutsch came from the University of Wisconsin to join Barker's staff. The department was later strengthened with the addition of Walter Prescott Webb in 1918, Charles Wilson Hackett in 1919, and Rudolph L. Biesele in 1925. In contrast to his predecessor, Barker was able to bring out-of-state scholars to the School of History and, what was more important, to retain them as permanent members of the faculty. Collectively, these men formed a remarkable group of historians —a group deserving special attention.

As noted before, Charles William Ramsdell joined the faculty of the School of History in September, 1906. Ramsdell, a native Texan, was born at Salado, Bell County, Texas, on April 4, 1877. After finishing the Salado schools, he entered the University of

[2] Barker to Frederic L. Paxson, October 5, 1911.

[3] Tom Bowman Brewer, "A History of the History Department of the University of Texas" (Master's thesis, University of Texas, 1957), 48.

Texas in 1900 and finished his B.A. degree in 1903. As an under-graduate, Ramsdell was an outstanding athlete and a stellar per-former on the Longhorn football team. Also a member of Phi Beta Kappa, he received a graduate fellowship in history and finished his M.A. degree in 1904. He spent two years in graduate study at Columbia University, and then returned to Texas. During his early years in the department, he taught courses in both European and American history. After receiving his Ph.D. from Columbia in 1910, he turned to the field of Southern United States history for a specialty and for the next three decades taught the courses in the Old South, the Civil War, and Reconstruction. From 1910 to 1938 Ramsdell served as associate editor of the *Southwestern Historical Quarterly*; he was a member of the editorial board of the *Mississippi Valley Historical Review* from 1930 to 1933. In the late years of his life (together with Wendell H. Stevenson, then of Louisiana State University) he initiated the multivolume *History of the South*.

Frederic Duncalf began a forty-year career on the faculty of the History Department in 1909. He was a native of Lancaster, Wisconsin, and completed his B.A. degree at Beloit College before entering the University of Wisconsin graduate school. Duncalf received his M.A. degree at Wisconsin in 1906 and his Ph.D. in 1909. After joining the faculty of the University of Texas, Duncalf experienced difficulty in deciding to remain at Texas. In 1910 he moved to Bowdoin College in Portland, Maine. He returned to the University of Texas as an instructor of medieval history in 1911 but resigned again in 1913 to accept a position at the University of Illinois. In 1914 he returned to Austin to stay. Frederic Duncalf became an outstanding scholar in the medieval field; the more significant of his publications include *Parallel Source Problems in Medieval History*, written in collaboration with A. C. Krey and published in 1912; *A Brief History of the War*, also written with Krey and published in 1918; and *The Story of Civilization*, written in collaboration with Carl Becker in 1938.

Frank Burr Marsh, a specialist in ancient history, was born in Big Rapids, Michigan, on March 4, 1880. He entered the University of Michigan in 1898 and received the B.A. degree in 1902.

Marsh spent the following year in Paris and returned to the University of Michigan graduate school in 1903. He received his Ph.D. in 1906 after a summer in Paris at the Bibliothèque Nationale. From 1905 until 1910 Marsh held an instructorship in the History Department of the University of Michigan. On June 4, 1910, Marsh wrote Dr. Garrison that "Your letter of May 31 offering me an instructorship, in the University of Texas, at a salary of $1000, has been duly received. It gives me pleasure to accept the appointment on the conditions offered."[4] Although he was a medieval historian by training, Marsh made the transition to ancient history and became an authority in the subject. His primary publications include *The Founding of the Roman Empire* (1922), *The Reign of Tiberius* (1931), *A History of the Roman World from 146 B.C. to 30 B.C.* (1935), and an edition of the works of Tacitus.

Thad Weed Riker was born at Stamford, Connecticut, on November 2, 1880. He received his education at Princeton University, where he completed his B.A. degree in 1903 and his M.A. in 1904. Riker then journeyed to England and enrolled at Queen's College, Oxford University. After a three-year study of history, he received the B. Litt. from Oxford. In 1909 Riker taught English history at Cornell and the following year George P. Garrison offered him an instructorship in modern European history at the University of Texas. Riker wrote Garrison, "I received your letter this morning and am pleased to accept your offer of the instructorship. The arrangement you suggest is entirely satisfactory. I shall probably arrive in Austin about the middle of September . . . to get a preliminary acquaintance with the library, not to mention finding a boarding house."[5] Although he always considered Texans rather provincial and regarded Austin as a frontier community, Thad W. Riker stayed on at the University of Texas to become one of the most colorful classroom lecturers of the Department of History. A member of the American Historical Association and the Royal

---

[4] Frank Burr Marsh to George P. Garrison, June 4, 1910.

[5] Thad Weed Riker to George P. Garrison, May 23, 1910. Biographical information on Ramsdell, Duncalf, Marsh, and Riker is based on Tom Brewer's excellent study, "A History of the History Department."

Historical Society, Riker served on the board of editors of the *Journal of Modern History* from 1928 through 1932; in 1932 he worked as the acting editor of the *Journal*. Riker's primary publications include *The Making of Roumania* (1931) and *A Short History of Modern Europe*, first published in 1935 and revised as *A History of Modern Europe* in 1948. In 1935 Riker was awarded the D. Litt. degree by Oxford University in recognition of his outstanding scholarship.

By the spring of 1912 the School of History was in the market for an instructor in medieval history. In his search to fill the position, Barker wrote to D. C. Munro at the University of Wisconsin, and Munro recommended Milton R. Gutsch for the instructorship. According to Munro: "Gutsch will suit you admirably. His interest is primarily Medieval History, but he would be glad to develop either the English side for his own special work, or the later period of the Renaissance or Reformation."[6] A few days later Barker replied, "We decided last night in a departmental meeting to offer Mr. Gutsch our instructorship in Medieval History."[7] Since Munro was of the opinion that the Texas offer "was the best opening . . . likely to come up this year," Milton Rietow Gutsch, a native of Sheboygan, Wisconsin, and soon to be a three-time graduate of the University of Wisconsin, arrived in Austin in September, 1912.

Many years later Dr. Gutsch remembered his arrival in Austin and his first meeting with Dr. Barker. Gutsch described the event:

I remember very clearly my first meeting with Dr. Barker. I can remember it with great distinctness not because of my trepidation and anxiety, more or less natural to a young instructor coming into personal contact for the first time with his department head, and not only because of my excusable curiosity to see the scholar and teacher of whom I had heard a great deal at the University of Wisconsin and with whom I had had some correspondence, but also because of the rather embarrassing circumstances under which the meeting occurred, circumstances which I must hasten to say were much more embarrassing to me than to him, but which nevertheless provided me with an opportunity to

[6] D. C. Munro to Barker, April 27, 1912.
[7] Barker to Munro, May 4, 1912.

observe one of those qualities that have endeared "the Chief" to many of us.

This meeting, which meant so much to me took place in September, 1912, at the University Club, where Mr. Duncalf and I had obtained a room, on the morning after my arrival in Austin. I had brought with me my life savings which amounted to about seventy-five dollars and which I considered quite a fortune. I had slept rather late that morning after my arrival. When I arose I found my clothes scattered on the floor and my fortune gone. I had been robbed. It was at that moment that Dr. Barker arrived to pay his respects. When he learned what had happened he assured me that this was not the customary Texas reception of strangers, and then he insisted that I accept from him enough money to "tide me over" until check day . . . And just as Barker "tided me over" on that day, so he "tided" many others over as the years went by. Student and teacher alike hailed him as benefactor and friend in need.[8]

Thus Milton R. Gutsch began a long career at the University of Texas, a career distinguished by his ability as an administrator and classroom teacher. After Duncalf returned to the University, Gutsch offered the advanced courses in English history. On his retirement in 1951, the Austin *American* commented on the fact that his lecture on Henry VIII was a classic and that he annually chose the last class day before the Christmas holidays to "demonstrate in his large voice the student drinking songs of the Middle Ages."[9] Professor Gutsch was further described in the following terms:

He was the stock martinet of the lecture hall, short in stature but strong in voice.

He had the gift and the determination to boom a knowledge and an appreciation of English history into the noggins of restless youngsters more immediately concerned with bulling, coking, catching dates, and slapping through their texts than they were with Egbert's ascension to the West Saxon throne or benefits the barons wrested at Runnymeade for posterity.[10]

[8] Milton R. Gutsch, March 26, 1942, Barker Papers, "Portrait of a Historian."

[9] Austin *American*, September 10, 1951.

[10] Ibid.

Charles Wilson Hackett was no stranger to the campus when he returned to the University of Texas as adjunct professor of history in 1918. In September, 1905, he had entered the University as a freshman student. As noted in the first chapter, Hackett credits Eugene C. Barker as the prime factor in an early decision to study history. Hackett, a superior student, became a student assistant in history in 1908–1909. He received the Bachelor of Arts degree in 1909, and after a year of graduate work at Texas, he followed Herbert Eugene Bolton to Stanford and California. Thomas E. Cotner has written, "From the University of California, Charles W. Hackett received the M.A. and Ph.D. degrees in 1914 and 1917, respectively."[11] During Hackett's years at California, Eugene C. Barker never lost sight of the young student; in 1918 he offered Hackett a position on the Texas faculty. When Charles Hackett returned to Austin in 1918 he began a thirty-one year association with the University. A persistent research scholar and writer, Hackett ended his lengthy tenure as distinguished professor of Latin American history and director of the important Institute of Latin American Studies.[12]

Walter Prescott Webb, a native of Stephens County, Texas, and a graduate of the University, joined the History Department on November 11, 1918. Webb had compiled a decade of experience in public school teaching and was brought to the University primarily to offer a course in the teaching of history. The need for a course such as the one proposed for Webb had been recognized by the Mississippi Valley Historical Association and the American Historical Association earlier in the decade. In 1911 the Mississippi Valley group established a committee to work with a similar committee of the American Historical Association in surveying the problem of the certification of high school teachers of history. A. C. McLaughlin, the president of the Mississippi Valley Association, appointed Eugene C. Barker to the committee.[13] The following August Frederic L. Paxson wrote Barker that

[11] Thomas E. Cotner and Carlos E. Castañeda (eds.), *Essays in Mexican History* (Austin, 1958), xii.
[12] Ibid.
[13] A. C. McLaughlin to Barker, June 28, 1911.

any scheme for the certification of teachers would "have to deal with the departments of pedagogy" and that one of the primary reasons impelling an interest in the problem was that the historians rather than the pedagogs should "define the qualifications of the teachers of our own subject." Paxson ended with the admonition, "If we don't do it, they will."[14] Therefore, the hiring of Walter P. Webb in 1918 culminated the University's quest for a person qualified to work with public school teachers. As time passed Webb moved beyond his early specialty to become one of the great American historians of his generation. Pioneering in the tradition of Frederick Jackson Turner, his major publications— *The Great Plains, The Texas Rangers,* and *The Great Frontier*— stand as significant contributions to American and global history. In a brief summary of Webb's distinguished career, Joe Frantz has written:

He was also moving insignificantly and at the lowest rank into a school he would serve full time for forty years, a school which would pay him its highest faculty salary, and whose faculty would name him to every elective committee before he retired. When in November, 1958, the University of Texas chose its four most significant living alumni, it named Congressman Sam Rayburn, the record-holding Speaker of the House of Representatives; Robert Anderson, at this writing Secretary of the Treasury; Ramon Beteta, currently Mexico's minister to Italy; and Walter P. Webb.[15]

After twenty years experience in the public schools of Texas, Rudolph L. Biesele joined the staff of the department in 1925. In 1931 he became a permanent member of the University faculty and supervised the multisection survey course in American history.

These were the men that comprised the "old department"— Barker, Ramsdell, Marsh, Gutsch, Riker, Duncalf, Hackett, Webb, and Biesele. From 1910 until 1927 Dr. Barker served as chairman of the department; in 1927 he stepped down to be succeeded by Milton R. Gutsch. It should be pointed out that Barker continued to be the strong man and the dominating personality of the department until the year of his retirement. Over the years other scholars joined the staff of the History Department for brief intervals. Among those who came to Austin and the campus of the University for shorter periods of service were A. C. Krey, William R. Manning, William E. Dunn, C. S. Boucher, and Isaac Joslin Cox. Because most of its members entered the department while they were young and chose to remain, the History Department of the University of Texas "has a history of its own that is perhaps unique among institutions of its size."[16]

It was during these early years at the helm of the department that Eugene C. Barker established his reputation for character and leadership among the University faculty. It was soon apparent to the University historians, however, that one strong man had succeeded another. Barker never let them forget who was running the department but he accomplished his task with diplomacy and benevolence. As the years went by, therefore, Barker's clear thinking, integrity, and courage made him a tower of strength on the faculty and perhaps the most powerful classroom teacher on the University campus. Although taciturn and severe, Dr. Barker was also kind and liberal in his administrative relationships. Frederic Duncalf once said that "this liberal quality of Barker's has been attributed in part to a reaction against the dogmatic methods of his predecessor."[17] In a longer narrative con-

---

[16] Ibid., 18. The austere economy involved in operating the School of History for the year 1914–1915 is revealed by a letter from Dr. S. E. Mezes to Barker setting up the History budget. The Mezes Budget included the following items: Professor of American History E. C. Barker, $2,500; Professor of History F. Duncalf, $3,000; Adjunct Professor of American History C. W. Ramsdell, $2,000; Adjunct Professor of English and Spanish-American History W. R. Manning, $1,800; Adjunct Professor of Modern European History T. W. Riker, $1,700; Instructor in Ancient History Frank B. Marsh, $1,500; Instructor in Medieval History M. R. Gutsch, $1,500; Instructor in Spanish-American History W. E. Dunn, $1,800; Archivist Mattie Austin Hatcher, $840; Texas State Historical Association, $180 (S. E. Mezes to Barker, April 30, 1914).

[17] Quoted in Brewer, "A History of the History Department."

cerning the early years of the Barker regime, Duncalf records the following:

Of the Muse of history he has been a devoted and faithful follower, but he has been an equally loyal son of his Alma Mater. In every crisis that has confronted the University he has always given his time and effort without hesitation and without fear. He has served on most of the committees which have shaped University policy. In the faculty forum he has championed every cause which favored higher standards of scholarship and instruction. A man of tremendous force of personality, with fixed principles of thoroughness in education, he has always scorned any compromise with sound teaching or academic freedom. When he is sure that he is right, his jaw sets, and his opponents well know that he will fight with all the power of his strong will, and to the end without quarter. When faculty debate has dragged on tediously and become aimless, it is usually Professor Barker who sums up the issue with a few terse and incisive sentences. And to this clear-minded exposure of all educational pretense and sham, the University owes much. In addition to being one of the most distinguished scholars on the faculty, no one has contributed more to the moulding of the ideals of the University than Professor Barker.[18]

In elaborating on the qualities relative to Barker's departmental leadership during the period of rebuilding "on broader foundations as befitting the growth of the University," Charles W. Ramsdell wrote:

His methods were characterized by rigid honesty, a strong sense of justice, generosity, the effort to obtain for each member of the department every opportunity for growth in scholarship and efficiency. He has always been loyal to the best interests of the University and the Department, and he expected the same attitude from others. He usually holds a conviction strongly, but he allows the same privilege to others. Discussions of departmental policy or measures have always been free and there have been many differences of opinion. It may surprise some to hear that he is very patient and considerate, and that he does not always have his own way but is sometimes voted down. If his is the strongest influence in the Department, and it is—it is because his quick

18 Frederic Duncalf, "The Scholar and the Achievement," *The Alcalde*, April, 1926; Barker, *Essays*, 290.

perception of the essential points of the problem, his clear-cut expression of his views, and his absolute integrity carry conviction. The net result is a very high departmental morale and mutual loyalty of which we are very proud.[19]

Before following Barker's career of service to the University of Texas in some detail, it is of significance to note that when A. C. Krey came to the University as a young instructor in 1910 he and Frederic Duncalf coined the title of "the Chief" for Dr. Barker because "had he been an Indian, he would have been a Chief, and he looked like one."[20] After that date, Dr. Barker was "the Chief" to those who knew him best. Frequently used as the salutation in letters to Barker, the nickname was no secret to the genial historian. As the years passed the title became widely used by graduate students and faculty members alike as a term denoting the greatest respect and admiration. It is appropriate here to examine some of the developments and events of the period from 1910 to about 1923 that made Dr. Barker "the Chief" to those who worked with him in the University of Texas. The most important of these events would include (1) the establishment of the Littlefield Fund for Southern History, (2) the efforts of Barker and Herbert Bolton to develop *The Southwestern Historical Quarterly* into a regional publication rather than a provincial local journal, and (3) the long and bitter controversy between the University of Texas and Governor James E. Ferguson.

Shortly after becoming chairman of the School of History in 1910, Dr. Barker began a correspondence with Major George W. Littlefield that was to result in the establishment of the Littlefield Fund for Southern History. A native of Mississippi and a resident of Texas most of his life, George W. Littlefield served with distinction in the Confederate Army during the Civil War. At the conclusion of the war he returned to Texas and shifted his interest from cotton farming to cattle raising. In the decades that fol-

[19] Charles W. Ramsdell, "Barker as a Historian," in Barker, *Essays*, ix.

[20] Quoted in both A. C. Krey to the President of the Texas State Historical Association, Minneapolis, Minnesota, January 6, 1962, and Walter P. Webb, "To the Chief," *Daily Texan*, October 24, 1956.

lowed, Littlefield accumulated a sizable fortune in West Texas cattle and lands. In 1890 he established the American National Bank in Austin, another successful enterprise. By the end of the century Littlefield was one of the wealthiest men in Texas. He became interested in state politics and in 1911 he was appointed to the Board of Regents of the University of Texas. Conservative and provincial in his political and economic philosophy, Littlefield soon expressed an interest in the content of the basic American history course at the University.[21]

On April 15, 1911, Major Littlefield wrote Barker to ask:

Do you use Elsons History of the United States in your teaching in the University? If not, then please let me know what history you teach from. Many persons over the state are anxious to know what history is being used in the University. Please let me hear from you promptly, and oblige.[22]

The Littlefield request was apparently motivated by a letter from a certain unreconstructed rebel named D. S. Sessions of Ennis, Texas. A few days earlier Littlefield had posed the same question to President Sidney E. Mezes of the University and Mezes also sought an answer from Barker. On April 12 Barker answered both Mezes and Littlefield by pointing out that while Elson's *History of the United States* was one of the books used in history courses it was not a textbook "in the sense in which Sessions understands the term," that Elson did not specifically refer to the Civil War as "the slaveholders war," that the author did not say that "John Brown was a man of high character and purpose," and that the book in question did not state in so many words that decent plantation owners and farmers of the South organized harems from their female slaves.[23]

Barker's frank reply was not wholly satisfactory to Major Little-

[21] For an excellent and detailed study of the life of George W. Littlefield see J. Evetts Haley, *George W. Littlefield, Texan*. A specialized study of the Littlefield Fund is found in Paul Walter Schroeder, "The Littlefield Fund for Southern History," *The Library Chronicle of the University of Texas*, VI (Spring, 1957), 3 ff.

[22] George W. Littlefield to Barker, April 15, 1911.

[23] Barker to S. E. Mezes, April 12, 1911.

field and his associates. Later in the year the adoption of the school textbook law brought the issue to a head. At the Twenty-First Annual Reunion of the Texas Division of the United Confederate Veterans Association, held at Austin in 1912, the historian of the ex-Confederates wrote:

For the fourth time, in 1911, a textbook law has been enacted which repeats again the requirement that United States histories for use in our public schools shall contain the construction of our Constitution placed on it by the fathers fairly presented. This is rendered imperative to avoid the false construction contained in the case of Texas-v-White in a decision rendered by Chief Justice Chase in 1868, and followed ever since in Northern authorities, that our government was founded on the plan of indestructable states in an indestructable Union. This is not history but bench-made law, made during the reconstruction period in violation of all law, and when the South was under military rule . . .[24]

Like many other Texans, Littlefield was a complete believer in the principles of states' rights and Jeffersonian democracy. He was also convinced of the righteousness of the cause of the Confederacy and was embittered by the events of Reconstruction. His convictions were shared by many of his friends in the Texas Division of the United Confederate Veterans. Other veteran groups in Texas regarded the John B. Hood camp (the veteran group of Austin) as a censoring agency for all textbooks presented for state adoption. As a result of veteran dissatisfaction no high school American history text was adopted in 1912. It was about this time that Dr. Barker wrote Major Littlefield seeking to enroll him as a member of the Texas State Historical Association. Littlefield responded with a check for life membership dues but appended the following note:

I wish to say to you as I believe you feel right towards Southern people, that a great many persons do not sympathize with movements of the University [sic], as a great many of the Professors and teachers employed there seem to prefer giving their support to Norther [sic] in-

[24] E. W. Winkler, December 18, 1941, Barker Papers, "Portrait of a Historian."

stitutions of this City. Not one, but dozens of times I have heard some of the best citizens say that the University needs a cleaning out, that it is politically rotten, and I hate to see such a feeling. The University is the biggest asset Austin can boast of. We are a Democratic State and a Democratic people and it seems to me those employed about the University should be in sympathy with the State and citizens . . .[25]

Barker's reply defended the personnel of the University as persons who were loyal to the best interests of Texas and the South.[26] In a subsequent letter to the old soldier, Barker pointed out that the fault was not with the historians, because nowhere in the South did scholars have access to source materials in Southern history, that those wishing to consult these materials were forced to travel to the Library of Congress or to libraries in New York or Boston, and that what was needed was a collection of source materials in Southern history in the South where they would be accessible to the students and scholars of the region. "The remedy for the situation," Barker wrote, "is perfectly simple. In the last analysis it is merely a matter of money to collect the historical materials of the South, and the time to use them." Barker reminded Littlefield that until such a collection was made "the resolutions and protests of patriotic societies against the misrepresentations of the South are 'as sounding brass and tinkling cymbals.' "[27] Although Barker only suggested to Littlefield that possibly some of the wealthy men of Texas might be willing to sponsor such a project, the Professor undoubtedly thought that George W. Littlefield would be just the man to underwrite such a collection.

A few weeks later Barker wrote two other letters. To Walter L. Fleming, the venerable professor of history at Louisiana State University, Barker explained that the state textbook board had failed to adopt a text for the Texas secondary schools because all available books seemed unfair to the South and that he had taken advantage of the opportunity "to point out to one of the Regents of the University himself a Confederate major that the South had done comparatively little to prepare for the writing of its own

25 Littlefield to Barker, September 10, 1912.
26 Barker to Littlefield, September 13, 1912.
27 Barker to Littlefield, December 5, 1912.

history."[28] On the same day Barker wrote a similar letter to Ruben Gold Thwaites, the superintendent of the State Historical Society of Wisconsin, to explain: "I have taken advantage of the occasion to stir up some of the University Regents and well to do Confederates on the subject of adequate library provision for the history of the South. . . . They are enough interested to want to know what it would cost, and I am writing you for help in forming an estimate."[29] Thwaites soon replied that no amount could be too large, that a good sum would be $200,000 to spend initially, and that it would hardly be worthwhile to start with less than $25,000.[30] As a result Barker subsequently mentioned $25,000 in his conversations and correspondence with Major Littlefield.

While Littlefield gave Barker's idea careful consideration, the proposal did not bear immediate fruit. In the spring of 1913 Littlefield complained about another Northern history with a remark to the effect, "There has grown to be a very great opposition to Channings [sic] History of the State among the veterans. Quite a lot has been said and written about the book being used by the University."[31] By the following spring Littlefield seemed convinced that if a library fund was to be established at all he would have to do it. On March 27, 1914, he called Barker to a conference designed to work out the details, and on April 24 the original endowment of $25,000 was accepted with gratitude by the Regents of the University of Texas. Thus the Littlefield Fund for Southern History came into being. As the final details were being worked out, Dr. Barker wrote E. P. Cheyney to comment that "perhaps Dr. Lingelbach has told you of a gratifying bit of luck I had the other day in securing a $25,000 endowment for Southern history. I had to phrase it in this way, though in general it can be used for almost anything in American history."[32] Between 1916 and 1920 Major Littlefield made many smaller donations to help with

28 Barker to W. L. Fleming, December 17, 1912.
29 Barker to R. G. Thwaites, December 17, 1912.
30 Thwaites to Barker, December 20, 1912.
31 Littlefield to Barker, April 30, 1913.
32 Barker to E. P. Cheyney, April 11, 1914.

the purchase of special items and upon his death in 1920 his will provided an additional $100,000.[33]

The establishment of the Littlefield Fund was only one of the important tasks that claimed Barker's attention during these early years. As Charles W. Ramsdell once phrased it, "In fact, it is partly upon his editorship of *The Quarterly* that Barker's reputation rests."[34] Of course Ramsdell was referring to the long association between Eugene C. Barker and the editorial offices of the Texas State Historical Association, a relationship that had its beginning during the early days of "Texas' oldest learned society." The Texas State Historical Association grew out of a meeting held in the Old Main Building at the University of Texas on the evening of February 13, 1897. Those attending this historic conference include Z. T. Fulmore, George P. Garrison, R. L. Batts, Charles Corner, Eugene Digges, Thomas Fitzhugh, Colonel John G. James, Major M. M. Kenney, Robert E. McCleary, and Lester G. Bugbee.[35] After a discussion of the objectives of the proposed organization, the group appointed a committee consisting of Dr. Garrison, Eugene Digges, and Charles Corner to draft a constitution and "to issue a call for a general meeting on March 2 to organize a historical association."[36]

On March 2, 1897, the second meeting was held in the rooms of the commissioner of agriculture, insurance, statistics, and history in the state capitol. The gathering was small—only twenty or thirty persons being present. After Judge Z. T. Fulmore was elected temporary chairman and Dr. George P. Garrison, temporary secretary, a draft of the constitution was read and adopted. An election of officers followed: O. M. Roberts was chosen president, and Dudley G. Wooten, Guy M. Bryan, William Corner, and Mrs.

[33] Paul Walter Schroeder, "The Littlefield Fund for Southern History," 10 ff.

[34] Barker, *Essays*, ix.

[35] H. Bailey Carroll, "A Half-Century of the Texas State Historical Association," *Southwestern Historical Quarterly* (extra number, February 1, 1947), 9.

[36] Ibid.

Julia Lee Sinks, vice presidents. Dr. George P. Garrison was made recording secretary and librarian, and Lester G. Bugbee was appointed corresponding secretary and treasurer. The first meeting of the executive council followed in May of 1897, and in July (about a month after the first annual meeting) the first number of *The Quarterly of the Texas State Historical Association* appeared in print.[37]

It will be remembered that at this time Eugene C. Barker was an undergraduate student at the University of Texas. In the April, 1898, number of *The Quarterly* the name of "Eugene C. Barker, Esq.," appears in the "list of new members" of the Association.[38] In July, 1901, *The Quarterly* carried a brief announcement by Dr. Garrison to the effect that,

> The members of the Association will regret to hear that Professor Bugbee, who has been Corresponding Secretary and Treasurer since its organization, and to whose diligent and faithful service much of its success has been due, has found himself under the necessity of resigning on account of ill health. His duties will be discharged, until his successor can be elected, by Mr. E. C. Barker. Professor Bugbee has obtained a leave of absence from the University, and expects to spend some time in New Mexico . . .[39]

Thus, Barker assumed a position in the editorial office of *The Quarterly* and the front office of the Association that would be his until his resignation in 1906 to attend the University of Pennsylvania; Charles W. Ramsdell then succeeded Barker as Corresponding Secretary and Treasurer. To Barker it seemed that the most important extracurricular work of Lester G. Bugbee was that which he did as secretary and treasurer of the Texas State Historical Association. In remembering these early years Barker wrote,

> It was the policy of the Association for many years to conceal its machinery of operation behind a screen of great names—mostly state

[37] Ibid., 11–12.
[38] *The Quarterly of the Texas State Historical Association*, I (April, 1898), 314.
[39] Ibid., V (July, 1901), 72.

political names—while the motive power was supplied by the staff of the history department of the University. Garrison was editor of the *Quarterly*, and more than once from his none too abundant means advanced money to pay for its printing. Bugbee, from even slenderer means, advanced money for labor and postage to solicit members by mail.[40]

In a review of the financial history of the Association Barker also recalled,

A review of early reports calls for mention of Bugbee's bookkeeping system: it was a combination of the primitive and (for that time) the ultra-modern. Daily transactions—receipts and expenditures—were recorded on cardboard slips about two inches square which he stuck on a spindle file; and membership payments were transferred from this file to 4" x 6" cards, spaced to take care of payments for twelve years. I inherited the system when I succeeded Bugbee as Treasurer in 1902, and Dr. Ramsdell took it over from me when I left the University on leave of absence in 1906. Sometime during his administration, which lasted until his death in 1942, Ramsdell bought a book and began keeping accounts in a bound volume.[41]

The inescapable conclusion to be derived from these facts is that during the formative period the success of the Texas State Historical Association and *The Quarterly* rested primarily on the energy and devotion of Garrison and Bugbee and Barker and Ramsdell. On Dr. Garrison's death in the early summer of 1910, Dr. Barker and E. W. Winkler edited the three remaining numbers of Volume XV of *The Quarterly*. In the following year Eugene C. Barker assumed the burden of editorship; a position which he retained for the next twenty-six years. During this period he not only edited the magazine, but he contributed to it article after article dealing with various phases of Texas history.

Long before Herbert E. Bolton departed Texas for California, he and Barker had discussed the possibility of expanding the scope of *The Quarterly* to cover scholarly articles not only from Texas but from the entire southwestern region of the United

---

40 Barker, *Essays*, 60.
41 Barker Papers, Speeches, undated.

States. Garrison's opinion of this development is not known. In June, 1911, Bolton wrote Barker:

The matter of re-organizing the Quarterly has been held in abeyance for some time. I am not sure now that my original suggestion, made while I was in Austin, is the best; namely, to continue the Quarterly as the organ of the Texas Association only, merely changing the name to the Southwest Historical Quarterly and electing the editorial board so as to have the Far Southwest represented. In this way the Quarterly would lose none of its support by the State Association, and the having of an editor in the Far Southwest would bring to it additional support. It deserves the wider influence which a broader title would help to give it. If you think it is a good plan, I would be willing to cooperate in any way, and to use my influence in extending or establishing, its circulation in this region. I am sure that I could bring it a good deal of support. . . . I should be willing to serve as co-joint editor with you or even as an associate editor (if it were to be considered desirable from the standpoint of Texas control).[42]

In complete agreement with Professor Bolton, Barker approached his executive council on the subject of enlarging the scope of *The Quarterly*, and on March 2, 1912, the council recommended that "the name of *The Quarterly* be changed to *The Southwestern Historical Quarterly*." Such an alteration, it was said, would permit as much "Texas material to be published as formerly" while "material on other portions of the Southwest" could be added. Professors Barker and Bolton were named as the editors of the publication.[43] The honest attempt of the editors to make the journal a regional historical review had great merit and resulted in a publication program which has long since been scuttled on the rocks of Texas provincialism.

During the two and one half decades that Eugene C. Barker edited *The Southwestern Historical Quarterly*, the arrangement worked out with Bolton in 1911 continued. During Barker and Bolton's editorship, contributors to *The Quarterly* included (in addition to the editors) Charles S. Chapman, Robert G. Cleland,

[42] Herbert E. Bolton to Barker, June 8, 1911.
[43] *The Quarterly of the Texas State Historical Association*, XV (April, 1912), 360.

William E. Dunn, Charles W. Hackett, Thomas Maitland Marshall, J. Fred Rippy, Charles W. Ramsdell, E. W. Winkler, William C. Binkley, John L. Waller, and C. C. Rister. It is of significance that during Barker's editorship the pages of *The Quarterly* were used for the publication of lengthy articles that frequently extended in serial form over several consecutive numbers of the magazine. Many of the articles of this nature were condensed versions of graduate theses which had been supervised by Barker and others at the University of Texas and elsewhere. At all times the level of scholarship remained high as the journal was directed toward a small reading public comprised for the most part of professional historians.

Another feature of Barker's directorship was that during the period from 1910 to 1937 the Texas State Historical Association was continually pressed for funds and membership. Barker once wrote that "translated into human emotion and viewed through the mist of tolerant memory the period was not too grim. There was always the strain of insecurity, with expenses treading on the heels of income." There was much talk of "turning the abundant patriotism of Texans into an endowment fund for the Association, but unfortunately those who readily perceived the usefulness of its work had no money to bestow and those who had the means lacked the interest."[44]

The many difficulties and problems facing Barker as director of the Association and editor of *The Quarterly* were summarized by "The Chief" in a frank letter to his friend, Samuel E. Asbury of College Station, Texas. Evidently Asbury had written a critical letter concerning the editorial policies of *The Quarterly* during the Barker era. Among other things, Barker had the following comments to make:

> You deplore the absence of articles on East Texas. Mr. R. C. Crane used to feel that I discriminated against West Texas. The truth of the matter is that there has been no planned policy of publication. In large measure, I published everything that came into my hands provided I myself could read it.—I mean provided it was written in intelligible form and provided it seemed to add fact or viewpoint to previous

[44] Barker Papers, Speeches (undated).

knowledge of the subject. I have solicited some articles, but not many. In the main I selected from the materials offered. Not infrequently I have published material that I thought of little value. Sometimes I did it because I had nothing else available; sometimes because it seemed desirable to gratify the writer or to please regional pride (or rather to placate a feeling that a region was being discriminated against) . . .

About the policy of electing officers of the Association: It is a fact that for many years I chose them. I did so because, apparently, nobody else would assume the responsibility. I shrank from the job, actually cringed with embarrassment every time I had to do it—and followed the line of least resistance by holding the same staff in office from year to year. That situation had some influence upon my decision to give up the editorship of the Quarterly. I simply felt that the direction of the Association was too completely a one-man affair. At the same time it was too laborious and time-consuming for me to divide the work and the responsibility. Therefore the proper and sensible thing seemed to be to get out from under and give others a chance to apply new (and I honestly believe) better methods—or methods that promise better development.[45]

Forced to the distasteful task of choosing the officers of the Association, pressed for time, and feeling that his direction was too much of a "one-man affair," Eugene C. Barker presented his resignation to the executive council of the Association at the Fortieth Annual Meeting on April 23–24, 1937. In a report of the business of the Association, *The Quarterly* announced that "Two meetings of the Council discussed plans for broadening the work of the Association . . . and accepted the resignation of Professor Eugene C. Barker as managing editor of *The Southwestern Historical Quarterly*."[46] Barker was succeeded by R. L. Biesele, Walter P. Webb, and Charles W. Hackett with Hackett as the "managing editor." At this time Walter P. Webb wrote that "Of the six million people in Texas fewer than five hundred individuals belong to the Texas Historical Association."[47]

[45] Barker to Samuel E. Asbury, February 4, 1938.
[46] "Affairs of the Association," *Southwestern Historical Quarterly*, XLI (July, 1937), 121.
[47] Walter P. Webb, "Historical Notes," *Southwestern Historical Quarterly*, XLI (October, 1937), 183.

While Barker attended the meetings of the national professional associations with some regularity, he "could never be called an association man." He was, however, a member of both the Mississippi Valley and the American historical associations. He served two terms on the Executive Council of the American Historical Association, 1915–1917 and 1938–1941; in addition, he served on one of its most important committees—the Historical Manuscripts Committee. With an interest in the Mississippi Valley Historical Association that coincided with its organization at Lincoln, Nebraska, on October 18, 1907, Barker was named to the first board of editors of the _Mississippi Valley Historical Review_ (along with Clarence V. Alvord, managing editor, Benjamin F. Shambaugh, Claude H. Van Tyne, Orin G. Libby, Archer B. Hulbert, James A. James, Walter L. Fleming, and Reuben G. Thwaites) at the Omaha meeting in May of 1913. During the year 1923–1924 Eugene C. Barker served as president of the organization.[48]

It was during this time that Barker's interest in both the Mississippi Valley Historical Association and the American Historical Association involved him as an interested spectator in the famous controversy among the members of the American Historical Association concerning the control of the organization by an "inner ring" of prominent American historians. As reported by E. D. Adams to Barker, Professor Dunbar Rowland launched the squabble at the Charleston, South Carolina, meeting of the Association in 1913 when he criticized the Executive Council and its control of the affairs of the Association. To be specific, Professor Rowland objected to "an inner circle control of the Association by the Executive Council, both as regards membership upon the Council, and editorial positions upon the _American Historical Review_, and to the methods followed in the election of officers in general." When J. Franklin Jameson, then the editor of the _Review_, seemed to defend the traditional and customary practices of the Association and Council, Rowland published a pamphlet titled _The Government of the American Historical Association_ in which he stated

---

[48] James L. Sellers, "The Semicentennial of the Mississippi Valley Historical Association," _The Mississippi Valley Historical Review_, XLIV (December, 1957), 502, 516.

(1) that the officers were not elected by ballot as the Constitution required but were chosen by the Executive Council, (2) that extreme power had been either lodged in or usurped by the Council, (3) that widespread discontent existed because of the "arbitrary and unconstitutional methods" employed by the Council, and (4) that ballots should be sent to members of the Association "some months before the meetings" in order that the membership might vote. Rowland also pointed out that "new blood has never been permitted in the Council in sufficient quantity as to affect the action of the Council or to alter the control of the 'inner circle.' "[49]

Apparently Dr. Rowland's point of view was shared by a substantial portion of the membership of the American Historical Association. In February, 1914, John H. Latane of Johns Hopkins University wrote an article for *The Nation* in which he expressed agreement with Rowland's position and described the entire matter as "an objection to the fact that the Association is run by a small clique or ring which controls the elections and divides the honors." It seemed to Latane that the honors of the Association excepting the positions of secretary-treasurer and managing editor of the *Review*, ought to be "passed around" among the membership. According to E. D. Adams, "very little defense has yet been expressed by any former member of the Executive Council."[50] At the 1914 meeting of the Association a committee of nine members was appointed to study and report on matters concerning the constitution, organization, and procedure of the Association and to examine the relationship between the Association and the *Review*. In due time this committee reported, and, as a result, the present system of mail ballots for election of members of the Executive Council and the nominating committee was adopted. In the meantime, however, C. W. Alvord, the editor of the *Mississippi Valley Historical Review*, was forced to seek the advice of his editorial board because,

[49] The information included in this paragraph is based on a rather lengthy letter from E. D. Adams to Barker, March 23, 1915, in the Barker Papers, Letters, 1899–1956.

[50] Ibid.

In a recent letter addressed to "All Reformers in the American Historical Association," Dunbar Rowland has signed himself as president of the
Mississippi Valley Historical Association and has placed himself squarely on the side of the reform movement led by Bancroft, Latane, and
himself. This communication appears, therefore, to have the sanction
of our own Association; but neither he nor anyone else has the power
to commit the men interested in western history. For example, the
members of the Board of editors of the Review are not united on the
reform issue that has arisen in the American Historical Association.
. . . Should there be an editorial in the December number of the Mississippi Valley Historical Review calling attention to the act of the
president of the Association, and pointing out that whatever his private
opinions may be he was not authorized to assume they were those of
his fellow members of the Mississippi Valley Historical Association.[51]

Refusing to be drawn into a major role in the conflict, Barker
replied to Alvord's query by expressing the belief "that Rowland
himself should print a brief note in the next number of the Review, explaining that he had no intention of implying that he
spoke for the Association . . ."[52]

Perhaps it may appear to the reader that Dr. Barker was rather
indifferent to the controversy that seemed so important to his colleagues in the two national professional organizations. If he was,
his lack of interest was due in part to the vast distances that separated him from the geographical center of the disturbance, and,
also, to the fact that more important matters were close at hand—
1915 saw the inception of the attack upon the financial structure,
the tenure, and the academic freedom of the University of
Texas by the governor of the state. The momentous events that
were to follow rank among the bitterest in the annals of Texas
politics and have been appropriately described by local historians
as "Ferguson's war on the University of Texas."

James E. Ferguson was nominated governor of Texas in the
Democratic party primary of 1914, elected to the office in November, and inaugurated on January 19, 1915. At the time he an-

51 C. W. Alvord to Barker, October 1, 1915.
52 Barker to C. W. Alvord, October 8, 1915.

nounced his candidacy, Ferguson was hardly known outside Bell County, where he had been a banker at Temple, Texas, for many years. He appeared as the champion of the downtrodden farmers, demanding a maximum rent law to protect the tenant farmer against landlords, a state warehouse system, and the prohibition of combinations to fix the prices of farm products. Ferguson's campaign of 1914 was the most spectacular of the twentieth century and he received the largest vote ever given a candidate in the primary election. It is possible that his margin of victory gave the new Governor a false sense of power. In office, he was soon to prove that he was petty, vindictive, and arbitrary. Only his relations with the administration and faculty of the University will be considered here, but this phase of the Governor's administration turned out to be a long and complicated affair—an affair that would threaten the destruction of the University and lead directly to the impeachment of Governor Ferguson.

When James E. Ferguson became governor of Texas, Dr. W. J. Battle, the scholarly professor of Greek, was serving as acting president of the University. Dr. Battle had replaced Sidney E. Mezes, one of the most popular presidents ever to serve the institution. Mezes had resigned a few months earlier. Three vacancies existed on the Board of Regents as the result of expired terms and Ferguson proceeded to fill these by appointing (with the consent of the Senate) Dr. S. J. Jones, Rabbi M. Faber, and Dr. G. S. Mc-Reynolds. On the surface, the Ferguson-University battle originated from a misunderstanding between the Governor and President Battle over the legislative appropriations for the University. It seems that the Thirty-Fourth Legislature made liberal appropriations for the University and Governor Ferguson signed the bill without change. The bill was itemized as previous bills had been and conflicting opinions arose when the comptroller expressed the belief that every item—several hundred of them— should be entered upon his books. Since such an itemization would interfere with "the changes and substitutions" that were a traditional part of the flexibility of University funds, President Battle requested that the comptroller enter the appropriation in his books as a lump sum. Such a procedure had been the custom in the past and the bill in question had provided that the appropriations were made "with such changes and substitutions within the total . . . for the University as the Regents may find necessary." Since previous bill had been itemized by the Legislature and lumped by the comptroller, Battle felt justified in making his request. To be more certain of this legal position, Battle requested an interpretation of the law from the attorney general. The attorney general ruled that the itemization might be lumped and expended at the discretion of the Regents. A few days later, on August 15, 1915, Governor Ferguson wrote to the Regents, and gave to the newspapers, a letter denouncing W. J. Battle as guilty of "sharp practice in a most culpable degree, . . . unworthy of the position which he holds," and declaring that he "should not be allowed in any manner to expend any of the money provided by the Legislature for the maintenance of the University." The war had commenced.[53]

In the meantime Eugene C. Barker became involved in an argument with Governor Ferguson concerning the proper qualifications of the state librarian. The Texas State Library and Historical Commission had been established by the legislature in

---

[53] [Eugene C. Barker], *Ferguson's War on the University of Texas, A Chronological Outline, January 12, 1915, to July 31, 1917, Inclusive,* Published by the Ex-Students Association of the University of Texas (hereafter cited as [Barker], *Ferguson's War on the University*). In a handwritten note in the copy of this remarkable pamphlet that is housed in the Texas Collection of the Barker Texas History Center at the University, Professor Barker explains his editorship as follows: "A Meeting of the Faculty appointed a committee to prepare for the minutes a record of Governor Ferguson's attacks on the University. As I remember (May, 1951) Professor Butte of the Law Faculty was Chairman. I was a member, and no doubt there were other members. Butte never seemed interested. I wrote this summary, and I believe it was inserted in the Minutes, but not as a committee report. I gave a copy of the manuscript to Mr. Will Hogg when he came to Austin to organize his movement for the Ferguson impeachment. The legislature had been called to meet a few days later and he had the article printed and placed a copy on the desk of each member of the legislature when it met. The printing was done by the A. C. Baldwin Company. Mr. Baldwin put a large portion of his staff to work on it and my recollection is that 5000 copies were done in 24 hours to be ready for the organization of the legislature."

1909 to supervise the Texas State Library. The Commission was originally composed of three members appointed by the governor and two ex officio members—the state superintendent of public instruction and the chairman of the School of History at the University of Texas. With Dr. Garrison's death in 1910, Barker automatically became a member of the Commission and shortly afterward he was elected chairman. Then, as now, the Commission was empowered, among other things, to control and administer the Texas State Library, to collect materials relating to the history of Texas and adjoining states, to publish manuscript archives, and to mark historic sites and houses.

Before Ferguson entered the governor's office he let it be known that he intended to replace E. W. Winkler, the state librarian, with A. F. Cunningham, a political friend and Presbyterian minister from Temple. It will be remembered that Winkler and Barker had been classmates on the campus of the University of Texas during the late 1890's; their friendship had deepened with the passing years and Barker was distressed that his friend might possibly be sacrificed to the exigencies of state politics. When the wishes of the Governor became known to Barker, he wrote Hugh M. Fitzgerald the following note:

It was the idea of the sponsors of the law creating the Library and Historical Commission that it should be removed from political patronage. It was for that reason that two members were designated by the statute, leaving the Governor the appointment of only three members. Few businessmen have any appreciation of the varied duties of a librarian. That is not to their discredit. It is just a fact. They don't need libraries, and so have no reason to become acquainted with them. I am sure that the Governor would look at the matter in quite a different way, if he realized the really important development of the library which he will be stopping by putting an inexperienced man in charge.[54]

Feeling that he was being coerced by the Governor, Barker agreed to an early meeting of the Library and Historical Commission. After a luncheon conversation with Dr. Alex Dienst of Temple, Barker also tactfully asked the Governor for permission

[54] Barker to H. N. Fitzgerald, February 15, 1913.

to write a letter to Cunningham to outline the qualifications for
the state librarian. Ferguson apparently had no objection to this
request, but the over-zealous Barker made the letter too strong.
He wrote Cunningham that "the object of this letter is to put
before you some of the facts and considerations concerning the
Office of State Librarian. I am writing it, frankly, in the hope of
dissuading you from accepting the position." Barker then went on
to inform Cunningham that a candidate for the position should be
a qualified historian with substantial knowledge of "general history and particularly state history." In addition, he should possess
a thorough knowledge of bibliography; he should be a qualified
editor; and he must, "if he is to fill the place efficiently, know
Spanish." Barker concluded with the statement that "No one but
a practical librarian has any conception of the complex duties of
such a position" and reminded the applicant that the law required
that the state librarian be "an experienced librarian." Stating that
"I do not know whether you possess these qualifications," Barker
reminded Cunningham, "If you do not, it would be a violation of
the law for the Commission to elect you."[55] When Barker mailed
the letter to Cunningham a carbon copy was sent to the Governor's office. On the following day Barker received Ferguson's
reply; it read:

> I am in receipt of your favor of the 19th, enclosing a copy of the let-
> ter you are writing for the purpose of intimidating Rev. A. F. Cunning-
> ham from accepting the place of Librarian.
>
> Just to keep the record straight, I want to say that I only consented
> for you to write Mr. Cunningham the legal qualifications for Librarian.
> I regard your letter to him an insult to him and me both. As you have
> entered into a long discussion of politics in the letter, I hope that you
> will not hereafter complain if your wishes are not carried out.[56]

With the candid observation that he had not noticed that his
wishes "had ever been regarded before," Eugene Barker joined
W. J. Battle in the professorial-occupied doghouse of the Governor of Texas. They were soon to be joined by others.

[55] Barker to A. F. Cunningham, February 19, 1915.
[56] James E. Ferguson to Barker, February 20, 1915.

Barker wrote a letter to the Governor explaining that he had "not the remotest thought of insulting" either Ferguson or Cunningham and expressed regret that "you have taken my letter as an insult."[57] On February 20, 1915, the Library and Historical Commission met at Austin. After a stormy session in which the names of E. W. Winkler and A. F. Cunningham were placed in nomination, the Commission found itself hopelessly deadlocked and adjourned without a decision. At the next meeting, on March 3, Dr. Barker found himself in a minority; Cunningham was elected state librarian and Barker submitted his resignation as chairman of the Commission. On the following day, Barker wrote Thomas M. Marshall:

Yesterday the Library and Historical Commission, which is an organization created by law some six years ago, met to elect a state librarian. The governor, who is as devoid of general education as he is of any historical appreciation, insisted on the election of a friend of his, a Presbyterian preacher, who had written a defense of the governor during the heat of the last campaign when the Governor (then a candidate) was being roasted by the other pulpit barnacles of the state. The man is more than usually ignorant and self satisfied, but since the Governor had the appointment of three members of a board of five, the man was elected.[58]

In a letter to Dr. Alex Dienst of Temple, Barker admitted: "I realize my inability to fathom the psychology of the political mind, and the only thing to do is to keep quiet hereafter."[59]

As the days passed the affairs of the University fell more and more under the sinister shadow of Texas politics. On October 26, 1915, Acting President W. J. Battle addressed a letter to the Board of Regents asking them not to consider him in the election of a University president. As a result, the Board did not elect Battle but continued him as acting president until April, 1916, when the Regents, without consulting the Governor, chose Dr. R. E. Vinson president of the University. Ferguson thought that he should have been consulted on the matter and soon revealed his anger.

[57] Barker to Ferguson, February 22, 1915.
[58] Barker to Thomas M. Marshall, March 4, 1915.
[59] Barker to Dienst, March 12, 1915, Barker Papers.

A short time later, Dr. Vinson, accompanied by Major George W. Littlefield, called on the Governor. Out of a clear sky, Ferguson expressed his dislike for Vinson and demanded that six members of the faculty be released from their positions without reason. With an arrogance all too typical of the Texas power structure, Ferguson explained to a member of the Board of Regents that "I am the Governor of Texas; I don't have to give reasons."[60] On September 5, 1916, after a summer of comparative calm, President Vinson, knowing that the Governor had not changed his mind concerning the demand for the dismissal of the faculty members, wrote to Ferguson to ask upon what grounds these men should be discharged. The Governor replied that he wished to make no charges against any of them but that he did desire the release of the six he had named earlier. In the meantime, Rabbi M. Faber, apparently disgusted with this new show of political force, had become reluctant to cooperate with the Governor and his plan. On September 11 Ferguson demanded Faber's resignation "unless I may be assured of your full and complete cooperation." On September 20 Faber replied,

I never dreamed that such an appointment has any political significance; nor that the appointee is expected to be a mere marionette to move and act as and when the chief executive pushes the button or pulls the string. . . . I cannot give you the assurance of my "full and complete cooperation" with your avowed plans concerning the internal affairs of the University of Texas without a thorough investigation into the merits of each individual case. I cannot pledge myself to follow the arbitrary will of any person, no matter how high and exalted, without being convinced of the justice of his demands. In my humble opinion, such action would disorganize and disrupt the University, the just pride of the people of Texas. It would produce untold harm to the cause of higher education and practically destroy the labors of a generation to bring up the University of Texas to the high rank it now occupies among the universities of the land. With all due respect to you, my dear Governor, I do not concede to you the right or the authority to interfere in the internal management of the University of Texas.[61]

60 [Barker], *Ferguson's War on the University*, 8.
61 Ibid.

On November 21, 1916, Rabbi Faber resigned from the Board of Regents. He was later replaced by W. R. Brents, a banker from Sherman, Texas. Prior to Faber's resignation, however, the Regents investigated Ferguson's charges of political activity, peculation, fraud, and outright theft against members of the University faculty. The investigation resulted in the acquittal of the accused faculty members, and the Board refused to dismiss them.

In the campaign of 1916 the people of Texas re-elected James E. Ferguson to the office of governor, and the battle for control of the University continued with increased intensity. Eugene C. Barker and his faculty colleagues on the forty acres kept a close watch as the Legislature assembled for its regular session of 1917. Several resolutions were introduced in the House requesting investigations of the Governor. The faculty of the University petitioned for a "full and complete investigation" of University affairs. When Representative Davis of Van Zandt County offered a resolution that looked forward to the impeachment of the Governor, Ferguson charged the "State University influence" with the responsibility for the attack on him and remarked to Davis that "T. N. Jones and the State University have conspired through you as a medium to affect [sic] my ruin. Well, the bridle is off. We are going to see whether the State University can maintain a lobby around this legislature and come here and try to ruin a public official . . ." Ferguson went on, "this is a fight of the State University on a Governor of Texas because he is not a college graduate and refuses to bow to their will."[62]

Thoroughly alarmed over the embarrassing situation confronting the University, Dr. Barker wrote W. E. Lingelbach,

Our situation here seems to be growing rather more critical. The Governor is entirely without conscience or scruple. He seems to have deceived the political wise men of the University into believing that he was going to let up so that since the investigation by the Regents nothing has been done until three or four days ago. Now it became pretty evident that his intention has been to keep the thing quiet until after the legislature adjourns and then carry out his intention of remov-

[62] Ibid., 19.

ing six or eight men through his control of the Board of Regents. Four new members of the Board are now before the Senate for confirmation, and these four with the henchmen that he already has on the Board would give him absolute control. We are now begging for a thorough investigation by the legislature and every influence that the University can control are insisting on an investigation while the governor's friends are trying to prevent the investigation.[63]

Three months later, Barker, obviously disturbed, wrote to a colleague at Harvard:

If you still read Texas newspapers, you know something of the confusion which the University has been in for the last year and a half. One irritation falls on the heels of another so fast that we are unable to settle down and do consistent work on anything. Your visit to Austin last summer no doubt put you in touch with the earlier stages of the controversy between Governor Ferguson and Dr. Battle. The quarrel—which was a one-sided one because Battle barely opened his mouth to defend himself—became acute in September when the Governor made most violent charges not only against Battle but against Mather, Lomax, Ellis, and several other members of the faculty. There was an investigation before the Board of Regents and all were acquitted, but the Governor announced that he would be heard from later, and, as you perhaps know, the complexion of the Board of Regents has now been changed very materially. I am not at all sure that the new board would have obeyed the Governor's orders and dismissed Battle, but we had no opportunity to find out because Battle resigned about a month ago to accept a place in the University of Cincinnati. I don't blame him for going.

After explaining that at the April 24, 1917, meeting of the Board of Regents, the president of the Board suggested a resolution dismissing from the service of the University all Germans who had not become naturalized citizens of America, and a resolution "dismissing all aliens" was adopted, Barker continued: "On the heels of this some old fool in the legislature is raising a row because University professors draw two salaries in the summer time, the second one for teaching in the summer school. My own im-

---

[63] Barker to W. E. Lingelbach, February 12, 1917.

pression is that Texas is politically about two decades behind Kansas of 'Sockless Jerry.' "[64]

In the beginning of the conflict, Governor Ferguson had named A. Caswell Ellis, John A. Lomax, C. S. Potts, W. T. Mather, and W. J. Battle as the University faculty members who must be removed from their positions. At a later date the Governor added W. H. Mayes, R. E. Cofer, George C. Butte, R. H. Griffith, and, of course, Dr. Vinson to the list.[65] Had the Governor been completely successful in his removal campaign, other dismissals would have probably followed. It was charged that A. Caswell Ellis, a professor of education, encouraged extravagance in the extension service; that John A. Lomax, the secretary to the University, had duties "confined to visiting the alumni"; that W. H. Mayes, of the School of Journalism, owned a Brownwood newspaper and drew a state salary "to skin Fergusons [sic] back from one end of the state to another"; and that R. E. Cofer, a professor of law, attended the Travis County political convention and helped send an anti-Ferguson delegation to the state convention. No specific charges were ever made against the others; apparently Ferguson simply disliked them.[66] After a bitter regular session of the Legislature that featured charges and countercharges, the appointments of J. W. Butler, W. P. Allen, and C. E. Kelley as new members of the Board of Regents were confirmed by the Senate on the eve of adjournment. In the subsequent special session, no controversy arose concerning the University. Both houses of the Legislature passed the University budget practically without change; the appropriations were minutely itemized in accord with the wishes of the Governor.

The crisis came when the morning papers of May 27, 1917, announced that Governor Ferguson had summoned the Board of Regents to meet in his office on the following morning. The rumor

[64] Barker to F. J. Dohmen, May 9, 1917.

[65] [Barker], Ferguson's War on the University; J. Evetts Haley, George W. Littlefield, 228; Ralph Steen, "Ferguson's War on the University of Texas," Southwestern Social Science Quarterly, XXXV (March, 1955), 356–362.

[66] Haley, George W. Littlefield, 228–229.

quickly spread about Austin that the Governor intended to ask the Regents to remove the faculty members as previously requested and to bar fraternities from the University campus. If the Regents refused to obey the Governor's command, the newspaper press intimated, Ferguson planned to veto the University appropriation. During the early evening of Sunday, May 27, nearly a hundred members of the University faculty assembled at the University YMCA to resolve that "the Regents should be a free and autonomous board" and to express the conviction that the University "would suffer far less harm by closing for two years than by keeping open at the expense of its independence and the independence of the Regents."[67] Eugene Barker remembered that "On May 27 a thunderbolt fell from a clear sky."

On the following morning, May 28, the students of the University held a mass meeting, and at the close of the meeting they marched in a parade through the streets of Austin and around and through the State Capitol carrying banners inscribed: "Kaiserism is a menace abroad and Kaiserism is a menace at home." The marching students broke up the conference between the Governor and his Regents at the very point where Ferguson began to read his recommendations pertaining to the dismissal of Dr. Vinson and the other faculty members and suggesting remedies for certain irregularities in University management. The timing of the student marchers was perfect and, needless to say, the Governor was furious. The meeting of the Regents was adjourned to the Regents' Room in the Library of the University so that an investigation could be held "to fix the responsibility of the student parade." The conclusion appears to have been that it was strictly a student idea without faculty inspiration but the name of R. H. Griffith of the English Department was added to Ferguson's list of undesirables because Griffith apparently led the marching students in singing "The Eyes of Texas." The Regents adjourned to meet at Galveston on May 31.[68]

In the short interval between May 28 and May 31, changes were

[67] [Barker], *Ferguson's War on the University*, 22 ff.
[68] Ibid.

made necessary in the composition of the Board of Regents when J. W. Butler, a banker of Clifton, and Dr. S. J. Jones resigned from the Board rather than be parties to the Ferguson plan. The Governor appointed J. M. Mathis of Brenham and Dr. J. P. Tucker of Galveston as their successors. Mathis was quoted as saying that he would "do his duty." It was quite apparent that drastic measures would be necessary to head off the Governor. On the afternoon of May 31, Travis County Attorney J. W. Hornsby was granted a restraining order by the Twenty-Sixth District Court enjoining Dr. Tucker from taking his seat on the Board of Regents on grounds that the Governor had no constitutional authority to remove a regent without cause established by trial. Several hours later the same court granted an injunction to John A. Lomax enjoining Regents McReynolds, Fly, Kelley, and Mathis from dismissing Lomax, President Vinson, or other members of the faculty on grounds that these four Regents had "conspired with the governor to dismiss certain members of the faculty." Many years later John A. Lomax could remember that "the suit to enjoin the Regents was brought in my name while I was out of Austin, nor do I know until this day who forged my name to the petition instituting this suit. I think that I would like to say publicly that someone did forge my signature."[69] Hobbled by injunctions, the Board of Regents adjourned to meet in Austin on June 11.

The big blow was soon to fall. On the evening of June 2, 1917, news spread through Austin that Governor Ferguson had carried out his threat and had vetoed the entire University appropriation. To Eugene Barker the Governor's action meant the "total destruction of the University of Texas." The veto message was carried in the newspapers of the state on June 3. Two days later Regents George W. Littlefield and W. P. Allen called on Dr. Vinson to suggest that if he and Lomax would resign the Governor would withdraw the veto in part and allow the University an appropriation of one million dollars for the next biennium. Lomax and Vinson refused to comply with such a request and a few

[69] John A. Lomax to Barker, January 22, 1940.

hours later (June 5) it was announced that the Governor's veto had been filed with the secretary of state and had therefore become final.[70]

During the dark days of June and July, 1917, Eugene C. Barker found himself drawn into the center of the Ferguson controversy. After Allen and Littlefield had called on Dr. Vinson on June 5 to seek a compromise, Barker conferred with his president. On the following morning the embattled University president received the following note of advice and encouragement: "Dr. Vinson— I'm afraid I forgot to say, *Don't you resign. Don't compromise.* Barker."[71] Four days later, on June 9, Ex-Governor Joseph D. Sayers presided over a mass meeting of the Ex-Students Association held in Austin to protest Ferguson's domination of University affairs. Barker attended the meeting; B. F. Pittenger, Frederic Duncalf, C. S. Potts, and Dr. Vinson were the only other faculty members present.[72] Judge Joseph C. Hutcheson of the United States Court of Appeals, Fifth Judicial District, remembers that,

the outstanding thing about Eugene in the Ferguson matter, as in all other matters of importance in his life, was that, instead of twittering and squeaking like a frightened bird as every other member of the faculty was doing, he not only stood out strongly against Ferguson but at one time made a public speech against him at a rally in Austin. . . . When I speak of Eugene's courage it was not of the kind exhibited by a bull on a railroad track springing from ignorance. It was the kind of which Socrates speaks springing from and based on knowledge and preparation.[73]

It seems that Barker's greatest concern during these difficult days was for the future of the University professors, including himself, who were about to be dismissed by the Governor. He expressed this concern in a letter to D. C. Munro of the University of Wisconsin, and Munro replied:

[70] [Barker], *Ferguson's War on the University,* 24.

[71] Barker to R. E. Vinson, June 6, 1917, R. E. Vinson Papers, Archives, University of Texas Library.

[72] Austin *American,* June 10, 1917, p. 1.

[73] Judge Joseph C. Hutcheson, Jr., to W. C. P., November 12, 1958.

I am extremely sorry to learn of the Governor's action. I hope that the regents will not give in, but I regret that this action should come just at this time. In any normal time, it would be easy to arrange some emergency positions that would be fitting for your better men to accept. Just at present, however, from what I hear from the various institutions, there seems to be little prospect of being able to secure such action.[74]

Two days after Ferguson's veto of the University appropriation, Barker wrote Herman V. Ames of the University of Pennsylvania to explain the turmoil in Texas and to ask Ames to keep him in mind as a possible unemployed historian. Ames replied:

Your letter came as a great surprise to me as I had not chanced to hear of recent developments in regard to the Governor and the University. The papers which you sent came yesterday and I read the same with great interest. Accordingly I do not wonder at the intensity of your feeling and the attitude of your faculty generally. Apparently you have a very stubborn man to deal with. . . . I do not believe that your personal fortunes will seriously suffer in the long run for your work is too well known to permit of your being left without a position more than temporarily. At any rate we should be glad to remember you if we hear anything of interest.[75]

As the Ferguson-University controversy overshadowed the excitement of the first week of World War I, Governor Ferguson toured West Texas to inspect sites for the proposed West Texas A. and M. college. In all of his many speeches he continued to villify "the University crowd" at Austin. At Kerrville, on June 10, the Governor told his listeners: "I have found far more disloyalty in the State University at Austin than among the Germans or the people of any other nationality."[76] Two days later, at Abilene, he declared that the University had attacked him because of his support of rural schools; he denied that he was against higher education and remarked that in his official career he had "found more corruption in the affairs of the University of Texas than in

74 D. C. Munro to Barker, June 11, 1917.

75 Herman V. Ames to Barker, June 9, 1917.

76 [Barker], *Ferguson's War on the University*, contains a chronological summary of statements made on Ferguson's West Texas tour, June 10–18, 1917.

all of the other departments of the state government." Other charges made by the Governor in his Abilene speech were that the expense accounts of members of the faculty were such as would cause the discharge of a section hand; that it took a teacher in the University three years to learn that wool would not grow on an armadillo's back; that the student body of the school was divided into fraternities which lived in "palatial houses" and poor boys, called "barbarians," who ate at "soup houses"; that the fraternity men were snobs and thought themselves "little tin Jesuses with little tin wings"; and that there was "no lie so black that these fellows [the University faculty] would not tell."[77] At Haskell, on June 13, Ferguson repeated the charge of disloyalty and added the new charge of *"high treason against the governor of Texas."*[78] At Lubbock, a few days later, he referred to the members of the faculty of the University as day dreamers, butterfly chasers, educated fools, and two-bit thieves. Two weeks later, on July 13, Ferguson addressed the Old Settlers' picnic at Valley Mills. It was here that the Governor told his audience that it was too much for the fathers and mothers of Texas to pay for "tailor-made clothes, ten dollar bouquets, automobiles, silk stockings, golf balls and highballs, poker chips, fraternity dues, frat pins, and mandolins, and a hundred other foolish and extravagant things which the rich crowd says is necessary to carry on this Belshazzar revel down at the State University. I say that not only are too many people going hog wild over higher education but that some people have become plain damn fools over the idea that we have to have an army of educated fools to run the government."[79]

While Jim Ferguson spoke at Valley Mills and Will Hogg looked forward to impeachment proceedings, the hand-picked Board of Regents of the University of Texas assembled at Galveston on July 12 to carry out the wishes of the chief executive.

---

[77] Steen, "Ferguson's War on the University of Texas"; [Barker], *Ferguson's War on the University.*

[78] Dallas *News*, July 14, 1917.

[79] Steen, "Ferguson's War on the University of Texas"; [Barker], *Ferguson's War on the University.*

On the following day, the Regents dismissed from the University faculty the following scholars and teachers: Lindley Miller Keasbey, professor of institutional history; W. T. Mather, professor of physics; W. H. Mayes, chairman of the School of Journalism; R. E. Cofer and George C. Butte, professors of law; A. Caswell Ellis, professor of education; and John A. Lomax, secretary to the University. Since W. J. Battle and C. S. Potts had already resigned, they were not listed among those dismissed. It is interesting to note that the motions for dismissal were made by Major George W. Littlefield, the self-styled friend of the University, and that Regents Littlefield, Love, Kelley, and Mathis (occasionally joined by Chairman W. P. Allen) were for dismissal, while Regents Brents, Cook, and Jones voted against the dismissal resolutions.[80]

Weeks before the Governor mounted the speaker's platform under the elm trees at Valley Mills, a reaction had set in against him that would eventually result in the impeachment proceedings of August, 1917. Realizing that the power of Fergusonism in Texas must be curtailed or the University of Texas would be destroyed, the ex-students of the University began to organize a campaign against Governor Ferguson as early as June 9, 1917. The impeachment of the Governor as a possible remedy was first publicly mentioned at the Dallas mass meeting on June 16 when Chester H. Terrell offered a resolution urging the Legislature to assemble for the purpose of bringing impeachment charges against Ferguson. Although the Terrell resolution was voted down, it reveals the thought of some of the members of the ex-student group. A few days later, Will C. Hogg also suggested impeachment as a solution to the problem. It is difficult to exaggerate the significance of the role of Will Hogg in the Ferguson controversy; only those who were close to him knew the full scope of his efforts. In his short biography of Hogg, John A. Lomax has written: "The University lay stricken and helpless until Will Hogg came to Austin, where, leasing a floor of the Driskill Hotel, he spent a long hot summer. He and Chester H. Terrell, his able

[80] Austin *American*, July 14, 1917, p. 1.

classmate of San Antonio, declared ruthless war on 'Farmer Jim.' No Governor could 'put his putrid paw of politics on the University of Texas.' "[81] Writing in appreciation of Hogg's efforts, Dr. Barker said: "His conduct in the series of investigations which disclosed the essential baselessness of the Governor's charge is a matter of record. His unofficial agency in the subsequent impeachment, conviction, and removal of the governor from office cannot be wholly apprehended or appraised, because nobody but Mr. Hogg knew, even at the time, the full scope of his powerful activities and influences."[82] The extent of Hogg's feeling in this matter was illustrated by a statement following Ferguson's Valley Mills speech; Hogg said:

To call our thimblerigging, swashbuckling, swaggering Governor a common garden liar would be the grossest flattery. . . . How far this cheerful and constructive autocrat will be able to travel the rocky road of his mad career is measured entirely by the forebearance and apathy of the best citizenship of the State. . . . Farmer Jim is a farce, and my prediction is that he is riding to the biggest fall, personally, and politically, in the short and simple annals of the misguided politicians of Texas.[83]

Hundreds of ex-students of the University throughout the state assisted Hogg in his anti-Ferguson crusade. The central core of opposition, centering about the Driskill Hotel in Austin, included, besides Hogg, John W. Brady, Dudley K. Woodward, Chester H. Terrell, Leon Green, Joseph C. Hutcheson, Jr., and Eugene C. Barker. Dr. Barker, always willing to fight for his beliefs, spent the last few days of July, 1917, gathering the information for his pamphlet titled *Ferguson's War on the University of Texas*. This concise and accurate account, so often cited in this narrative, was completed and passed on to Will Hogg for publication. As noted previously, it was published in haste by the A. C. Baldwin Company of Austin and distributed to the members of the Legislature as they organized for the Ferguson impeachment. Barker's work

[81] John A. Lomax, *Will Hogg, Texan*, 17.

[82] Barker, *Essays*, 73.

[83] *Will C. Hogg, An Interview*, 1–3; Lomax, *Will Hogg, Texan*, 18.

consisted of a chronological outline of the entire Ferguson controversy with the author's comments included in bold-face type as answers to the Ferguson charges. In brief, Barker dismissed the fraternities as insignificant, pointed out that the University was "not composed of rich men's sons and daughters," and emphasized the following points:

Every friend of the University—and this certainly includes the faculty, students, and ninety-nine per cent of the ex-students—favors most liberal support of city, town, and rural schools. Aside from an enlightened desire for the general spread of education, they perceive, much more closely than the Governor can possibly do, that the highest development of the University can come only through the general diffusion of high school education.

Note that no one could object to the Governor's appointing his friends regents, provided they are qualified for the office; but surely no one could believe that a man is fitted for that office merely because he is Governor Ferguson's friend.

As to President Vinson: The President of the University does not teach. No president of the University has ever taught classes. His alleged deficiency in this respect, therefore, even if it were a fact, which it is not, would have little bearing on his efficiency as president of the University. Concerning his lack of education it is hardly necessary to speak. No one who knows him or who has ever heard him speak, has any doubt on this point. The charge that he mismanaged the Austin Theological Seminary and left it in a bankrupt condition is a gratuitous distortion of fact. . . . He is a Presbyterian preacher. During the term of his presidency he has preached six sermons. At the time when the Governor declared that he had preached 186 sermons, he had really preached only five. Far from arousing the antagonism of other denominations President Vinson has been specifically and emphatically endorsed by the principal denominations. Some of his most earnest and able defenders are Catholics. . . . President Vinson is emphatically *an educated Christian gentleman*. . . .

Faculty leaves of absence: The Board of Regents which have controlled the University for the last thirty-four years have at times granted leaves of absence to members of the faculty for a few months, and in some instances for a year, and have allowed them to draw a part of their salaries while on leave. This is a matter of common practice in all first-class universities. Some institutions compel their members to take

one years leave every seven years and pay them full salaries while absent. They believe that the increased efficiency gained by fresh study
is a profitable return on the investment. If this is illegal and unconstitutional in Texas, it should be stopped, but the issue has never been
raised in the past. . . .

As to the professors who do less than fifteen hours work a week: It
is probably true that very few professors or instructors do more than
fifteen hours a week of actual class teaching. The most burdensome
part of a teacher's work, however, is not in the class room but in reading papers, directing the work of individual students, serving on committees, looking after the details of administration in his department,
and keeping up with educational progress in his special field. Counting
this, very few professors and instructors work less than ten hours a day.
To consider only the hours spent in the classroom is as unfair as to
declare that a lawyer is working only while in the court room, or a
doctor while he is visiting a patient.[84]

Following the Galveston meeting of the Board of Regents, the
anti-Ferguson forces moved to destroy the power and influence of
the Governor of Texas. On July 23, Speaker F. O. Fuller of Houston called the House of Representatives to meet at Austin on
August 1 to consider impeachment charges against James E.
Ferguson. Governor Ferguson gave his consent by issuing the
call for a special session. Four days later (July 27) the Governor
was indicted by a Travis County grand jury. On August 24, 1917,
the House of Representatives, after an investigation that extended
over four weeks, voted twenty-one articles of impeachment
against the Governor—charges fifteen through nineteen touched
the University by asserting that the University is expressly established by the Constitution and that in seeking to destroy it by
vetoing the entire appropriation the Governor violated the Constitution, that the Governor had sought to set aside the Constitution and the law which vested the administration of the University
in the Board of Regents, that he had sought to remove members
of the Board without due cause, that his villification of the faculty
amounted to conduct unbecoming to a governor of the state, and
that he had sought to influence the vote of a member of the

---

[84] [Barker], *Ferguson's War on the University of Texas.*

Board by remitting a bail bond of $5,000 which the regent would otherwise have had to pay to the state.

On receipt of these charges, the Senate resolved to convene as a court of impeachment on August 29 to hear the evidence and give judgment. The trial continued until September 22, when the Senate voted to sustain ten of the charges made by the House. On motion of Senator Bailey it was then resolved to pronounce the formal judgment of the Court of Impeachment at 12 o'clock, Tuesday, September 25. In the meantime the judgment was prepared by the Senate's Committee on Civil Jurisprudence. In due time this committee presented a majority and a minority report. The majority report recommended removal from office and disqualification from holding any office or position of public trust in the future. The minority report sought to punish simply by removal from office. After defeat of the minority report, the majority report was adopted by a vote of 25 to 3, and James E. Ferguson was removed from office.

Eugene Barker's indignation over the whole sordid Ferguson episode is probably best revealed in a letter to Dr. Alex Dienst of Temple; at the close of the letter, Barker added the postscript: "I merely wish to say that if your friend is not dead, he ought to be and I wish he were." Dienst has noted in the margin that "this reference is to Governor James E. Ferguson."[85] A few days later, Barker answered a Dienst query with the remark, "I suppose my postscript was more than half serious, but I am not going to let that person's memory worry me very much. If the decent people of Texas can't prevent that sort of vermin from feeding on the State I shall get out; but I am making no preparations yet."[86] After Ferguson defied the impeachment order and announced as a candidate for governor against Will Hobby in 1918, Barker wrote William E. Dunn, who was then in Veracruz, Mexico, in search of archival material:

You may be interested in some of our political affairs. The special session of the legislature, which adjourned about a month ago, has passed

[85] Barker to Alex A. Dienst, February 20, 1918, Claude Elliott Collection.
[86] Barker to Dienst, March 1, 1918, Barker Papers.

laws which establish prohibition in zones with ten mile diameters sur-
rounding army camps and stations. This puts the saloon out of business
in every large town of the State. . . . Our black beast (translate this
into French) is now making a considerable stir in the state, and seems
convinced that he will be re-elected Governor. All contestants practically have withdrawn from the race except Hobby, and I believe most
people who have a right to an opinion feel fairly certain that Hobby
will win.[87]

Since the years of the Ferguson episode coincided with the
years of the First World War, it was only natural that the problems of a nation at war should occupy a considerable part of Dr.
Barker's time and thought. The observation may be made that
Barker regarded the crusade to "make the world safe for democracy" as "a righteous war, free from the slightest taint of selfish-
ness." Desiring to get into the conflict, Barker filed his name with
"the National Intelligence Committee of the University of Pennsylvania to serve in any capacity which may be useful to the
Government, even to fighting in the trenches." But it was not to
be Barker's lot to fight in the trenches; he was declared to be
over the age limit for military service. As a result, his activity
was confined to lectures in American history and "Americanism"
at military installations near Austin. In a letter written to F. J.
Dohmen in the early weeks of the war, Barker explained (with
humor) that "about eighty-five or ninety members of the faculty,
some of them over fifty years of age, formed a company for military drill some three weeks ago and are drilling three days a week
under the direction of Captain J. L. Henderson. Since only three
or four of them have any intention whatever of going into military service, it seemed rather foolish to me." Barker also revealed
that, along with "about two dozen others," he took up a vacant
lot of about two acres to plant "sweet potatoes and peas and other
things." Barker was of the opinion that the garden "might be
foolish, too."[88] Foolish or not, it was in this manner that Dr.
Barker passed the months of the war.

Before moving on to Professor Barker's accomplishments of

87 Barker to William E. Dunn, April 16, 1918.
88 Barker to F. J. Dohmen, April 9, 1917.

later years, it is significant to note that as he closed his second decade as a member of the University of Texas faculty he could look with pride to the History Department that he had been instrumental in building, to the excellence of the *Southwestern Historical Quarterly*, and to his active role in the battle to keep the University from becoming a pawn in the hands of the politicians of Texas. In his quiet manner, he probably realized that his efforts constituted a job well done; furthermore, his future on the faculty of a growing state university looked bright indeed—the golden decades were just ahead.

Barker and the Forty Acres

As the years passed, semester by semester, Eugene Campbell Barker became a legend on the campus of the University of Texas. To many students, graduate and undergraduate, he seemed to be the personification of the typical professor. To a large extent, his reputation, based primarily on his scholarship and the breadth of his knowledge rather than on his forensic skill in the classroom, was well established by the mid-1920's. During the 1930's and 1940's the Barker legend continued to grow as additional generations of young Texans fell within the sphere of his influence and came to know and understand the great significance of his presence on the campus. Looking back over the years, Dr. Barker modestly remembered that his success as a scholar and teacher had been derived from the fact that he had been allowed to do what he wanted to do in the way that he wanted to do it. To him "the place of the individual, in the academic world particularly, is rarely of supreme importance. Common honesty and a decent respect to the opinions of mankind impel him to discharge his duties creditably. In the field of history, for example, his duty has been to do an efficient job of teaching certain accumulated knowledge of the past and to increase that knowledge by his own industry and investigation."[1]

Eugene C. Barker was revered by student and professional colleagues alike, and he made a profound impression upon all persons with whom he was associated. "Time and time again," wrote

[1] Barker, *Essays*, 21.

A. C. Krey, who knew Dr. Barker as early as 1910, "the whole campus would be echoing with some remark of his which had served to deflate aimless and vapid faculty discussion."[2] During the postwar years of the late 1940's, near the close of his career the same remark could still have been made. J. Evetts Haley recalls that Barker's courage and honesty, "his rugged nature, his strong individualism, and his brave realism were tempered at the forges of labor, where only honest workmanship would stand the test of time. His big rough and expressive hands, continually hunting in his pockets as he fumbles his social obligations with a rough and ready grace, but not without self-conscious embarrassment, were fashioned, like his rugged views, at the anvils of hard work."[3] It is probably an understatement to observe that in more than fifty years of active life on the forty acres Dr. Barker left his mark and brand on the campus of the University of Texas. The time has come to record this mark and brand. Ofttimes during the years between 1895 and 1952, Dr. Barker's friends and associates found occasions to compose character sketches in which they described the characteristics of the historian. Three University professors of the present generation describe Dr. Barker, admitting frankly that "great as [was] his scholarship, sound as [was] his teaching, both were equalled or surpassed by his strength of character":

Physically he was tall and angular, rugged is the word for him. His eyes were keen, his nose aquiline, his forehead high. He had about him an unconscious austerity, the sort found in generals and Indian chiefs. . . . To those who knew him best, this austerity was but a crust to cover a great heart, to hide his compassion for those less fortunate than he. It is doubtful if any individual who ever went to him in personal distress, failed to receive aid. He lent money to any needy student, never took a note or required any proof other than the individual volunteered to give. All this money, he once said, was paid back, sometimes twen-

[2] J. Evetts Haley, "The Eugene C. Barker Portrait: Presentation, Acceptance, and Acknowledgment Addresses," *Southwestern Historical Quarterly*, XLVI (April, 1943), 306.

[3] Ibid.

ty years later. Nobody ever forgot to pay one so austere and so kindly generous. . . .

This is one side of Dr. Barker, but there was another. While he was tolerant of individuals whatever their frailties, he was intolerant where principles were involved. He hardly knew the meaning of the word compromise when an issue he thought important was at stake. In faculty controversy he would first present his views quietly in a few words, but if the opposition persisted, he would unfold his six feet and move from his seat, now a different man. His eyes were no longer kindly nor his manner considerate. He destroyed the opposition in language that was sometimes intemperate. Once when some colleague suggested that academic courtesy should prevail, he retorted that what passed for courtesy in a faculty was often damned cowardice.[4]

Several years earlier, Dr. Webb remarked that at times Dr. Barker had reminded him "in his combination of power and kindliness of a great Newfoundland dog moving a little awkwardly and with tolerance among the nimbler breeds around him. I have seen him at other times as an Indian chief. If he could be induced to don a Sioux war bonnet he would pass for a chief anywhere." On other occasions Dr. Barker appeared to Webb "as the general of a great army, directing relentless, hammer-like blows at the enemy. His analytical ability and eye for fundamental and essential things would have made him an iron commander."[5]

Dr. Webb also pointed out that it had been difficult for him to harmonize Dr. Barker's personal philosophy with his social philosophy; while Barker's acts of personal charity were legion among those that knew him best, he was adamant in his opposition when it came "to applying this same principle to suffering humanity in mass, by the government." In short, Webb, could not understand how Barker could lend a helping hand "to all individuals who could reach him—some of them quite worthless—

4 Walter P. Webb, Robert Law, and Joe Frantz, "Report of the Special Eugene Campbell Barker Memorial Committee," Documents and Minutes of the General Faculty, 6919.

5 Barker Papers, "Portrait of a Historian." Unless otherwise stated, "Portrait of a Historian" has been used as a source for the remainder of the first two sections of this chapter.

and at the same time condemn a government that does the same thing." Barker commented on Webb's reference to his opposition to the New Deal program with a marginal note to the effect that "I don't think Webb ever realized that it was not the aim of the government that I deplored but its ruinous methods."

Dr. Barker's striking personality made a similar impression on many others in the University community. Dr. William J. Battle, the veteran of a multitude of academic and political fights at the side of Barker, recalled that "Dr. Barker's outstanding qualities as a man seem to me to be honesty, courage and kindliness. His honesty appears in his every act and word. He has no toleration for pretense. . . . Along with his honesty goes a courage that does not hesitate to speak out, always forcefully, often with vehemence, occasionally with temper."

Roy Bedichek, who knew Dr. Barker as a student in the late 1890's, remembered "a face already grim but kindly." Barker appeared to Allen B. Cole as a typical Texan, "rangy and vigorous" with "the skin of a plainsman, and eyes which must have often searched the horizon." E. C. Barksdale, who claims to have been one of Barker's "problem students," described Barker as "a long, lean, lank Texan with granite face, deep-set, honest eyes, and a mind like a surgeon's scalpel, the exterior of an incensed porcupine, and a warm heart soft with sympathy for all humanity." Dr. W. C. Binkley recalled that "behind his reserve lies a strong and fearless character, quick to condemn injustice or sham or equally ready to extend friendly aid and encouragement." In a comment on Barker's temper, William R. Hogan noticed that Dr. Barker's "righteous wrath" was rarely vented unjustly and was often directed "against the follies of the crackpot educational theorists who infest the modern academic world. His restrained impatience with hypocrisy and stupidity reveals power which impresses all with whom he comes into contact." Dean A. P. Brogan was impressed with Dr. Barker's "rugged honesty and sincerity of character" and referred to him as "an outstanding leader of our faculty." Perhaps the greatness of Dr. Barker may best be summed up in the cryptic phrases of his friend and associate, J. W. Calhoun: "Historian, Author, Research Scholar, Distinguished University

Professor, Fearless Citizen, Hater of Sham, Lover of the Genuine, Philosopher of Reality, Scorner of Pollyanna, Transparent Specimen of Honesty, Embodiment of Sincere Highmindedness—all these and more."

Despite his austere exterior, Eugene C. Barker's sterling qualities of character made him an exceedingly popular departmental chairman. Since there was nothing of the promoter in him (he would have scorned promoter activities), his success as leader of the history faculty must be explained in other terms. Dr. Barker built the Department of History at the University largely by setting an example of industry and consistent work which in turn influenced those about him to work. He never told anyone in his department to do anything in addition to routine duties, but what is more important he never forbade anyone to do anything that he wanted to do. As far as investigation and independent research were concerned, Dr. Barker believed that the individual scholar should be free to go anywhere that his intellectual curiosity might lead. The idea of an individual pre-empting a field of history to the exclusion of all others was repugnant to Barker; perhaps he learned this lesson well as the result of his early unhappy experience with Dr. Garrison. But Barker, like Garrison, never let one forget who was running the department.

Dr. Frederic L. Duncalf spoke for all of the members of the "old department" when he summarized Dr. Barker's long career as departmental chairman with the following statement: "We know and understand the quality of that strong, reasonable, tolerant leadership. Through many years, different as we are, we have become knit together in pleasant and intimate comradeship. More than we realize that has been done by the Chief, and neither he nor we can explain the process by which he has worked upon us." To Dr. Duncalf, the History Department of the University of Texas was Barker's "greatest creation." In Berkeley, California, Dr. Herbert Eugene Bolton agreed with Duncalf; Bolton wrote that "Barker has played a leading part in making the University of Texas one of the great institutions of learning. The dream of the founders (a university of the first class) has come true, and Barker has contributed devotedly and mightly toward transforming the dream into an accomplished fact."

Dr. Milton R. Gutsch, who succeeded Dr. Barker as chairman of the department, was, to a large extent, referring to Barker's leadership within the department when he wrote:

There are those who consider Barker cold and difficult to approach. Those, however, who have worked with him or under him soon realized that the forbidding exterior concealed an unusually warm and sympathetic personality. They came to trust him; they confided in him. He comforted them in their sorrow and helped them in their misfortune. No task was too irksome, no labor too severe. Yet his charity has never been indiscriminate. If he thinks a person undeserving, he frankly and bluntly tells him.

He has always placed the interests of the University and of the department above his own. No other person that I have known has been so thoroughly unselfish. I have heard him say more than once that he would be willing to have his own salary cut if it would benefit some of the members of his staff whom the administration seemed to have overlooked. I know of another occasion when he consented to forego a salary increase in order to preserve University tranquillity.

If there is one characteristic that stands out more prominently than others, it is courage—the courage of his convictions. He has always been willing to fight for his beliefs and when he does he fights hard and does not pull his punches. His blows usually expose the weak spots of his foe. His argument, whenever written, is a model of logic; but when oral and impromptu, its clarity is sometimes obscured by invective and its effectiveness by temper. More than once when the University's very existence seemed to be threatened by politics, and a courageous and forceful leader was needed, the faculty turned to this man; and he did not fail them.

Dr. Gutsch recalls that Barker always strove to consider University matters objectively, but "friend as well as foe has felt the sting of his lash for loose thinking, false conclusion, impractical proposals, and wasteful suggestions"; the Chief "never hesitated to dissect his colleagues without any anesthetic, uncovering their weaknesses, but he has always invited a similarly thorough examination of himself. What he said often hurt, yet we all realized that much of it was true." Nevertheless, Dr. Barker's verbal blasts probably irritated many of his faculty colleagues—especially those from departments distantly removed from the School of Arts and Sciences—beyond any hope for renewed friendship; Barker never seemed to let this bother his basic philosophy in the least.

It is significant, however, that two of Barker's close associates wrote with awe concerning his brusqueness of manner. H. Bailey Carroll pointed out that Barker's intellect was so sharp that when a student went to his office with three questions, he usually "came away with two answers that had come with such swiftness that he later realized that he had entirely forgotten to ask the third question." This brusque manner prompted Dr. Walter P. Webb to remark: "Dr. Barker was the kindest man in the world, but almost fierce in his shyness. . . . He could look at me and unnerve me, even though I knew he was kind. If I went to his office with three things on my mind, I would have to make three trips to remember them all."[6] If Dr. Barker had such an effect on Carroll and Webb, one might inquire about the effect that this gruffness and shyness might have on the graduate and undergraduate student. H. Bailey Carroll remembered:

I first met Dr. Barker about the time the little patch of grey hair on the back of his head was about the size and shape of a half-dime. From that time to the present I have been among those who affectionately watched it through the years assume the proportions of a silver dollar. In these years, particularly as an assistant in History 15, I believe that I have picked up from the Sophomores a number of, to me, the most interesting characterizations of the man. Some of these ran about as follows. "This new teacher of ours certainly looks like Abraham Lincoln, doesn't he?" "He's a fraternity man, but he doesn't like fraternities." "He doesn't like football or football players." Numbers of them called him "the Great Stone Face," while yet others called him "Chief Joseph," which was several times explained as, "Boy, you wrap a blanket around him and he looks like the chief of the Sioux." "With a coat that long he ought to be a preacher." "I hear he used to be a blacksmith." "Well, he looks like it, but somebody over at the house

6 Walter P. Webb, *An Honest Preface and Other Essays*, 19.

"We might see a 'granite monolith,' a sturdy man in tweeds, striding across the campus, each step a firmly planted and decisive one. He grimly clutches a bundle of notes and looks not to right or left, but straight ahead with a dogged determination not to be diverted by the pleasant inane life that ripples around him."

TEXAS BETA

1896   1897

"In Phi Delta Theta Barker formed lasting friendships."

"The Main Building occupies a position at the center of the campus, facing south. University Hall is situated east of the Main Building. The Chemical Building is a substantial ediface, two stories in height."

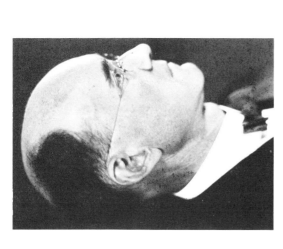

WILLIAM J. BATTLE: "A stimulating and inspiring teacher."

LESTER G. BUGBEE: "A man utterly free of pretense, whose judgment and character can be trusted."

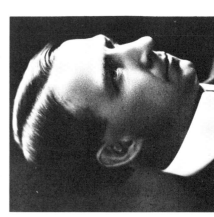

H. E. BOLTON: "Bolton had

HARRY YANDELL BENEDICT: "Revered by students and faculty alike."

The campus (circa 1920).

Courtesy of the Barker Texas History Center.

Dr. Barker, Mrs. Barker, and their son David.
Courtesy of the Barker family.

Dr. Barker and his grandchildren at the dedication of the Barker Texas History Center, 1950.

The Old Library Building, which later became the Barker Texas History Center.

said he used to be a brakeman." Thus did the Sophomores try to pierce the veil of that challenging and somewhat baffling personality. Like numbers of others they usually failed, but wound up with a summary which has been rather universal on the part of his students: "Well, one thing about it you can understand what he is talking about."

In graduate study I seem to remember him best in two widely varying instances. One was his great difficulty with social history. Long before the half-hour mark he would reach his conclusion: "Social history slips through your fingers." Then that massive right hand with fingers extended would go up and the fist would clinch so that the veins would stand out. "You squeeze it and it all goes through your fingers, not much left. That is all today." The other instance regards a special problem I was working on in which I needed a particular government document. I searched and searched and solicited the assistance of the library staff in vain. Finally, I went to Dr. Barker with the matter. He said that he believed I would find the reference in a certain volume on a certain page. It was there. The expression for which I remember him best is, "The study of history is a curious mental exercise."

Another report regarding Dr. Barker's impact on the average undergraduate student comes from an anonymous, uninhibited sophomore—a member of one of Dr. Barker's wartime American history survey sections—who fearlessly wrote,

In our class we called Dr. Barker, "Chief Standing Bull." Sophomores are not very respectful, and we thought he looked like an Indian. I guess we weren't alone in that for I later learned that his co-workers called him "The Chief." And too, we thought he had no more emotion than a cigar store Indian until one day he got red in the face and yanked off his glasses and bawled out everyone in the room because someone else had slipped out. The slip-out happened back of me and I sat blissfully through it, but I testify here and now that I was never before or afterward half so scared as when the bomb went off. I remember Dr. Barker because he gave me the biggest scare of my life. But honestly, I liked him better after he exploded.

Later on one of the boys saw him bathing a fox terrier out in his front yard. We liked him better for that. The human side gradually came in more and more as someone saw him walking with his little boy and someone else knew a fellow he had loaned money to so he could continue going to school. In spite of ourselves we almost began to get interested in the things he had to tell us, and even more surpris-

ing we found ourselves liking the man. Certainly Dr. Barker doesn't
know it (because they would all be too afraid of him to show it) and
possibly he wouldn't even care, but lots of his undergraduates think
he is a grand old man.

Much of the humor related to Dr. Barker's career evolves from
episodes that occurred in his Old Main and Garrison Hall classroom; in fact, it became tradition on the campus for students
enrolled in History 35 to warn the neophytes in History 25: "Don't
disturb his class, he won't take it—and when he gets red in the
face and reaches up and pulls off those glasses, it's the next thing
to the San Francisco earthquake." There is little doubt that many
of these stories are pure legend, and it would be inappropriate
and unwise to repeat others; on the other hand, a rather large
number are either true or approximately true. As a general rule,
students got into trouble with Dr. Barker by either chewing gum
in class, reading unauthorized materials during the lecture
(enough to arouse the ire of the most passive type), or slipping
out of or talking in the classroom.

Dr. Fritz L. Hoffman, now at the University of Colorado, remembers that one morning in Dr. Barker's History 25 class a
graduate student continued to converse with a pretty girl sitting
next to him. Suddenly and without warning Dr. Barker got up
from the high stool that he liked to perch on to lecture and went
to the door. The members of the class of about 125 students
thought that he had forgotten something in his office. But when
he opened the door, Professor Barker turned to the offending
student and said, "Now damn it, I'm teaching this class, and if
you want to talk, I'll leave, and you can take over. Or else you
can get out. There is the door." After a meek response indicating
the student's desire to remain in class, Dr. Barker slowly returned
to his stool; a grin came over his face and the class breathed a
collective sigh of relief. Needless to say, the student kept quiet
after the embarrassing experience—as did the rest of the class.

Miss Ruby Mixon related a similar experience:

It is a long way from the lecture desk to the back rows in Dr. Barker's
Garrison Hall lecture room. Competition between the Spearminted

lovelorn and the social lions for the rear seats has through the years laid a trap from which no professor worthy of his title can escape. I still can feel the warmness of embarrassment when I recall an outburst one morning, provoked by a member of the rear guard. A hundred and fifty of us sat breathless, if not paralyzed, while Dr. Barker vented his wrath upon a talker who for weeks, no doubt, had violated the respectful attention which a teacher has the right to expect. Too stunned by such an explosion from one usually so mild left us so self-conscious that no one dared turn around to watch the culprit sneak by order from the room [*sic*]. With pen and pencils poised, we sat in silence. . . . I guess the others dreaded the next day as much as I did. But Dr. Barker entered the next morning with his usual firm step and business like mien. The answers to the roll call had a frosty-morning, military precision. Then with a slightly squinted left eye and the shadow of a sardonic grin, Dr. Barker swept the back of the room and signed off the previous days chastisement with this forgiving remark: "If a student has no self-respect he ought to be ashamed to make a fool of his professor."

Rupert N. Richardson commented on Dr. Barker's temper by recounting that "once or twice I have fairly trembled at an explosion when he was vexed with some student. I recall that once he stopped in the middle of a lecture to blister a fellow student with a word-lashing. Later I asked the student what he was doing that so provoked the professor and learned that he was reading a magazine." Richardson could not understand how a man who seemed so considerate and gentle could react so severely to a minor offense until he learned how Dr. Barker hated sham and pretense. A student who could not learn called for his sympathy; a "trifling fellow" who would not study was tolerated, but "for the student who could claim credit for class attendance while he was mentally absent," Barker had nothing but contempt.

Miss Winnie Allen, the beneficiary of a long and pleasant association with Dr. Barker, remembers that one day in Dr. Barker's class he became annoyed because of the inattention of a young lady near the rear of the room. When the breaking point came, Barker turned his wrath on the boy who sat next to her and said, "What is your name?"

The young man answered, "My name is Joyce Cox."

The annoyed Barker then demanded, "Will you repeat to me what I have just been saying?" Joyce Cox began very pleasantly at the beginning of the lecture, which had lasted almost half an hour and told the whole story, including a joke or two that Dr. Barker had added. Barker's anger soon gave way to chagrin, and his face passed through various stages of coloration until it showed a sheepish smile as Cox finished his narration. "Well, you ought to be ashamed of yourself for making such a fool out of me," was the classic Barker remark that closed the episode.

Miss Allen also relates the story of a woman who was busy writing a social history of the Republic of Texas. One day she returned from Dr. Barker's office in tears and announced that she never expected to go back again; she had been mortally offended and would not subject herself to further comments that Professor Barker might make. With some urging from Miss Allen, she described how during the lecture Dr. Barker directed his remarks toward women's patriotic organizations—the Daughters of the American Revolution, the United Daughters of the Confederacy, and the Daughters of the Republic of Texas. "These," he said, were organizations for the perpetuation of war and were," he thought, "a social menace. But there was no way that he could see to obliterate them, however, except to declare a moratorium on girl babies for about fifty years."

E. C. Barksdale likes to relate a story on himself. It seems that during his younger days Dr. Barksdale was more interested in campus life as it existed in the vicinity of Beck's Pond than he was in the history of the United States as presented by Barker. Accordingly, a few minutes after Barker had finished calling the class roll, Barksdale would slip out the rear door and head toward his favorite rendezvous. His retreat had been successful on several occasions and Barksdale came to believe that Professor Barker had not noticed his departures. One day, however, Dr. Barker pointed to his hasty retreat with the remark: "If that young man must go every day, I wish that he would not slam the door in leaving." There was a rather sound basis, therefore, for the legendary comment to the effect that Dr. Barker was "Half sabre-toothed tiger and half St. Francis of Assisi."

But, on the other hand, Barker's kindness made a great impression upon everyone associated with him. Dr. R. N. Richardson remembers an incident that revealed to him "the most pronounced quality of the man, sympathy." It seems that Richardson entered Barker's office one day and found the Chief greatly disturbed. Thinking that Barker was in an angry mood, and not wishing to antagonize him further, Richardson began a quiet retreat; but Barker stopped him and explained the source of his trouble. He had just completed a conference with a student, an elderly woman who had been on the verge of starvation in order to spend a year in school and complete a M.A. degree. In order to get rid of her, her superintendent had insisted on an advanced degree, probably knowing that she did not have strength or ability to do the work. Dr. Barker had just told her that she could not graduate at the end of the semester and that the odds were against her ever completing the thesis. Barker's pain over the incident was so obvious that Richardson remarked that he "had never seen him so troubled."

A similar incident was never forgotten by William R. Hogan, who remembered the small seminar that met in Dr. Barker's office in which "one candidate for the master's degree, nervous almost to the point of psychopathy, collapsed" of hunger. Hogan subsequently learned that Barker "provided the funds and the encouragement" that made it possible for the student to finish the year and get his degree. As the years passed, such incidents as the two related above made Barker's kindness another familiar story on the campus of the University.

Dr. Barker's early morning arrival on the campus of the University and his preclass routine (always following more or less the same pattern) have been described by W. Turrentine Jackson and J. Evetts Haley:

In retrospect, we might at mid-morning see what Roy Bedichek calls a "granite monolith," a sturdy man in tweeds, striding across the campus from the west, each step a firmly planted and decisive one. He grimly clutches a bundle of notes and looks not to the right or left, but straight ahead with a dogged determination not to be diverted by the pleasant but inane life that ripples around him. He gruffly barks a good morning" to an associate as he swings through Garrison Hall to his office. . . .

Let us observe his pre-class routine: With the door of his office but slightly ajar to tempt the timid soul to enter, he sits before a jumbled desk. With his hat pulled low over his eyes he scans the mail while the waste-basket seems to heave an expectant sigh. The personal stuff finds a revered depository among the musty accumulation of days. A bit of bibliography from a dealer's catalogue, falling within the well-ordered field of his historical interests, challenges his attention. Picking up a much-used manila envelope that had been oft-addressed to him, he sparingly dips his stub pen in a bottle of ink dug out of the recesses, scratches out his own name and finely chisels thereon: "E. W. Winkler." With his usual redundancy he scratches his message to the University's bibliographer alongside the title of the book, and Mr. Winkler later opens the worn envelope to read: "Get it. ECB."

He unties the books that have come for review, and carefully stores the string away against the day when the Japs should shut us off from the jute of India and Java. Then he spreads his notes before him for a brief review. Instead, he takes time off to give frugal but pointed advice to the students who ease through the door to disturb his unhappy peace. At last, anticipating the roll-call, he fishes from his desk a gapped, broken, and rusty knife that any youth would have scorned to own, and somehow chops a point on his stubby pencil. At the gong he gathers his notes and with the grim look of a man who will die for duty heads across the hall.

And then, as W. Turrentine Jackson has so vividly said: "at two minutes past ten . . . he sauntered into the class room wearing his square cut coat reaching almost to his knees. Without a word he would approach the lecture table, place his half-page notes on the lectern, and with a sweep of his right arm pull a four foot stool under him. As the arm reached out for the stool, the Chief always started to sit, and with perfect timing he never missed a landing. Methodically he removed one pair of glasses, took a metal case from his upper coat pocket containing his reading glasses, carefully adjusted them and his notes, and the lecture began."[7]

In the classroom "his meticulously prepared lectures have flowed, like a well-written book, through the departmental cours-

[7] Haley, "The Eugene C. Barker Portrait," 5–6.

es" for a period of five decades. Dr. Barker's lectures were always concise and well organized. Perhaps it should be pointed out that he never was a showman in the classroom. Apparently he never considered himself as an actor playing a part on a public stage. In other words, Barker believed that entertainment was not within the scope of his ability. His lectures, therefore, were scholarly but not especially colorful, except when Dr. Barker—who was the master of a kind of wit that was a combination of sarcasm, satire, and humor—decided to be clever; the unsuspecting student never knew when to expect such a display of humor. During the late years of his career, Dr. Barker was especially effective with not infrequent sarcastic remarks about historians and history, Franklin D. Roosevelt and the New Deal, and Bernard de Voto and *Harper's* "Easy Chair." When he was in the midst of one of these rare good moods, Dr. Barker's face would redden slightly and he would frequently break out in a low chuckle as he told his story; on these occasions it was well worth while to be a listener.

It is quite possible that the average underclassman never came to know the great heart and kind disposition of Eugene C. Barker. His austerity and grimness—traits that are easily exaggerated—were just severe enough to be a barrier to a close student-teacher relationship on the lower levels of university instruction. It should be emphasized, however, that Dr. Barker's wrath was never aroused without reason. He once said that he had extreme patience with the slow student who had honest difficulty with history; on the other hand, he could not tolerate the loafer who was looking for something (a university degree) for nothing. Nevertheless, Dr. Barker frightened a large number of young students. It was in the graduate seminar in the company of mature students that Barker probably did his most effective teaching. It was in this learning situation that all of his fine qualities of character and scholarship became evident for all to observe. Even in the seminar Professor Barker was the master of brevity, and he expected the same skill on the part of his students. These seminars were conducted as a learning experience in which the most significant element was a mutual exchange of information between the students and their professor; it was here that the scholarly skills of Dr.

Barker were impressed forever in the minds of all students fortunate enough to sit around his table.

In addition to the basic survey course, Eugene C. Barker tra-
ditionally taught three advanced courses: History 25, The History
of the United States, 1750–1829; History 35, The History of the
United States, 1829–1860; and History 87, The Anglo-American
Southwest, 1803–1850. The first of these courses, History 25, covered the following topics: the background of the American Revolution, beginning with the establishment of the English colonies;
the political and diplomatic history of the Revolution; the origins
of American state government during the years of the Revolution;
the government under the Articles of Confederation; the formation of the Constitution and the struggle over ratification (with
detailed attention to the errors and implications in Beard's *An
Economic Interpretation*); the Federalist period; the Jeffersonian
system, with emphasis on the diplomacy of the Louisiana purchase; the diplomatic background of the War of 1812; John Marshall and judicial review; and a detailed study of the background,
content, and reception of the Monroe Doctrine. The course was
organized around selected readings from, primarily, the several
volumes in Albert Bushnell Hart's *American Nation* series. Thus
Dr. Barker made frequent assignments in G. E. Howard, *Prelimi-
naries of the American Revolution*; A. C. McLaughlin, *The Confederation and Constitution*; John Spencer Bassett, *The Federalist
System*; Frederick J. Turner, *The Rise of the New West*; and others. Edward Channing's *History of the United States* and John B.
McMaster's *History of the People of the United States* were also
used extensively. Barker would not infrequently point out that
Channing's history was "a notable work and an authoritative
secondary source" written by a man who was "a thorough scholar
and notable teacher." McMaster's work was sometimes described
as "a crude sort of social history." In addition to the *American
Nation* series, Charles Warren's *The Making of the Constitution*;
Max Farrand's *The Framers of the Constitution, The Fathers of
the Constitution*, and *The Records of the Federal Convention*;
Homer Hockett's *Constitutional History of the United States*; and
William McDonald's *Documentary Source Book of American His-*

tory were combined with the writings of Charles A. Beard and J. Franklin Jameson to round out the basic readings.

Beginning with the reorganization of political alignments in the United States and a survey of the significance of the western movement, History 35 included a detailed study of the following topics: the Jackson administration, with emphasis on the tariff, public lands, internal improvements, the United States bank, Indian lands, and slavery; a continuation of the story of western expansion, with special attention to the frontier movement into Texas, 1820–1848; the causes of the Mexican War; the diplomacy and significance of the Treaty of Guadalupe-Hidalgo; the Compromise of 1850; and the breakup of the Union as reflected in the Kansas-Nebraska Act, the Dred Scott decision, and the Pacific railroad question. As was true with History 25, the basic readings for History 35 included the individual volumes of the *American Nation* and *Chronicles of America* series. Since Barker devoted considerable time to the causes of the Mexican War, the works of George L. Rives, Jesse Reeves, E. D. Adams, and Justin H. Smith were used extensively.

It is noteworthy that not all of Dr. Barker's time was spent in activities related to classroom teaching and scholarship. His recreations consisted of golf, fishing, and reading in the quiet dignity of his home. On the golf course, he played the game with the same seriousness that he exhibited while lecturing on the economic interpretation of the Constitution or chasing down a slanderer of Stephen F. Austin. He was a good golf player with a score in the low 80's or, on exceptional days, in the high 70's. For many years Barker frequently played with the same foursome; the group consisted of Barker, Theophilus S. Painter, Dr. Caleb Perry Patterson, and Hal Armstrong. When duties detained one of the four at his University desk, Dr. J. L. Patterson would substitute for the missing person. Dr. Barker's golf game has been described by Caleb Perry Patterson:

For more than a decade I have fished and played golf with him . . . In sports he is always a strong competitor and constantly a joy to his associates, dispensing the rarest sort of wit and humor. In golf he is known to his pals as "Bobby" or "Old Pipe Line." He drives a long straight ball. In fact he always knows that his ball will be within a few feet of its usual place. He is indisputably the "Bobby Jones" of the foursome.

Dr. Barker's second love in the way of outdoor life was fishing. His fishing expeditions began during his youth when he would frequently accompany Bates McFarland and his brother, Paul Barker, to Aransas Bay and the Trinity River. In later years, after Bates McFarland moved away and Paul Barker met an untimely death in a railroad accident, Dr. Barker was joined by Dr. Charles W. Hackett, Dr. Caleb Perry Patterson, and Hal Armstrong in frequent trips to Aransas Bay. In an effort to fill in the details, Dr. Patterson points out that the group always traveled to Captain George (Florida) Roberts' place at Port Aransas. Captain Roberts had been driven out of Florida by frequent hurricanes; he came to Texas and settled at Port Aransas, where he had three or four cottages. Dr. Patterson frankly admits that all three of the University professors involved in these Port Aransas weekends tried to arrange their class schedules so that their lecture courses fell on Monday, Wednesday, and Friday—this would free them for a long weekend on the Texas coast. Dr. Barker eventually loaned Florida Roberts the money to build a large ocean-going boat; when the boat was completed, the captain would take his Austin guests out to the edge of the continental shelf for better fishing. Both Dr. Hackett and Dr. Patterson have recorded their experiences with Barker and Armstrong on these trips; Charles W. Hackett recalls,

> For twenty-three years I have been associated with Dr. Barker as a member of the Department of History of the University of Texas. During the past seven or eight years of that twenty-three year period, Professor Barker and I have been members of what might be called a "fishing foursome"—this group going at frequent intervals through out the year to fish in the Mexican Gulf out of Port Aransas, Texas. It is on these trips that I have come to regard Dr. Barker as an intimate friend and to appreciate to the fullest his sterling qualities as a human being. I have fished with a good many people in my life, but I have never seen anyone, who[,] when he went to fish, made fishing the prime

and sole object of endeavor as consistently as does Dr. Barker. I have seen him draw in on a hook a flounder—a most unusual fishing stunt. I only wish that when he landed this two or three pound flounder, I had had the equipment to record his spontaneous and hearty chuckle. I have seen him catch sheephead, red fish, trout, croakers, kingfish— much to his disgust—and even hook a tarpoon, which was more to his disgust than the hooking of a kingfish. In all cases, except when he hooks a kingfish or a tarpoon, his chuckle is worth any red-blooded man's money to hear. On the other hand, I have seen Dr. Barker experience the general bad luck which sometimes attends a fishing party, but even on such occasions he does not waver in the serious business of fishing. One day we had fished all morning and not one of the four of us had caught a single fish. About 12:30 P.M., just before time to go into port for lunch, and after some of the others in the party had drawn in their lines in perfect disgust, Dr. Barker rebaited his hook, "Well, when a person is fishing, I just don't know of anything for him to do but to fish." That illustrates his philosophy of life, as I understand it, for any task upon which he is engaged.

On these fishing expeditions, our fishing foursome can only fish during certain daylight hours, and the long evenings have to be accounted for in some way. This is usually accomplished by playing dominoes, and Dr. Barker makes the playing of dominoes as much the business of the hour as he does fishing when he is fishing. He had the reputation during his student days, so I have often heard, of not being very good in mathematics—in fact, I think it is very common gossip that he almost specialized in mathematics! Therefore, while Dr. Barker is a splendid domino player, and has become more and more proficient in that gentle art during the past few years, the rate of playing would be speeded up somewhat if someone could devise a little adding machine for his use when most of the dominoes are in an elaborate and extended cross design on the table before us. But even when he has had a "Brainstorm" trying to add up "counters" toward the end of a hand, he has been consistently lucky and frequently has made a play which has netted him and his partner as much as 25 or 30 points without his discovering that fact before it was called to his attention. On such an occasion, it is worthwhile to hear him say: "Well, I didn't realize that."

Writing at a different time and place, unknown to Hackett, Dr. Caleb P. Patterson tells a similar story about the Port Aransas trips; Patterson remembers that,

In fishing "Bobby" is equally skilled in the art as in golf, but he is also lucky. If he doesn't catch the first fish, and he generally does this, he always catches the biggest one. Whether he as a matter of science knows the best casting place, or has that delicate touch which dictates the moment to jerk the rod, or whether he is just naturally lucky, is a matter of debate among his colleagues. We are inclined, for perfectly obvious reasons, to think that it is luck.

One of the things that caused us to regard Bobby's expertness in fishing as a matter of luck is the frequent charges which Captain George Roberts, our boatman, brings against him. At frequent intervals Captain Roberts cries out: "Dr. Barker, why in hell don't you jerk that rod? For years I've been telling you how to do this. You must remind yourself of some of your University students." The conversation that follows one of these outbursts of the Captain is irreproducable. Only an expert at shorthand could get the language.

In dominoes "Bobby" is uncanny. He will make twenty-five or thirty and profess not to see it, leaving it to his honest and chagrined opponents to call attention to the matter. This is always followed by one of "Bobby's" chuckles. It is believed by his opponents that these tactics are only very suttle [*sic*] methods of punishment, and frequently lead to the remark that in dominoes there is no place for brains.

Dr. Charles S. Potts, one of Barker's friends of long standing, also remembers fishing with the Chief and recalls with great pleasure "the half-dozen fishing trips to Lake Medina with Barker, Milton R. Gutsch, Ed Miller, 'Rube' Lewis, and E. J. Matthews." And again reference was made to Barker's outstanding luck as a fisherman. On another occasion, Dr. Barker and Dr. L. W. Payne took Potts fishing on the Colorado River near Austin; Potts recalls the incident as follows:

> Also vividly impressed on my mind is the time when he and Dr. L. W. Payne took me out to fish in their favorite spot about the size of a barrel head in "Laguna Gloria." Their long poles enable them to drop their hooks into the "barrel," as they called it, and they soon caught a dozen or two nice ones. My short pole and shorter arm left me a foot or two short of "the happy hunting ground." I felt exactly like Aesop's fox that was invited to dine with the crane from the contents of a long-necked jug. But in the end, I fared better than Br'er Fox, for that night my family and I enjoyed a nice mess of fish with the compliments of ECB and LWP.

From these reminiscences related to sport and recreation, the conclusion is apparent that Dr. Barker and his friends fished all of the waters and played most of the golf courses within easy driving distance of Austin. Mr. Hal Armstrong summarized the lighter side of Dr. Barker's personality when he remarked that "because of Eugene's shyness, many people thought perhaps he missed a great deal of the simple pleasures of life. But this is not true; with his keen sense of observation, Dr. Barker missed nothing on the lighter side of life."[8]

The Town and Gown Club, a dinner and discussion group composed of University faculty members and Austin professional men, was another source of pleasure for Dr. Barker. It was here that the academic mind and the professional-business mind of the community met to exchange ideas and information. On occasions the program would be of a serious nature and on other nights humor would be the main feature of the meeting. On one such occasion, the meeting of January 12, 1932, Oliver Douglas Weeks spoke on "The Recent Presidential Election" and Roy Bedichek's announcement of the meeting read as follows:

The post mortem will be conducted by a skilled political diagnostician. There were plenty of doctors predicting even before November that something was the matter with the Grand Old Party. Senility, over-feeding, dropsy, arteriosclerosis, prohibitionists, water on the brain, protectionists or locked bowels, concealed abscesses, rheumatism (and other diseases one might find named in medical dictionaries) have been charged with the responsibility for the demise of the late unlamented . . .[9]

The meeting (as usual) was to be at the Driskill, the menu included simply "ducks," and the program was arranged by Dr. Joe Gilbert and Charles Ramsdell.

It was at the conclusion of one of the meetings of the Town and Gown Club during which the membership had listened to a lengthy discourse given by a University professor of sociology that Dr. Barker, when it came his turn to make a critical remark during the discussion period, waved his massive hand in the air and said, "Words, words, words. Nothing but words." Barker made his statement with such finality that the discussion period ended immediately. On another occasion a member of one of the patriotic societies inquired about the possibility of combining the State and University libraries. In a reply to the query, Barker remarked: "I am by that as Van Buren was about the annexation of Texas. I don't know whether it would be constitutional, and I don't want to find out."[10]

Besides the fishing hole and the golf course, Dr. Barker's other retreat from an irritating world came when he reached the quiet dignity of his oak-shaded, rock home at 2600 San Gabriel. It was there, as reported by Evetts Haley and Laura Lettie Krey, that Barker found peace and quiet at the close of the day:

Within his study he reads the daily news with mounting passion, and then sooths his adrenalin glands with Perceval Gibbon's stories of the African veldt, or Eugene Manlove Rhodes' plots of western cowboys. And when he steps from that study for supper he is in a quiet and peaceful world, dominated by a well-poised nature moving with the cultured grace of another day and a gentler land. No masculine hand could do her justice. Laura Krey has come to my help.

"As I look back over the years that I have known both him and Mrs. Barker," she wrote, "I am conscious that my debt to her is no less great than to him. For, long ago . . . when I was trying to determine what qualifications . . . I might have for being the wife of a University professor, I recall paying her a visit. Never, I think, had I met her before that lovely spring night, but as soon as I saw her I knew at once . . . that she was, herself, that rare and exquisite creation which we used to call a lady. I have wandered far and wide since then, and have heard it proclaimed that such as she really never existed except in novels, or, if so, that too high a price was paid in the South for her special kind of beauty and graciousness . . . I remain immune to any such heresy . . . In building so lovely a home and garden she has reminded us all on what strength any nation must finally rest."[11]

---

[10] Roy Bedichek to W. C. P., August 10, 1957; Haley, "The Eugene C. Barker Portrait," 10.
[11] Haley, "The Eugene C. Barker Portrait," 10.

It was in such surroundings as these that Dr. Barker found the beauty and renewed strength so essential to intellectual survival in the modern world; and it was in these pleasant surroundings that David Barker, Eugene and Matilda Barker's only son, grew to manhood.

With reference to his personal philosophy of history, Dr. Barker once remarked that "every earnest history teacher faces now and then the depressing question of his reason for existence. Why does he teach history? What are the objectives of history teaching, and in what measure does he attain them?"[12] Admitting that he had no answer to these questions, Barker recalled that he once wrote in a seventh-grade textbook that "history is the story of what men and women have thought and done in the past. It tells how they have lived and struggled and worked. It tells how they have suffered from errors, false ideas, and misfortunes. But it also tells how they have continued for many thousands of years to make the world always a happier and more comfortable place in which to live." The writer of history, according to Barker, attempts "to learn the truth as nearly as it can be ascertained" and "to relate this small segment of truth to the whole fabric of history." Pointing out that the historian can never learn the whole truth about anything, Barker liked to contrast what he called the "Old History" with the "New History" of the twentieth century. It seemed to Dr. Barker that the "old" historian submitted himself to severe discipline in training for his task. He approached his investigations without preconceived notions and opinions; as a result, he collected all the evidence available and formed his deductions and conclusions with a critical mind free of bias of all sorts. He tried to present to the reader a picture of conditions and events as they actually were, with their causes and consequences. When he did allow himself the luxury of an opinion or a conclusion he labeled it plainly as personal opinion and gave both sides of the argument. In other words, the historian of the "old school" tried to be honest, though no *honest historian ever be-*

[12] Eugene C. Barker, "The Changing View of the Function of History," *The Social Studies*, XXIX (April, 1938), 149 ff.; *Essays*, 225 ff.

lieves himself wholly unbiased, impartial, and objective. He merely tries to be."[13]

On the other hand, the "new history"—originating when Professor James Harvey Robinson published his conviction that "the
uses of sealing wax and cabbages are history as well as the doings
of kings"—marked the beginning of what Barker referred to as
"a crusade to reform the written content of history." It seemed to
Dr. Barker that Robinson himself was not affected by his theory,
but "the same cannot be said, however, of his disciples and of
others who practiced what he preached." The New History of
Robinson, Barker pointed out, stimulated "the production of books
chiefly in the fields of economic and social history."[14] Barker's
doubt with regard to the value of the economic and social emphasis of the New History stems, of course, from the fact that he was
primarily a political historian who drew his conclusions from a
great mass of documents, preferably official documents.

In search of additional arguments to support his thesis, Barker
turned to the report of a committee of the American Historical
Association, published in 1899 and titled *A Study of History in the
Schools*; in Barker's mind the committee's conception of the value
of history to general education was that "it equips pupils with
some knowledge of the past and the relation of the present to the
past; it teaches orderly thinking in the analysis, coordination, and
arrangement of facts; and it develops the scientific, or historical,
habit of mind"—a quality defined as "the habit of approaching
every question without prejudice and of examining it with candor
and honesty."

It was of great significance to Dr. Barker that another report
was published in 1934 by a similar committee of the American
Historical Association in which the earlier concepts were either
abandoned completely or altered to a marked degree. While the
1934 report declared that the purpose of education and history
(and the other social sciences) was to fit boys and girls for the
duties of citizenship, Barker thought that any similarity with the

---

[13] Barker, *Essays*, 226.
[14] Ibid., 227.

1899 report ended right there. "In confusing language and with many contradictions," wrote Barker, "the committee seems to say that the objective of society is a collectivist democracy—whatever that may be—and that it is the aim of historical study and the duty of the schools to prepare citizens who will work harmoniously and unselfishly for the attainment of that happy end as speedily as possible."[15] In describing the universal goal of the committee, he reported that, among other things,

> In the Utopia of its dreams, the committee sees "a society in which no man, woman, or child can be exploited by another"; where "aquisitive individualism with all its cruder manifestations in gambling, speculation, exploitation, and racketeering, is subdued to the requirements and potentialities of the emerging society"; where "the establishment of a higher and finer standard of living may be expected to free people from absorption in material things and enable them to devote greater attention to ideals of spiritualism, scientific, and cultural development"; where "individualism in economy" will be curbed on the one hand and on the other there will be a "reservation to the individual of the largest possible measure of freedom in realms of personal and cultural growth, and the preservation and development of individuality in its non-acquisitive expressions as the finest flower of civilized society."[16]

To Eugene C. Barker, the significant thing about the 1934 report was that the committee advocated a dynamic program of propaganda in which "history teachers are urged to abandon the outworn shibboleth of judicial detachment and blow the horn and beat the drum for the advancement of the committee's prophetic vision; in short . . . one should amuse himself as much as he likes with such sterile pastimes as research, publication, and scholarship, but when he is tired of emulating the freedom of the 'Wild Jackasses of the Wilderness' he will return to the party fold, accept the platform, and lead the nation to ever grander and more glorious freedom." Asking that the teachers of history lend themselves neither to a campaign of propaganda for the maintenance of a *status quo* nor to one for the establishment of a Utopia, Barker remarked that "Perhaps one teaches as an act of faith, hoping to

15 Ibid., 231 ff.
16 Ibid., 232.

contribute to habits of straight thinking, intellectual honesty, good judgment, tolerance, and independence, while imparting some knowledge of the culture and experience of the past which has helped to make the present and which in some form will undoubtedly help to shape the future."[17] This statement is an accurate summary of Eugene C. Barker's own philosophy about teaching history.

In the spring of 1939 Dr. Barker read a paper titled "Three Types of Historical Interpretation" to a group of Texans assembled to dedicate the San Jacinto Museum of History. After pointing out that the library and museum on the old battleground would, in time, become the "storehouse of books, manuscripts, and artifacts . . . for the accurate writing and interpretation of history," Barker set the theme of his address with a remark to the effect that "there is too much inaccuracy in both writing and interpretation—and particularly in interpretation. I have no quarrel with differences of conviction growing out of the honest consideration of all the facts that an honest investigation can discover. Such differences are inevitable. It is the careless interpretation, founded upon incomplete assimilation of the facts, and the contrived interpretation based upon falsification, against which we need to guard."[18]

Following an example of an honest difference of opinion based on honest facts, Barker told his audience,

The other two types of interpretation which I have mentioned are not so innocent or amusing. As an example of the interpretation that is more or less contrived to deceive, I venture to cite the expositions that we have been reading in the papers and hearing on the radio for the past few years of the origin of the Constitution and the function of the Supreme Court of the United States. All of this language has not issued from the historian, but he has laid the groundwork for it, and in a measure is responsible, therefore, for the license of the expositors.[19]

17 Ibid., 234.
18 Eugene C. Barker, "Three Types of Historical Interpretation," *Southwestern Historical Quarterly*, XLV (April, 1942), 323 ff.; Barker, *Essays*, 236 ff.
19 Ibid.

Neither Barker's central theme nor his general tone of criticism had changed when he addressed the Phi Beta Kappa chapter of The Rice Institute the following spring. Selecting the obligation of the historian as his topic, Barker told the Rice audience that "the obligation of the historian is to tell the truth about the particular phase of the past that he is discussing, and as much of the truth as he can." Barker continued, "Having chosen his subject for investigation and narration, it is the duty of the historian to make an honest effort to find out all that he can about it and to state his findings as fully as the scale of his narrative permits and as objectively as his human limitations allow him to do. There are many difficulties in the way, and at best his finished picture will fall short of reality—or go beyond it." Concerning historical truth, Barker reminded his listeners that in the effort to learn the truth the historian must "rid his mind of bias—personal, emotional, social, economic, sectional, and national. As far as possible, he must turn himself into an impersonal intellectual machine with the sole aim of gathering the facts and describing them as they were."[20]

Thus Dr. Eugene C. Barker's philosophy of history and historical scholarship was clearly and concisely stated on several occasions during the late years of his long and fruitful career. In summary and review, he charged historians (1) to learn the truth by impartial investigation free from preconceived opinion and to tell the truth about the particular phase of history under investigation and as much of the truth as possible; (2) to shy away from the use of history as propaganda for either the maintenance of the *status quo* or the establishment of a Utopia; (3) to strive, in their teaching, to promote habits of straight thinking, intellectual honesty, good judgment, tolerance, and independence while imparting knowledge of the past and its relationship to the future; and (4) to avoid the careless interpretation founded upon incomplete facts, and the contrived interpretation based upon the falsification of facts. It is significant to note that these were not mere platitudes for lip service; Dr. Barker, lived, taught, and wrote history in conformity to his code of ethics.

[20] Barker, *Essays*, 278 ff.

On the seventy-fifth anniversary of the University of Texas, J. Frank Dobie remembered that "courses in Education spelled with a capital E, were regarded as snap courses as early as 1914," but "they were so boring that few students of that kind were willing to pay the price for that form of a snap." Professor Dobie also recalled that Eugene C. Barker, "professor of history and master of sardonic realism, used to define education as 'the unctuous elaboration of the obvious.' " According to Dobie, Barker modestly claimed this to be a quotation from someone else, but it was Barker who received credit for originating and popularizing the barb.[21] In complete agreement with Professor Dobie, Eugene C. Barker was extremely critical of both the intellectual aridity of professional education courses and the professional educators who practiced the false ideas contained therein—Barker and his liberal arts colleagues called these "educators" by the scornful title of "peedoggies."

It seemed to Barker that about the same time that James Harvey Robinson pronounced his theory of the "New History" the professional educators were "amusing themselves by assaulting common sense with the doctrine that equal effort produced equal value in education regardless of the nature of the subject upon which the effort was expended." Years later Dr. Barker, taking notice of the effect of the theories of the professional educators on the teaching and writing of history, deplored the fact that "in response to the demands of educational theorists, most of whom neither write or teach history—even if they know it—textbook writers have tried to substitute the delightful pastime of doing 'activities' for the painful drudgery of learning facts."[22] On another occasion Professor Barker made a trip to Lubbock, Texas, to speak at the inauguration of William Marvin Whyburn as president of Texas Technological College. In enumerating the various developments that the new president might expect, Barker, in a pointed reference to the education department, remarked:

Representatives of a huge department which had its origin not so

---

21 *Daily Texan*, March 28, 1958.
22 Barker, "The Changing View of the Function of History," 152.

long ago as a teacher of method without substantive content, will want authority, and money, to add a professor, three instructors, and a laboratory assistant to measure the immeasurable and weigh the imponderable. Their department has grown like Jonah's miraculous gourd—and many of their colleagues wish that it might suffer the same fate. The avowed object of their request is to put into effect a "mandate" . . . laid down by the legislature in a law that it did not understand, but which it passed under the misinformed impression that it was doing something to further "democracy" in education—democracy quoted.[23]

In the same address Barker scored the educational administrator by warning President Whyburn that, in the discharge of his off-campus obligations, he would have to attend conferences of fellow presidents and other "administrators" and listen to their talk "on whatever topic might be absorbing their temporary yearning to make a better world." Barker called attention to the fact that in such meetings,

It really makes little difference what you say about these subjects. Before the debate is ended, the "leaders" of the profession will be in full cry after another list of panaceas. The manner of your saying, however, is very important. Never let innate honesty betray you into an effort to express your thoughts in comprehensible language. There is a jargon to be used at such meetings, and a style of unctuous profundity, both designed to conceal platitudes and puzzle simple souls, who really are, perhaps, as we have heard from a high authority, "too damned dumb to understand." Impious scoffers may jeer that there is nothing there to understand, but be not misled by such sacrilege; perseverance and sedulous cultivation of appropriate style and vocabulary can make any man an educational "leader." Unfortunately you cannot devote all your time to mastering the art of verbal confusion, but it cannot have escaped your observation that very respectable standing in the lower ranks of leadership can be attained by paraphrasing the obscurities of others. In the last resort, there are "ghost writers."[24]

After the frank reminder to Dr. Whyburn that "One of the two essential elements in any school is the faculty, and . . . the presi-

[23] Barker, *Essays*, 7.
[24] Ibid., 8–9.

dent is not the other," Barker concluded his Lubbock speech with the reminder that "a strong college of arts and sciences is fundamental in a scheme of sound general education" but "it has everywhere lost its integrity" because,

Some fifty years ago President Eliot of Harvard, a man to conjure with then but astonishingly dead now, mounted a hobby and rode it furiously, crying the educational virtues of free election. Professional educationists, calling themselves pedagogists then, put their own brand of lunacy on Dr. Eliot's nag and began asserting that all subjects were of equal educational value if studied with equal labor. Though nobody really believed them—and they did not believe themselves very long—they hypnotized enough recruits to vote out the rather solid requirements of the B.A. degree and substitute a curriculum that enabled them to clothe their vagaries about the democratic equality of all types of learning with the aristocratic prestige of the ancient A.B. Since then the college of arts has traveled in a wilderness without compass or guide, yielding to every varying wind of vocationalism and fallacy of educational theory.[25]

Thus, Dr. Barker joined the ranks of the "impious scoffers" who pointed to the self-evident truth that there was nothing to understand concerning the barren theories of the professional educationist—the teacher of method without substantive content. But unhappily for Dr. Barker and his fellow historians the cult of progressive educators did not suffer the same fate as Jonah's gourd. On the contrary, they have continued to measure the immeasurable and weigh the imponderable to the detriment of American education in general.

As the Ferguson controversy raged about the campus of the University of Texas, the faculty of the History Department, as previously noted, included Eugene C. Barker (chairman), Frederic Duncalf, Charles W. Ramsdell, William R. Manning, Thad Weed Riker, Frank Burr Marsh, William E. Dunn, and Milton R. Gutsch. The graduate assistants during these years included Mattie Austin Hatcher, Thomas J. Calhoun, Asa Kyrus Christian, and Charles A. Gulick, Jr. Manning and Dunn, both specialists in the

[25] Ibid., 12.

Latin American field, departed Austin during the war years and did not return. As noted previously, Charles W. Hackett and Walter P. Webb were added to the staff in 1918 to round out the personnel of the "old department."

The years following the conclusion of the Great War were years of growth and expansion for the University of Texas. These were the years and days of the "roaring twenties" with memories of Beck's Pond, Dillingham's pasture, the Blunderbuss, "hot rocks," the pushball contest on each March 2, and the "H. A. team." The 1920's also witnessed the ascendancy of "king football" and E. J. Stewart, Clyde Littlefield, Mack Saxon, Mortimer E. Sprague, Joe Ward, Oscar Eckhardt, and others were the Longhorn heroes of the hour. The years between 1923 and 1925 witnessed the fund-raising drive to build Memorial Stadium as a monument to Saturday's children. It seems that the years of "normalcy" produced a poor setting for the academic mind; yet in the autumn of 1927 the College of Arts and Sciences, presided over by Dean Harry Yandell Benedict, consisted of eighteen departments "teaching about forty major subjects of human knowledge." From the small beginning in 1883, when 6 professors comprised the entire faculty, the instructional staff had grown to 111 professors of all ranks, 81 instructors, and 114 tutors and assistants. The Arts and Sciences enrollment had reached 3,400. The campus of the University was growing in another way and in the spring of 1927 the *Cactus* reported that,

The day of shacks on the campus of the University is at last passing; a year or two ago most classes met in these temporary buildings, and it began to appear that they were temporary only from a point of view of style; but upon the building of Garrison Hall most of the shacks on "shack row" were abandoned by classes and given over to the Curtain Club, the Band, and the Men's Gym.[26]

During these years Eugene C. Barker and his faculty colleagues continued to meet their classes day after day so that another generation of Texans could receive the rudiments of a university education. Aside from his classroom duties in Old Main and Garrison

[26] Ibid., 103. See also ibid., 20.

Hall, Dr. Barker's university-wide interests during the 1920's included his opposition to the proposal to move the University campus to the north bank of the Colorado River, his efforts to build the archives and the general library of the University, his opposition to the selection of Governor Pat M. Neff as president of the University, his concern about the quality of an expanded Graduate School, and his desire to see the University become a "university of the first class."

One of the major controversies of the early 1920's was related to the proposal to abandon the original "forty acres" in favor of a new University campus. During the winter of 1920–1921 the students of the University and most of the administrative staff endorsed and addressed "a memorandum to Governor Neff and the 37th Legislature" requesting that the campus of the Main University be moved to the 496-acre Brackenridge tract on the Colorado River near Lake Austin. President R. E. Vinson, who favored the plan, called the request "the most radical announcement ever made in the history of the University of Texas."[27] The idea of removal to the Brackenridge tract soon gained enough publicity to become the topic of the day in and about Austin. President Vinson threw his support behind the effort, but the property holders in North Austin were opposed to the proposed move. Eugene C. Barker was one of the many to voice his opposition to such a plan. On January 29, 1921, Barker expressed his opinion in a letter to John Lomax; the Barker opinion had been requested by Lomax for publication in *The Alcalde*. Barker showed the letter to Vinson before mailing it and the University president was much opposed to its publication; Vinson wanted to know why Barker did not "get behind and push." In this letter Barker pointed out the disadvantages of the Colorado River site as the location of the new university—the tremendous cost and the probable difficulties of securing new building funds—and remarked:

Let us look for a moment at the possibilities of the present site. We have upon it nine brick and stone buildings, including two dormitories.

[27] *Daily Texan*, March 28, 1958.

The rest of the campus is covered with shacks. The shacks have an average class room space of five rooms each. One modern building three stories high would take the place of six shacks. Two buildings would remove every shack from the campus and leave much space for additional buildings. . . . No University that I have ever heard of has "scrapped" its old buildings because they were not fireproof and modern. It may be at once admitted that a campus of forty acres is not large enough for all future development, but I cannot conceive of any legitimate reason to argue that five hundred acres, not to say eight hundred, is necessary or even desirable.[28]

Dr. Barker believed that a most generous estimate of the cost of additional acreage bounded by "Nineteenth Street, San Antonio Street, and the gulch north of Twenty-seventh Street" would fall inside of a million dollars; this figure, he reported "would be considerably less, if Austin business men had the intelligence and enterprise of a village of Digger Indians, and would go out with a bag of silver dollars buying options." Barker also announced that Dr. Vinson, in his enthusiasm for this entrancing vision, "neglects some very practical realities" in that "he is persuaded . . . that the University can be moved and adequately equipped with 'little or no cost to the taxpayer.' If he can accomplish that feat, the alchemist's quest is ended. The philosopher's stone is found."[29]

Since he was directly and personally involved in the opposition to the removal proposal, Dr. Barker was highly pleased when the Texas Legislature voted to extend the boundaries of the University property in North Austin rather than to build a new campus on the north bank of the Colorado River. There is evidence in the Barker papers to show that, during the controversy concerning the Brackenridge tract, Dr. Barker used all of his skills in oral and written persuasion to influence his friends in the Legislature. He apparently leaned heavily on the strong political arm of Edgar

---

[28] Barker to John A. Lomax, January 29, 1921.
[29] Ibid.

E. Witt; after the issue had been closed, Witt wrote Barker the following note:

I want to thank you for your letters of appreciation and congratulation and assure you that I appreciate your thoughtfulness in writing me very much. Candor and frankness, as well as pride in my achievement, compels me to admit that I did play a considerable part in the enactment of the University legislation. And I also take pride in the fact that I probably influenced the governor in securing his approval, because in his message he gives the very reasons for approving the University bill that I urged upon him by letter and by formal resolutions adopted by the McLennan County Ex-Students Association.[30]

Since his early years on the University faculty, Eugene C. Barker had been interested in building the archive collection of the University library; this specialized interest was, of course, in addition to his equally strong interest in the general library and the Littlefield collection. As the years passed by, therefore, Barker became the greatest ally that Mattie Austin Hatcher and Winnie Allen had in their efforts to collect the archival materials related to the history of Texas and the Spanish borderlands. Among the early members of the History Department, it was Barker who clearly saw the advantage of collecting and housing archival materials pertaining to the history of Mexico and adjacent lands. Beginning in 1906—building on a foundation laid by Lester G. Bugbee, George P. Garrison, and young Barker—the University regents made a modest appropriation of $500 for the purchase of transcripts of archival materials from the libraries of Mexico. At this particular time, Herbert Eugene Bolton was in the process of making the transition into the new field of Latin American history and the $500 was to be spent by Bolton (already engaged in a survey of Mexican archives) in making transcripts for the University library. As the years passed, this modest appropriation was continued and increased, finally, to $1,000 annually. The figure remained $1,000 until the item was dropped from the University budget as an economy move in 1921.[31]

[30] Edgar E. Witt to Barker, April 5, 1921.
[31] Barker to H. Y. Benedict, January 6, 1923.

Between 1910 and 1921 those engaging in the Mexican enterprise presented many vouchers to Dr. Barker for his approval as chairman of the department. Barker approved expenditures made by William E. Dunn, C. H. Cunningham, Charles W. Hackett, and Carlos E. Castañeda—all pioneer Latin American historians who journeyed to Mexico at their own expense during the summer vacations to select the materials to be copied. After the selection had been made, a list of the items desired would be left with qualified copyists. The actual copy work would then be completed during the academic year. The following summer would witness a repetition of the process. Dr. Barker joined in the venture on several occasions, working especially with the documents of the legislature and other departments of the former Mexican state of Coahuila y Texas at Saltillo. The complex financial system followed by the state of Texas concerning the handling of University funds—no payment could be made until the materials were actually delivered—made it necessary for those directing the copy work to make the original payment from personal funds; they then billed the University in their own names. It was in this manner that the significant collection of documentary source materials in the history of Mexico and Latin America was originated and built—a remarkable tribute to the industry of a few interested historians.[32]

During the winter term of 1920–1921, the library staff discovered that the University could acquire, through purchase, the valuable private collection belonging to Genaro García (1867–1920), a distinguished Mexican historian and bibliophile. The García collection included large portions of other famous libraries as well as the archives of Mexican presidents, statesmen, and diplomats. On January 21, 1921, Dr. Vinson appointed a committee consisting of Barker, John A. Lomax, and H. Y. Benedict to handle all matters related to the acquisition of the García library. A few days later Barker wrote E. W. Winkler, who was in Mexico City, to explain that "the president finds himself so occupied with his ambitious project of moving the University that he can give

[32] Ibid.

no attention to raising money for the library. He has, therefore, passed this rather large buck to a committee consisting of Benedict, Lomax and me.[33] Fortunately for the University, the committee members (working through Winkler in Mexico City) were successful in raising the necessary money; within a few months the García collection had been purchased and added to the University of Texas library.

In the early spring of 1923, Robert E. Vinson resigned as president of the University of Texas to accept a similar position in the administration of Western Reserve University of Cleveland, Ohio. Dr. Barker's high regard for Dr. Vinson was expressed in a letter of appreciation written for publication in *The Alcalde*:

> Dr. Vinson has for seven years paid the people of Texas the compliment of believing that they actively desire a "University of the first class," that vague abstraction of the constitution of 1876, and all his waking moments (and one suspects most of his dreams) have gone into his effort to realize his own fine vision of such an institution. That he has spent himself unselfishly and without stint no one doubts who has seen him at the task.[34]

To Barker, who described himself as a "disillusioned realist," Dr. Vinson's greatest strengths were his desire to secure a properly trained faculty "working under conditions conducive to the highest efficiency," his recognition of the necessity for adequately equipped laboratories and libraries, and "his belief in a democratic administration for the University of Texas." "Dr. Vinson," said Barker, "won the amazed admiration of his faculty within three months of his election by his astonishing defense of the University in the Ferguson controversy, and he has held their loyalty and affection (including that of the disillusioned realist) as no president before him has ever done." This was high praise from an individual such as Barker, who sincerely felt (along with a great majority of the rest of the faculty) a severe loss when Vinson announced his decision to move to Western Reserve.[35]

[33] Barker to E. W. Winkler, January 26, 1921.
[34] Eugene C. Barker, "An Estimate of Dr. Vinson," *The Alcalde* (July, 1923), 273.
[35] Ibid.

The search for a successor to President Vinson produced an annoying situation which was rather typical of Texas politics. It was soon evident that the management of the University remained under the shadow of the capitol dome when Pat M. Neff, then governor of the state, decided that he would be a candidate for the vacant University presidency. Angered beyond description, Dr. Barker again marshalled his energy for a "bear fight"; he was determined to bring all of his talent and influence into play against the selection of Governor Neff. Barker was not alone in his opinion concerning the governor. Charles W. Ramsdell remarked,

> I am very much worried over the situation of the University just now. The general legislative attitude would alone be enough, but to have this question of the presidency up at the same time brings grey hairs in a hurry. From what I hear there is much talk of Butte and— Neff! Is it possible that there is real danger of the Board selecting that damned politician? I think that our great Board might do anything, almost, because few of them have any sense; but it seems incredible to me that the friends of the University over the state would allow that to threaten without a protest that would jar them into something like a sense of their duty and responsibility. If they even dare to think seriously of that they ought to be shaken over the pit of Hell.[36]

In May of 1923 Barker wrote A. C. Krey to explain, "as you know we have lost Vinson and are in eminent danger of getting Neff to succeed him. I think the faculty for once is a unit in opposing the appointment of any politician, but being a unit in opinion means nothing as to the method of procedure and action. As a matter of fact, we are doing nothing."[37] But Barker was not to be a do-nothing faculty member; as early as March, 1923, he was busy writing letters to R. H. Baker, Burke Baker, and Joe Hutcheson of Houston to urge them to bring the pressure of the powerful Houston Ex-Students' Association into the battle to secure an academic man instead of a politician as president of the University. Again Barker was partially successful. Within a few

---

36 Ramsdell to Barker, March 4, 1923.
37 Barker to A. C. Krey, May 15, 1923.

days he wrote Dean K. C. Babcock of the University of Illinois, "There is a committee of the faculty at the University of Texas to collect information concerning persons suggested to the Regents for the Presidency of the University. While the Regents requested the appointment of this committee, I do not feel very confident that they will pay any attention to the information which we collect."[38]

The Barker committee met at frequent intervals; after screening various suggestions, they recommended that the new president be chosen from the following list: Guy Stanton Ford, dean of the Graduate School, University of Minnesota; Herbert Eugene Bolton, professor of history, the University of California; George Norlin, president, the University of Colorado; E. H. Lindley, the chancellor of the University of Kansas; Harry Yandell Benedict, dean of the College of Arts and Sciences, the University of Texas; and George Butte, professor of law, the University of Texas. Months passed and while there was much talk nothing was done. In the meanwhile Dr. Barker had been greatly disturbed by a letter of resignation from a friend and colleague in the History Department.

Shortly after the First World War, Dr. C. S. Boucher had accepted a position on the history faculty at the University. Boucher was a fine scholar in American history and Barker wanted to keep him. On May 12, 1923, Boucher wrote Barker from Chicago to offer his resignation so that he could accept a position on the University of Chicago faculty. According to Boucher, he had never been happier than he had been with conditions within the University of Texas, where he "had gained great respect for and confidence in his colleagues of the history faculty, where the library equipment in the field of American history was excellent, and where the administration had also been excellent. . . . But there are two determining reasons, somewhat birds-of-a-feather," Boucher wrote, "why a man who receives a call from another university is almost compelled to accept it," especially when the institution has the standing and the secure position of the University of Chicago:

[38] Barker to Babcock, June 4, 1923.

In the first place, persistent rumors have come to me from many sources that there is a strong probability that the appointment of the new President of the University is to be too much mixed up with the politics of the state for the good of the university; that it is to be determined too much as a part of a political deal. If this is so it would, of course, be likely to have disastrous results upon the institution. Then, too, there is too much of the "buy-it-made-in-Texas" spirit that is likely to be a determining factor in part of the selection of a president. That in itself, of course, would not necessarily be ruinous, if a man with the proper academic standing were chosen, for I can think of two men who are connected with the institution and native Texans who would make good presidents, and certainly far better than an outsider and a politician. The institution must be kept out of politics, as far as its direct and intimate management is concerned, or it will be ruined in standing as an institution of higher learning.

In the second place, there is another form of political interference which is real and threatens worse. This is found in the attitude of a controlling majority in the Legislature. During the debates in the special sessions of two years ago many speeches were made which were a positive disgrace to the state. And in the final action by the Legislature, not simply in cutting salaries and thus breaking many contracts which had been made by the President and the Board of Regents, but in itemizing the budget to the last instructor and thus robbing the administrative authorities of power properly theirs, the university was seriously crippled. I understand that in the present status of the University Appropriation Bill though a slight increase in salaries is provided for, it is on the pernicious horizontal basis, and again the fatal principle of itemization is insisted upon. The legislature has thus entered a field of direct university administration about which it knows nothing, and has made impossible dozens of readjustments within the salary scale and the meeting of dozens of emergencies to hold the faculty together. . . . I honestly believe that the University will have increasing difficulty in getting men of proper training and standing to fill positions above the rank of instructor, because of this interference on the part of the Legislature, and the general dragging of the University through the mire of politics every two years.[39]

Barker was in complete agreement with Boucher on the point that the University was worthy of "far better treatment and a far

[39] C. S. Boucher to Barker, May 12, 1923.

better fate than now seems to be in store for it." A few weeks later A. B. Wolfe, who had recently resigned from the economics faculty at the University to accept a similar position at Ohio State University, wrote Barker that with regard to the Ohio move "the deciding factors were the uncertainty as to the presidency, and still more, the uncertainty as to the kind of financial support the University can look forward to." Wolfe also wrote, "had I stayed I would have been glad to see you [Barker] in the presidency— though I would not wish that thankless job on anybody."[40]

Despite the determined opposition of the University faculty and Ex-Students' Association, the Board of Regents on the afternoon of May 16, 1924, offered Pat M. Neff the presidency of the University. Governor Neff, feeling the antagonism of interested groups, reluctantly declined the position. In the meanwhile Will C. Hogg, in a wire to J. Lutcher Stark, expressed his indignation at the action of the Regents in giving their primary consideration to Governor Neff.[41] On the same afternoon, the Regents elected Guy Stanton Ford, graduate dean of the University of Minnesota, to the Texas presidency. On the following day Dr. Ford declined the position. On May 28 Herbert Eugene Bolton was selected for the job. Bolton tentatively accepted but, after a trip to Austin on June 13–14, he, too, refused the offer. Finally on July 5, Walter Marshal Splawn accepted the University presidency and the long search came to an end.

During the early months of the summer of 1924 there had been much speculation among the members of the University history faculty that Splawn would finally be the choice of the Board of Regents. In a letter to "the Chief," Frederic Duncalf expressed the opinion that "Splawn is Neff's man and appointed by Neff's regents probably at his dictation."[42] Frank Burr Marsh, in Michigan for the summer, wrote Barker, "He is not the man I would have picked for the place but I don't think he is a very bad choice."[43] More pessimistic, Duncalf wrote, "I have no confidence

40 A. B. Wolfe to Barker, June 9, 1923.
41 *Daily Texan*, May 17, 1924; May 18, 1924.
42 Duncalf to Barker, [1924].
43 Frank Burr Marsh to Barker, July 21, 1924.

in him and with the power he will have he can do much damage."[44] A week later Duncalf reported, "I must say that I have been doing some serious thinking. The future at Texas looks more uncertain than it ever has to me."[45] Thad W. Riker wrote from Chicago, "We hear unofficially that Bolton is not coming and there is a rumor that Splawn has already been elected. I told Freddy last winter that we were going to get him. I can picture our colleague's [Hackett's] despair if or when he learns that Bolton is not coming after all. Is it the sp(l)awn of the Devil, I wonder?"[46] In spite of his reservations, Dr. Barker wrote the new president a letter of congratulations and promised to cooperate to the fullest to make his administration a success.

Turning from the turmoil of University politics to academic concerns, we find that one of the school activities that placed severe demands on the time and energy of Professor Barker during the years of the mid-1920's stemmed from his great interest in the establishment of a strong graduate school. The Graduate School of the Main University had been created by the Board of Regents in 1910. From the time of its creation down to June, 1925, the Graduate School had been administered through a presidentially appointed committee known as the Graduate Council. In response to demands upon the University for an expanded program of graduate teaching and research, the Board of Regents requested the 39th Legislature to make possible the creation of a Graduate Faculty. The Legislature responded by appropriating the necessary funds for graduate professorships, research fellowships, and other items essential to the operation of a graduate studies program. In the summer of 1925, therefore, a new era dawned for the University. The Graduate Faculty was organized during the summer months and met in its first formal session on November 11, 1925, under the able direction of Dean Henry Winston Harper.

Interested in the problems and progress of the past in the realm of graduate studies, Eugene C. Barker, a member of the original Graduate Faculty, was keenly aware of the promise and problems

44 Duncalf to Barker, July 16, 1924.
45 Duncalf to Barker, June 23, 1924.
46 T. W. Riker to Barker, July 29, 1924.

of the future. Invited to address the Ex-Students' Association of
Harris County on March 2, 1925, Barker chose the expanded
graduate program as the theme of his Houston speech. In the address Barker pointed with pride to the fact that of the 5,011 students had enrolled in the Main University during the 1924–
1925 winter term, 776 had been graduate students. He then told
his Houston audience that at last the Graduate Faculty was ready
to start and "in general we know where we want to go." Frankly
asserting that "an institution [should] carry students to, or nearly
to, the boundaries of knowledge . . . and set them in the path that
leads beyond the boundary," Barker reported that "the aim of all
graduate training is to make one's self a master of some branch
of learning, with an intelligent comprehension of its relation to
other branches of knowledge." In this respect, he thought, the
ex-students of the University should remember that money alone
was not sufficient "because (1) outstanding scholars will not
work under restraint, (2) they are not to be 'hired and fired'
and muzzled, (3) they will not submit their competency to a test
of student and ex-student opinion or consent to hold or resign
their position at the smile of a petty member of the legislature
just out of their classes." On the contrary, continued Barker, these
people demand, "and in the great universities of the country they
get, (1) permanence of tenure, (2) freedom of thought and
speech, and (3) a peaceful and undisturbed atmosphere in which
to work."

With reference to the situation on the Austin campus and in
answer to the question "where do we stand?" Barker told his listeners, "As to the stability and atmosphere of peace and quiet,
the least said the better. As to permanent tenure, I have known a
full professor to be dismissed for no reason ascertainable by an
outsider other than inability to keep a neurasthenic wife happy;
and I have known more than one full professor of national reputation in his field, and after years of service in the University of
Texas, to be hounded into an involuntary 'voluntary' resignation
by a deliberate persecution on the part of personally unfriendly
ex-students." Admitting that thought was free and that "there has
been a good deal of free speech," Barker left the strong implica-

tion that the deplorable conditions which he had discussed would have to be remedied before the University could become a first-class institution. The remedy, he felt, would depend on the insular Texans' ability to realize (1) that the University of Texas was but a small unit in a large university framework and must conform to established convention or suffer the consequences, and (2) that the tactics of an efficiency expert cannot be applied to the management of a University faculty.[47]

Obviously irritated by conditions that he considered detrimental to faculty morale, Eugene C. Barker soon had another opportunity to express his frank opinions in public. The formal inauguration of W. M. W. Splawn as president of the University of Texas was scheduled as a part of the forty-second annual commencement exercises on the evening of June 8, 1925, in Memorial Stadium. Among the several speakers at the impressive ceremonies was Eugene C. Barker as the chosen representative of the faculty of the University. On Monday evening, June 8, the academic procession assembled at the south entrance to the campus under the direction of Joseph Lindley Henderson for the march across Waller Creek to the stadium. After the invocation by James B. Tidwell of Baylor University and a student address by young Cecil R. Chamberlain, Dr. Barker rose to present his faculty address. As quiet fell over the large audience, Barker began an historic speech, titled "Academic Freedom." In part, he read the following challenge:

MR. PRESIDENT:

It may occur to some that the faculty on such an occasion, like good children in our grandmother's time, "should be seen and not heard," but the committee which arranged these exercises assigned it a speaking part. On reflection this must seem fitting. The relations of a president and faculty are reciprocal and direct. To no other group of men and women in Texas is your inauguration of such vital interest and importance; but conversely the loyalty and trust and sympathetic understanding of no other group is so nearly indispensable to your own successful labor. . . .

Our purpose, I take it, yours and ours, is the same—to realize that

[47] Barker Papers, 1925 (outline of Houston speech, March 2, 1925).

vague, dim vision of the Constitution, "A University of the first class." The attainment of that goal lies through one single channel—a first class faculty. It can be reached through no other route, and it is your principal function to develop conditions that will enable you to obtain and hold such a faculty. This in part is a matter of money. University professors, like business men, lawyers, and other highly trained experts, respond to the law of supply and demand. As a class the best are to be found where the best salaries are paid, and can be attracted only by higher salaries. But money alone is not sufficient. Outstanding scholars will not work under restraint. They are not to be "hired" and "fired." They will not submit their competency and their fitness to any test but the verdict of their professional peers. They will not consent to hold or resign a position at the smile or frown of student or ex-student opinion.

Such men demand, and in the great universities of this country and Europe they have—and the universities are great because they have—(1) Permanent tenure; (2) Freedom of thought and speech, restrained only by taste and good sense; (3) a peaceful atmosphere of assured stability in which to work. Great universities impose no restrictions on the intellectual independence of their faculties, and their governing boards tolerate no interference with them by others.

We have not had these conditions here. It could serve no useful purpose to particularize, but it is no secret to my academic colleagues here or anywhere that a call to the University of Texas arouses no thrill of elation, but only hesitation and doubt, and that for a long time we have been losing more good scholars than we are replacing. No doubt this is an ungracious thing to say. We Texans are much given to talking of the "Great State of Texas"; its primacy in agriculture and exports; its great mineral resources; and its rapid strides in manufacturing. We are smugly self-satisfied, blind to our insularity, and the University is the victim of our smugness. For the real University—not the stately mirage that floats in our admiring vision—is judged by standards which we do not set, and which are little affected by what we think. The University of Texas is part of a university world and must conform to its standards and conventions or suffer the penalty. The penalty is that we must recruit our faculty from the young and untried or from the ranks of tried and proven mediocrity. We are not exempt from the economic law of diminishing returns, and so long as we are content to occupy marginal ground in the university commonwealth we must accept the sort of service that goes with that position.

Dr. Barker then remarked that "there is little the faculty can do about this situation except look to the future with such cheerfulness as experience has left us. . . . We do look to the future," said Barker, "despite the blasting assurance of the chairman of the Board of Regents at a recent faculty meeting that for us 'the future is here.'" And in the end Barker told Splawn: "We look to you, Mr. President, for the development of the spirit that is inseparable from 'a university of the first class.'"[48]

In a comment on Dr. Barker's "remarkable demand for academic freedom," the San Antonio *Express* reported, "the University commencement exercises are over but the echoes of Professor Barker's speech are by no means stilled. In dignified, but direct language, Professor Barker told President Splawn that the members of the University faculty expect conditions different from those which, he intimated, have prevailed."[49] An unidentified member of the faculty was quoted as having said: "This speech, delivered with great vigor, and weighed with the strong personality of its author, made a great impression on the entire University community. It presents so tersely, forcibly, and accurately the views of the faculty on one of the most important problems of the University that it deserves wider publicity than it has received."[50] But the news of Barker's speech did circulate in academic circles. As the word spread, Dr. Barker's daily mail brought a shower of compliments from far beyond the borders of Texas. From Ohio State University, A. B. Wolfe, commented, "We have 9,000 students on the ground but I doubt if we are a university of the first class. We can't even beat Red Grange!"[51] From the University of Wisconsin, the distinguished historian W. T. Root wrote:

You are a man after my heart—I hurry to tell you while the spirit is moving. Thanks for a copy of your address. I read it once, I read it

48 Barker Papers, 1925 (longhand copy); Barker, *Essays*, 3–5.
49 San Antonio *Express*, June 14, 1925 (a carefully preserved clipping in the Maury Maverick collection).
50 Ibid.
51 A. B. Wolfe to Barker, November 23, 1925.

twice; then I thought it over. They picked you to do the job; that was a good "pick" and you gave the stuff straight. Every word is true; every thought is sound; it is well expressed. How glad I am to hear one say the truth soberly and squarely. I've heard enough about Birge who goes out as president here and Frank who comes in that it makes me sick. I heard so much about the "Wisconsin Idea, of Wisconsin progress," that I almost was forced to the conclusion that the University had a monopoly of ideas and progress. And so I was in a receptive mood when I read your address.[52]

Perhaps it should be pointed out that Governor Miriam A. Ferguson was on the speaker's platform on the fateful evening and followed Dr. Barker on the program—without doubt, he also spoke for the benefit of the governor.

When President Splawn recommended the elimination of advanced courses in the field of Latin American history for the school year 1926–1927, Dr. Barker rallied to Hackett's defense by pointing out to the president that the University of Texas was recognized as one of three or four institutions in the United States best prepared for work in that field; that abandonment of advanced courses in Latin American and Spanish southwestern history would injure the department for many years to come; and that the elimination of these courses would be highly inconsistent with the emphasis about to be placed on graduate work at the University. Obviously angry, Barker made it clear to his president that,

The development of a well articulated department is a matter of time and much effort, and, to some degree, of happy circumstances. Many years of exceptionally harmonious thought and effort have gone into the development of the history department. It is by no means what we should like to have it, but it would be meek humility to deny that we have been proud of its standing here and especially abroad. With all due respect to you, we must protest, that, in our judgement, the internal organization of this department cannot be wisely administered from the President's Office. Nor, as a matter of general administration, do we believe that progress will come by weakening a strong department. We beg of you to reinstate the provision which the legislature

[52] W. T. Root to Barker, June 23, 1925.

made for Professor Hackett's work, and, since departmental plans are involved in the matter, we hope that you will inform us of your decision promptly.[53]

It is of the greatest significance that Dr. Barker won his point and the work of Charles W. Hackett in the Latin American field continued with even greater emphasis than before.

President Splawn's tenure in the presidency of the University was of short duration; in the early part of the year 1927 he resigned effective September 1 of that year. Carefully preserved in the Barker papers is an undated newspaper clipping, yellowed with age, carrying the story that the University of Texas would not go outside the state in search of a president to succeed Dr. Splawn. It was reported that four men on, or formerly on, the faculty were being considered; the names listed were Dean Harry Y. Benedict, Professor Eugene C. Barker, Dean Thomas U. Taylor, and Dr. George C. Butte. After a mention of the fact that Dr. Benedict, current dean of the College of Arts and Sciences, would serve as acting president during a brief absence from the campus by Splawn; that T. U. Taylor was a senior member of the faculty and dean of the College of Engineering; and that Dr. George C. Butte was currently serving as the attorney general of Puerto Rico; the unknown journalist remarked that "the attitude of Dr. Barker toward the presidency is not known."[54]

There is not a single piece of evidence, either in the Barker manuscripts or in his vast letter collection, to indicate that he was actively seeking the office of president at this time. There can be little doubt, on the other hand, that Barker would have accepted the position if it had been tendered to him. In May, 1927, he received a copy of a letter written by Arthur Lefevre to Robert L. Batts to the effect Lefevre was writing Judge Batts "as an old friend and not at all as a member of the Board of Regents"; Lefevre pointed out that "I simply want you to know personally that in my opinion Professor Barker is the best qualified man who could be called to the Presidency. Barker understands the essential

[53] Barker to Splawn, May 25, 1925.
[54] Barker Papers, undated newspaper clipping.

principles of university administration better than any incumbent of the Presidency that the University has heretofore had. . . . I believe him to be a good judge of men. . . . the prime requisite for successful administration. . . . He is a lover of truth and justice and has true courage."[55]

Perhaps the Lefevre letter was a complete surprise to Dr. Barker, perhaps not. It is definite that there was a move to make Eugene C. Barker president of the University and that this movement centered in Houston. And there was some concern among the members of the University faculty who feared the Barker honesty and courage, that Barker might be the choice of the Regents. On June 6, 1927, for example, Dr. Barker received what he described as "my first anonymous letter," addressed to Mister E. C. Barker, Esq., 2660 Saint Gabriel Street, and containing a newspaper clipping announcing that Dr. Butte had been proposed for the presidency of the University; and underneath the pasted clipping, in a childish scrawl, the writer had commented: "Hee! Hee! Ha! Ha! Ha! Not You; Thank God!"[56] This anonymous correspondence stands as proof that at least one member of the University community took a rather dim view of Barker's possible elevation to the front office. When the time for decision arrived, the Board of Regents chose Harry Yandell Benedict, revered by students and faculty alike as "Dean Benny." Benedict had entered the University of Texas in 1889; he graduated in June, 1892, and took an M.A. degree the following year with a major in mathematics. After finishing his Ph.D. at Harvard, Professor Benedict joined the University faculty as an instructor in mathematics in September, 1899. He and Barker became steadfast friends early in the history of the institution. There is no evidence to indicate that Dr. Barker was disappointed in 1927 when Benedict was chosen president.

The days with Harry Yandell Benedict at the administrative helm of the University were to last for ten years. For Dr. Barker these were among the happier years of his long service on the

[55] Arthur Lefevre to R. L. Batts, May 21, 1927, in the Barker Papers.
[56] Barker Papers.

faculty; he had great admiration for Benedict and, following the president's untimely death on May 10, 1937, he remarked in a brief statement of appreciation,

Though his administration as president of the University of Texas was identified with its gratifying physical growth, his supreme interest was centered in its spiritual and intellectual growth. He strove to build an institution of superior teachers and fruitful scholars, and to create an atmosphere of vital learning which would penetrate the civic character of the State. He labored faithfully, against recurrent disappointments, to co-ordinate the various educational institutions of the State into a harmonious system, advancing from the elementary grades of the public schools to the graduate school of the University. He set and maintained a standard of intellectual independence that was an inspiration to all who knew him. He practiced in all sincerity the much abused doctrine of academic freedom, and was zealous in its defense. His regard for the rights of the faculty was so sincere and so unobtrusive that the ease and security which was its fruit were accepted by its beneficiaries as a commonplace of University administration. . . . In personal relationships, Dr. Benedict had a rare gift of friendship. It was a quality not easy to analyze. Fundamentally, it was the product of a truly sweet and gentle character. He was tolerant, patient, judicial, considerate, and always self-controlled. Withal, he was genuinely democratic. His broad knowledge and lively interests attracted men and women in many fields of activity. They admired his unpretentious learning, enjoyed his shrewd humor, and loved his steadfast character.[57]

As the eventful years of the Benedict administration passed, the golden prosperity of "normalcy" gave way to the bitter depression of the 1930's. A stunned nation watched depression spread over the land. While economic conditions in Texas were generally better than the national average, distress and suffering were both real and severe as the gradual collapse of agricultural prosperity during the 1920's finally brought an unbelievable low to prices paid for farm products and a subsequent increase in farm mortgage foreclosures. Entire families, displaced agrarians, wandered about the countryside in search of work; hitchhiking by road and by rail and residing in crude "Hoovervilles" on the out-

[57] Barker, *Essays*, 75–76.

skirts of Texas cities, the vast army of unemployed added to the bleakness of the era. In 1931 Eugene C. Barker watched with interest as the state Legislature discussed a multitude of proposals to reduce the salaries of state employees. Although the debate was lengthy, no salaries were cut, however, until the legislative session of 1933; at that time the Texas lawmakers reduced practically all state salaries by 25 percent. A conservative by nature, Dr. Barker was dismayed by the victory of Franklin D. Roosevelt and the New Deal in the national election of 1932. However, before moving on to a detailed study of this phase of Barker's life, we will examine and evaluate his more significant contributions to the field of American history.

The Historian at Work

As has been noted in a previous chapter, Dr. Barker believed that a historian should approach his scholarly investigations without preconceived notions or opinions, that he should collect all of the available evidence and then present to the reader a picture of conditions and events as they actually were, with their causes and consequences. All personal opinions were to be plainly labeled as such with both sides of the argument clearly presented. In this fashion the special subject being investigated should be related to the whole fabric of history. This was Dr. Barker's simple formula of historical investigation and writing. His style of writing, once described by Barker as heavy and undramatic, was actually straightforward, compact, and logical. The facts were presented and allowed to speak for themselves "without verbal display [seldom a wasted word], highflown rhetoric, or soap-box oratory."[1] In a statement pertaining to Barker's *Life of Austin*, Dr. Charles W. Ramsdell caught the essence of the historian's style when he said: "The reader cannot fail to be struck by the style of the narrative. It is Barkeresque. Everyone who has been associated with Barker knows what that means. It means absolute precision and clarity of expression in a natural, easy, direct, yet vigorous, pungent diction. The reader is never in doubt as to what he means. He strips his sentences clean of superfluous words."[2] It

[1] L. W. Payne, "Professor Eugene C. Barker's Life of Stephen F. Austin," in Barker, *Essays*, 297.

[2] Charles W. Ramsdell, "Barker's Austin as Viewed by the Historian," in Barker, *Essays*, 252 ff.

would not be an exaggeration to say that the style of all of Barker's writing was Barkeresque.

Eugene C. Barker's greatest contribution to the field of American historical writing came in the area of Texas history; in this respect he did more than any other historian to show the influence that Texas exerted in shaping the destiny of the United States. But Barker would have been the last person in the world to describe himself as a Texas historian and only a Texas historian. His active mind was not limited by provincialism; his basic nature was not insular. In a report to a group of Rocky Mountain historians, Barker, while at the very height of his career, said: "It happens that nearly all of the independent investigation that I have ever tried to do in American history has impinged upon the motives and methods which have operated in the acquisition of the West."[3] In the mind of Professor Barker, therefore, the history of Texas was primarily the story of the pioneer farmers who followed the fur traders into the trans-Mississippi West from their log-cabin homes in Missouri, Arkansas, Tennessee, Kentucky, and neighboring states. He pointed out that the prime character in the development of the lands beyond the Sabine River was the typical American frontiersman, a self-reliant, democratic individual, rich in experience, poor in material wealth, but indoctrinated with a restlessness inherited from generations of pioneering forefathers. When these men crossed the Sabine and Red rivers they found the mission stations, ranches, puebloes, and presidios of the Spanish-American. As the aggressive Anglo-American pioneers over ran this vast domain, the history they left behind provided the setting for Dr. Barker's special field of study. A survey of his bibliography, however, reveals that most of Barker's scholarly investigations were related directly to the field of Texas and Mexican history. By way of explanation, it should be pointed out that the primary materials available to the resident historian west of the great river concern the story of the Spanish borderlands. When

[3] Eugene C. Barker, "On the Historiography of American Territorial Expansion," *Essays*, 205 ff., reprinted from J. F. Willard and C. B. Goodykoontz (editors), *Trans-Mississippi West*. The Barker article was prepared to be read at a conference of American historians held at Boulder, Colorado.

Eugene Barker entered the field of American history in 1899, these materials remained unexplored and unused by the professional historian. Barker simply worked with the materials at hand, and the total product of his labor was extensive.

In 1926 Charles W. Ramsdell remarked that "a prominent scholar in the field of American history once referred to 'the Texas school of American historians.'" Ramsdell was of the opinion that the *Texas school* was a proud title that included within its scope "the names of Garrison, Bugbee, and Bolton, and by no means least, Barker."[4] To a large extent Eugene C. Barker's decision to explore the sources of the history of Texas and the Spanish borderlands had been made long before he entered the University of Pennsylvania to complete his graduate studies. These formative years, as noted previously, were shaped primarily by George Pierce Garrison and Lester G. Bugbee, and Bugbee's influence was the stronger of the two.

Many years after the death of Bugbee, Barker called attention to the fact that "although the total volume of Bugbee's publications was not large, their influence was significant. They changed the tone of American historical writing concerning the colonization of Texas, the Texas revolution, the annexation of Texas, and, in a large measure, the Mexican War."[5] Barker was of the opinion that Bugbee's most significant publication was his essay entitled "Slavery in Early Texas," published in the *Political Science Quarterly*, September and December, 1898. Prior to the Bugbee essay the traditional view of the immediate cause of the Texas revolution had attributed the rebellion to Anglo-American resentment of Mexico's efforts to abolish slavery in the province of Texas. Barker believed that "Bugbee so completely proved the fallacy of the charge that it was never subsequently repeated by a recognized historian."[6]

Barker's future was also conditioned by the professional and scholarly interests of Dr. George P. Garrison, the new-found in-

---

[4] Charles W. Ramsdell, "Barker as a Historian," *Essays*, vii.
[5] Barker, *Essays*, 55.
[6] Ibid.

terests of Herbert Eugene Bolton, and, at Pennsylvania, the teaching and skills of the venerable John B. McMaster.

Less obvious but no less significant is the fact that Dr. Barker was influenced to a remarkable degree by the early writings of Frederick Jackson Turner. A keen reader, Barker became familiar with the Turner thesis as expressed in "The Significance of the Frontier in American History" at an early date in his career, and, although its presence is not always easily seen by the reader, the frontier hypothesis outlined by Professor Turner is the underlying theme of the great majority of Barker's scholarly investigations and subsequent writings. In *The Life of Stephen F. Austin*, Dr. Barker uses a quotation from the writing of Baron Carondelet, the Spanish governor of the Louisiana territory who had a keen appreciation of the menace to the Spanish empire in the westward push of the American frontiersmen. With picturesque accuracy Carondelet recorded,

A carbine and a little cornmeal in a sack is sufficient for an American to range the forests alone for a month. With his carbine he kills wild cattle and deer for food, and protects himself from the savages. Having dampened the cornmeal, it serves in lieu of bread. He erects a house by laying some tree trunks across others in the form of a square; and even a fort impregnable to savages by building on a story crosswise above the ground floor. The cold does not fright him, and when a family grows tired of one place, it moves to another, and establishes itself there with the same ease.[7]

Barker's source for this statement was Louis Houck, *The Spanish Regime in Missouri*, published in Chicago in 1909. Houck's source is unknown, but the letter from Baron Carondelet, governor of the provinces of Louisiana and West Florida to his captain general, was secured for the Draper collection of the Wisconsin State Historical Society in 1883, translated by Professor W. F. Giese of the University of Wisconsin, and edited by Frederick Jackson Turner in the *American Historical Review*, April, 1897, with the title, "Carondelet on the Defense of Louisiana, 1794."[8]

---

[7] Barker, *The Life of Stephen F. Austin*, 7.
[8] Everett E. Edwards and Fulmer Mood, *The Early Writings of Frederick*

In organizing his narrative on the life of Austin, Barker traces the fortunes of Moses Austin on the Missouri and Arkansas frontiers, describes the origin of the Texas colonization scheme, takes Stephen F. Austin into Mexico, and, in a chapter entitled "The Establishment of the First Colony," returns to the frontier theme proper with the following statement:

> The colonization of Texas began at an auspicious time. As Professor Turner has so effectively described in his illuminating studies, the current of population set westward with the establishment of the first English settlement on the Atlantic coast. For a century and a half the movement was necessarily slow, up the rivers beyond tide-water, into the piedmont. The broad parallel ranges of the Appalachian Mountains served as a dam to hold venturesome frontiers-men back from the country beyond. By the beginning of the American revolution, however, they had begun to trickle across the barrier into Kentucky and Tennessee.[9]

Several years later Barker teamed with Walter P. Webb and Henry Steele Commager to write a textbook for use in the American history classes of the secondary schools of the nation. The three historians divided their task, and it fell to Barker to cover the period from 1789 to 1845. One of his chapters was entitled "The Growth of the Nation," and Dr. Barker began this specific unit with "the characteristics of the westward movement."

In 1893 Professor Frederick Jackson Turner, a discerning student and a great teacher, published an essay entitled, "The Significance of the Frontier in American History." It is one of the most famous and effective pieces of writing ever done in the field of American history. In it Professor Turner described the movement of pioneers across the continent from the Atlantic Ocean to the Pacific, analyzed the motives which sent them on their migrations, and indicated the effects of the Westward movement upon the development of United States history. After calling attention to the fact that "the motives which carried settlers westward were substantially the same as those which cause

Jackson Turner (Madison, Wisconsin, 1938), 242 (the bibliography was compiled by Everett E. Edwards).
[9] Barker, *The Life of Austin*, 89.

people to move today," Barker emphasized the continuity of the frontier movements and pointed out that,

the frontier was a mixing place. Professor Turner called it the melting pot. Wherever encountered, frontier conditions were much the same, and emigrants exposed to them, no matter from what section they came, tended to grow into a common type. As a rule frontiersmen were independent, self-reliant, and democratic. They had a way of demanding social and political equality. Frontier communities and frontier states had a great influence in doing away with restrictions on voting and holding office which the early state constitutions imposed and in substituting the democratic practice of manhood suffrage and eligibility to office. To combat the double attraction of cheap public land and liberal political privileges in the new states, the old states were compelled to liberalize their own constitutions. Other influences besides those of the frontier moved in the same direction, but the freedom of the West was always a powerful stimulus to liberalization.[10]

Barker's acceptance of the Turner frontier thesis was also demonstrated in the classroom. In his advanced courses at the University, Dr. Barker would introduce the topic of westward expansion with a concise interpretation of Turner's essay on the significance of the frontier in American history. After pointing out the several stages in the geographical advance of the frontier, he would call attention to "Turner's fine simile: Stand at Cumberland Gap and watch the procession of civilization marching single file across the continent. The buffalo following the trail to the salt licks; the Indian following the buffalo; the hunters and fur traders following the path of the Indian; the pioneer cattle raiser and rancher creeping along in the path of the trader; and the farmer following the rancher, pushing the whole procession farther west—and the frontier had passed by." Distinguishing between the several frontiers—the trader's frontier, the rancher's frontier, or the miner's frontier, and the farmer's frontier—Barker then called the attention of his students to the fact that "Texas represents a typical frontier state" in that the region was settled as a result of individual initiative. To him, the result was "marked

[10] Barker Papers, miscellaneous manuscripts.

individualism"—one of the major products of the Texas frontier.[11] Therefore, Barker was being consistent with his general philosophy of American history when he began work on the life of Stephen F. Austin, a typical American frontiersman.

An analysis and evaluation of Eugene C. Barker's contributions to the historiography of the American West should properly begin with *The Life of Stephen F. Austin, Founder of Texas, 1793–1836: A Chapter in the Westward Movement of the Anglo-American People*, published in 1925 by the Texas State Historical Association. The story of Barker's book begins long before the year 1925. When Lester G. Bugbee became interested in the Austin papers in 1892–1893, the vast collection was the property of Colonel Guy M. Bryan, grandson of Moses Austin and the nephew of Stephen. For over a half a century Colonel Bryan had stored the papers in a tower room of his home at Quintana to protect them from inundation by gulf storms. When Bugbee, who desired to write the life of Stephen F. Austin, requested permission to use the papers in 1893, Colonel Bryan replied that he would be absent all summer and could not permit use of the papers except under his own supervision. Bugbee had to depart for New York and Columbia University without seeing the manuscripts.

On his return to Austin in 1896, Bugbee's interest in the Austin papers was delayed by a trip to Mexico City. The following Christmas he spent a portion of his vacation at Quintana and so completely won the confidence of Colonel Bryan that he was permitted to spend the summer of 1897 working through the papers without supervision. Bugbee promptly pushed his proposed study of the Massachusetts Loyalists during the American Revolution into the background; a more interesting and more important field had opened for him. In December, 1898, Colonel Guy Bryan moved to Austin; the Moses and Stephen F. Austin collection was stored in the basement of the capitol, and the papers

---

[11] Barker Papers, class notes: History 35. These notes, carefully written on half sheets in typical Barker fashion, appear on the back side of stationery belonging to the Texas State Historical Association during the years when Z. T. Fulmore was president of the Association.

were made available to graduate students of the University. As a senior and graduate student, Barker had free access to the Austin papers.[12] In June, 1899, the elderly Bryan wrote Bugbee to ask, "When can you commence to write the life of Stephen F. Austin?" In the early part of 1901, Bryan made a similar query. But the days of both Bryan and Bugbee were numbered.[13] After Colonel Bryan's death the papers "which he had so long and so faithfully held in trust for the history of Texas were given by his children to the University of Texas."[14]

In 1926 Dr. Barker recalled,

Then by a species of hereditary succession the trust devolved upon me. Even before the Austin Papers came to the University Lester G. Bugbee had done much work in them, and contemplated writing the life of Austin. Three striking articles, great volumes of notes, and two or three paragraphs of a chapter on Moses Austin remain to show how excellently he would have done it. More than any other historian I have ever known, Bugbee seemed to me to possess the power to make the past live—to present it simply and vividly in all its complex relation. Bugbee died in 1902. Had he lived he would have been now just fifty-seven years of age, and he would have been now one of the great historians of the United States.

Then Dr. Garrison turned to the task. His *Texas* appeared in 1903, his *Westward Extension* in 1906, the first volume of his *Diplomatic Correspondence* in 1909. He had already begun to canvass the Austin Papers when he died in 1910. Whether he had in mind a comprehensive history of the colonization of Texas or a life of Austin, I do not know. They are almost one and the same. Dr. Garrison was a keen, cultured, broadly trained scholar. His study of either would have been definitive.

I loved Bugbee; I love his memory. I revered Dr. Garrison. And as the academic heir of Bugbee and Garrison and the appropriate representative of the University, I had to undertake this work, whether I wanted to or not (But I wanted to).[15]

---

[12] Barker, "The Historian Explains," *Essays*, 18–19; "Lester Gladstone Bugbee," *Essays*, 49–51.
[13] Bugbee Papers, Letters, 1899–1900; 1900–1901.
[14] Barker, "The Historian Explains," *Essays*, 18.
[15] Ibid.

Having "fitted his shoulders well into the collar," Eugene Barker went to work on the life of Stephen F. Austin. Barker had been somewhat of a prophet in 1906 when he wrote Hallie Bryan Perry, "I am still grubbing away on the period of the Texas Revolution, and the more I learn of the period the more I am impressed with the thorough greatness of Austin. I hope someday to see an exhaustive biography of him with a complete collection —so far as it is possible—of his letters and writings. It would be a magnificent monument to his greatness."[16] Shortly after the realization dawned on Barker that the life of Stephen F. Austin would be his to complete, a letter arrived from W. S. Robertson asking for information about the Austin papers:

I write to you in regard to a matter which I mentioned to you when we met at the American Historical Association meeting at Indianapolis. For some time I have been interested in the career of Stephen F. Austin, partly because I am investigating some related topics in Mexican history, and partly because of a genuine interest in Austin himself. Would you, therefore, be good enough to tell me something about the general character of the Austin MSS. in Texas? I should also like to know whether or not you know of anyone who is at present seriously at work investigating the career of Stephen Austin.[17]

Barker answered Robertson's questions without delay; he wrote,

The Austin MSS. at the University of Texas are almost entirely calendared, and are in good condition for working.

· · ·

Your next question causes me some embarrassment. Certainly nobody is at this time working seriously on the life of Austin unless it be I, and I am afraid that I can't honestly claim that I am. I have looked upon him with the eye of desire but it is only within the last year that the way has opened for me to get at the subject. During the present year I have been too much pressed by other things, mostly administrative work and teaching, to do anything. . . . There are few things I like less than seeing a man sit on a good thing and keep others off, and there

[16] Hallie Bryan Perry Papers, Letters from Eugene C. Barker, Archives, University of Texas Library.
[17] W. S. Robertson to Barker, May 28, 1911, Barker Papers, Letters 1899–1956.

is no reason why my intention to do a piece of work should bar you from it. At the same time, I frankly confess that I should hate to see you start this. The conditions are somewhat peculiar. The Austin MSS., which are indispensable to the subject, are the property of the University of Texas, and I, a member of the faculty of the University of Texas, am working in the field of the papers. It would look bad locally to have someone else take the cream.[18]

Several months later Barker received a generous and understanding letter from Robertson saying, "Thank you for your frank letter. I shall leave the subject alone, for the time being at least, trusting that you will exploit it. . . . For some time I have been collecting data for a biography of Agustín de Iturbide."[19]

Perhaps the Robertson correspondence prompted Barker to remark, "since it was known that I had begun, no one else could ethically take up the investigation, and so I came under obligation to Austin's memory. If I prevented others from building his long overdue monument, I must in decency build it myself."[20] At any rate, Barker went to work. The University provided the money for copying manuscripts, and the Littlefield Fund furnished the means for obtaining all available background material. As the years passed, Dr. Barker devoted as much time as he could spare to the Austin project. First, he arranged all of the Moses and Stephen F. Austin letters and writings in order, made brief but careful editorial notes, and submitted the collection to the Historical Manuscripts Commission of the American Historical Association for publication. The initial volume of *The Austin Papers,* covering the years 1789–1827, appeared in print as a part of the *Annual Report of the American Historical Association for the Year 1919.*

The second volume of *The Austin Papers,* published in 1928 as a part of the *Annual Report of the American Historical Association for the Year 1922,* contained the papers "belonging to the

[18] Barker to W. S. Robertson, May 31, 1911.

[19] Robertson to Barker, October 15, 1911 (Robertson's work on Iturbide was published by the Duke University Press in 1952).

[20] Barker, "The Historian Explains," *Essays,* 19.

years 1828–1834." Barker commented that it was "during these years that Stephen F. Austin was driven from his attitude of loyalty to Mexico and began to give thoughts to the future of Texas, either as an independent State or as a member of the United States of the North."[21] In the meanwhile, the third and final volume, containing the papers of Austin from October, 1834, to January, 1837, had been published by the University of Texas Press—a task finished in 1927. Thus the end came to a laborious and tedious research project. As the result of patient editorial work, stretching over the better part of two decades, Barker made a significant contribution to the understanding of Anglo-American Texas, the background of the Texas revolution, and contemporary conditions in Mexico and the United States.

As work progressed on the papers, Barker began the task of writing the life of Austin. He read a paper titled "Stephen F. Austin" at the 1917 meeting of the American Historical Association at Philadelphia. This introductory work was subsequently published in the *Mississippi Valley Historical Review* and the *Southwestern Historical Quarterly* and marks the completion of Barker's first effort toward a biography of Stephen F. Austin.[22] Delayed by his great diversity of duties on the campus, Barker made slow progress during the months that followed. A painstaking scholar who left no stone unturned in his search for the truth, he wrote Hallie Bryan Perry in December, 1921, that he would have to spend time in Saltillo "next summer working on the Robertson Colony." Barker was certain that most of the necessary documents were in the possession of Mr. Sterling Robertson of Temple, but "I shouldn't like to borrow from him, even if he would lend, because the facts will prove Robertson (and John Henry Brown) such a bilious liar that I shouldn't want to be under obligation to him."[23]

---

[21] Eugene C. Barker (ed.), *The Austin Papers* (3 vols.; Washington and Austin, 1924–1928), II, vii.

[22] Eugene C. Barker, "Stephen F. Austin," *Mississippi Valley Historical Review*, V (June, 1918); *Southwestern Historical Quarterly*, XXII (July, 1918).

[23] Barker to Hallie Bryan Perry, December 12, 1921, Perry Papers.

In the spring of 1923 another letter to Mrs. Perry reveals progress on the manscript; Barker wrote,

> The Life is started and moving with considerable momentum—a
> few hundred words every day. I plunged into the Texas part of the
> story, leaving Connecticut, Pa., Va., and Mo. for later labor. I did this
> because I found that sort of a mental hazard, as we say in golf, was
> holding me back from the beginning in that phase, so I decided to
> jump the whole period and get down to what after all is the main show.
> I have three chapters done—The Beginning of the Texas Venture—
> Stephen in Mexico, 1822–1823—the Establishment of the First Colony.
> Sometimes I have the uneasy feeling that the innocent by-stander, for
> whom the book is presumably written, will find too much detail, will
> feel that it is much to do about little, and that I will not succeed in
> making Stephen's problems and his great character and ability in
> handling them for all to see who read. . . . Sometimes I think I'll get a
> good stenographer and dictate roughly the story of the Robertson
> colony so that if I should happen to leave you before getting through
> with the chapter at least the main facts would be in shape for any
> intelligent student to polish off.[24]

In the autumn of the same year, Barker reported: "I got in some
good licks this summer, and have my schedule arranged to allow
a good deal of uninterrupted time this session so that I hope to
make good progress. I have something more than 80,000 words
done, and when I get one more chapter done (which I am just
starting) I'll have it all typed and see what you think of it. I am
afraid it has no soul."[25]

The finishing touches were applied to the manuscript during
the year that followed, and *The Life of Stephen F. Austin, Founder of Texas, 1793–1836: A Chapter in the Westward Movement
of the Anglo-American People* was published by the State Historical Association in 1925; Barker had made a major contribution to
the history of western America. As Herbert Gambrell read Barker's
estimate of Austin, the story of the Great Stone Face was called
to mind, and Gambrell asked: "Wasn't it possible that, through
living with Austin all these years, Barker had subconsciously tak-

24 Barker to Hallie Bryan Perry, March 9, 1923, Perry Papers.
25 Barker to Hallie Bryan Perry, October 10, 1923, Perry Papers.

en on Austin's characteristics?"[26] While there may or may not be something in Gambrell's theory, the reverse might as well have been true; perhaps Barker's Stephen F. Austin took on the characteristics of his biographer.

In a lengthy review of his accomplishment, Dr. Barker remarked,

In writing my *Life of Austin*, I was blessed with an abundance of material, a figure of first class importance, and a wholly virgin subject. One needed only patience, industry, and persistence to accomplish an important result, because, Austin's work being what it was, no first biography of the man could be unimportant. Looking back on my long association with Austin, I find nothing to regret on the score of patience, industry, and persistence. I set no time limit for the completion of the job. I spared no pains in collecting material without neglecting daily duties—I hope. I tried to enforce a self-imposed rule to write at least a few words every day; and it isn't an easy rule to live by, as anyone may learn.

. . .

. . . I have sometimes wished that my limitations were fewer and different. I lack dramatic and romantic appreciation; I am emotionally tongue-tied, writing or speaking. The result is a heaviness that need not exist, for there was plenty of drama in Austin's career, and possibly romance for one who chooses to find it. One of my graduate students once told me that the book was hard reading, and I can well believe him. I see no reason why anybody should read it except for information. Seekers of sober knowledge should be grateful for two qualities of style: there are no cryptic, truncated sentences and not a single *former* or *latter* in the book.[27]

In 1924 Frederic L. Paxson surveyed two decades of the historiography of the southwestern frontier and remarked, "Eugene C. Barker, the worthy successor of Garrison in the University of Texas, has traversed the whole early history of the State in the *Quarterly* of the Texas State Historical Society, now continued as the *Southwestern Historical Quarterly*. Garrison and his pupils,

---

[26] Herbert P. Gambrell, December 18, 1941, in Barker Papers, "Portrait of a Historian."

[27] Eugene C. Barker, "Reflections of a Biographer," Barker Papers.

Barker and Bolton, founded a distinctive school of investigators of southwestern history."[28] Many years later, Walter P. Webb, one of Barker's pupils, pointed out that through books and articles concerning the influence of the Texas question and Texas history upon national development (and especially western expansion), Dr. Barker "exploded some pet hypotheses that had gained wide acceptance. One was that the westward expansion of the United States, the acquisition of Texas and the Mexican cession of 1848 resulted from a conspiracy of southerners to expand slave territory; another was the idea that in the Texas Revolution and Mexican War all the fault was on the Mexican side."[29] With these statements in mind, it would be well to examine in detail the more significant contributions of Eugene C. Barker to the historiography of the southwest. For the sake of simplicity the following subtopics will be reviewed: (1) the colonization of Texas, (2) the Texas Revolution, and (3) the annexation of Texas and the Mexican War.

Under the general heading of the colonization of Texas, Eugene C. Barker attacked the conspiracy theory with such vigor that it is now apparently a dead issue to American historians. Following the evidence assimilated by Lester G. Bugbee, Eugene C. Barker became interested in the fallacy of the conspiracy theory at an early date in his career. In 1911 he wrote,

Earnest patriots like Benjamin Lundy, William Ellery Channing, and John Quincy Adams saw in the Texas revolution a disgraceful affair promoted by sordid slaveholders and land speculators. Even to the critical ear of the modern historian their arguments sound plausible, and it is not strange that in a period distinguished by sectionalism they were accepted by partisans at full value. The fundamental defect of these arguments lay in the fact that their authors knew too little of contemporary opinion in Texas. The truth is, so far as one may judge from the absence of discussion of the subject in Texas, that slavery

---

[28] Frederic L. Paxson, *History of the American Frontier*, 303.

[29] Report of the "Special Eugene Campbell Barker Memorial Resolution Committee," Documents and Minutes of the General Faculty, March, 1957. The resolution was prepared by Walter P. Webb, Robert A. Law, and Joe Frantz.

played no part in precipitating the revolution; while it is certain that land speculation, of which there was unquestionably a great deal, tended rather to retard than to hasten the outbreak.[30]

Speaking as the president of the Mississippi Valley Historical Association at Louisville, Kentucky, on May 1, 1924, Barker returned to the conspiracy theory for his subject. Beginning with the origin of the idea, he reminded his fellow historians that "Benjamin Lundy published in 1836, at the close of the Texas revolution, a pamphlet entitled: *The War in Texas; A Review of Facts and Circumstances, showing that this Contest is the Result of a long Premeditated Crusade against the Government set on foot by Slaveholders, Land Speculators, etc., with the View of Re-establishing, Extending, and Perpetuating the System of Slavery and the Slave Trade in the Republic of Mexico*," in which the author announced in the course of his argument "it is susceptible of the clearest demonstration that the immediate cause and leading object of this contest originated in a settled design among the slave holders of this country (with the land speculators and slave traders) to wrest the large and valuable territory of Texas from the Mexican Republic in order to re-establish the System of Slavery, to open a vast and profitable Slave Market therein, and ultimately, to annex it to the United States." Barker then explained that Lester G. Bugbee in 1898 "discussed this question with a breadth and penetration that leaves little to be added. The present study, which is a by-product of a biography of Stephen F. Austin uses a considerable volume of sources that Mr. Bugbee did not have . . . but it confirms his main conclusions."[31] Barker pointed out that he had covered other features of the problem in works on the colonization of Texas, relations between the United States and Mexico, and a study of President Jackson and the Texas revolution. After a detailed examination of slavery from the point of

[30] Eugene C. Barker, "Public Opinion in Texas Preceding the Revolution," *Annual Report of the American Historical Association for the Year 1911*, I, 219.

[31] Eugene C. Barker, "The Influence of Slavery in the Colonization of Texas," *Mississippi Valley Historical Review*, XI (June, 1924); *Southwestern Historical Quarterly*, XXVIII (July, 1924), 1–33.

view of the settler in Texas, asking the question: Did he regard himself as a crusader to perpetuate slavery and the slave trade in Mexico and to bring Texas finally into "the United States of the North"? Barker could report that the essential results of his investigation were,

(1) While at the beginning of Texas colonization the government reluctantly tolerated slavery, it was consistently and persistently hostile to the institution.

(2) Slaveholders contemplating emigration to Texas, manifested, naturally, a good deal of anxiety concerning the status of slavery there; and after settlement opposed abolition and evaded the government's efforts to prevent the further introduction of slaves. Their reasons were twofold: they wished not to lose their property and they were profoundly convinced that the development of Texas, and consequently their own prosperity, depended upon an abundance of slave labor.

(3) But there is no evidence of purpose on the part of the emigrants, or of the slaveholding leaders of the United States, to wrest Texas from Mexico to enlarge the slave area of the south; and, so far as the absence of evidence may prove the negative, it seems that there was no such purpose.

And, finally, (4) it does not appear that anxiety concerning the status of slavery played an appreciable part in producing the Texas revolution.[32]

If the conspiracy theory has little to recommend it, what were the factors motivating the colonization of Texas by American frontiersmen? In his Garrison Hall classroom, Barker answered the question rather simply by pointing out to his students that Texas was settled as the result of (1) the westward movement, (2) the change in public land policy in 1820, (3) the effects of the panic of 1819, and (4) the reorganization of the United States Bank in 1819 under the direction of Langdon Cheves—marking the origin of a rigid, stringent financial system that accentuated economic distress along the frontier. In answer to the question: Did the Missouri Compromise affect immigration into Texas,

---

[32] Barker, "The Influence of Slavery in the Colonization of Texas," *Mississippi Valley Historical Review*, XI (June, 1924), 35.

Barker said, No! He then remarked that the theory began to be expressed about 1837 and grew because of repetition. "The Chief" would then trace the conspiracy theory as set forth in Hermann von Holst's second volume of *Constitutional History*; he omitted nothing.[33]

Turning from the colonization of Texas to the Texas revolution, Dr. Barker's work was directed toward an explanation of the causes of the revolution and toward an explanation of the role of the United States in the war. Although his writings on the general causes of the rebellion in Texas cover the entire span of his fruitful career, in the year 1928 the Graduate Faculty of the University of Texas selected Dr. Barker to deliver a series of research lectures on the causes of the Texas revolution. At the appointed time, Professor Barker presented a series of four papers on the assigned subject; he then added a fifth and much earlier paper on the topic of public opinion in Texas on the eve of the revolt and published the results of his labor under the title *Mexico and Texas, 1821–1835*. This small volume contains a concise narrative which represents a condensation of Barker's immense storehouse of knowledge on the complex causes of the Texas revolution.

In the introduction of his *Mexico and Texas*, Barker explains that "the causes of the Texas revolution are more than a study in local history," because "it is the misfortune of the United States to have acquired three-fifths of its continental territory from Spain and Mexico."[34] In the first paper, entitled "The Racial and Political Background," he takes his cue from Dr. Garrison's *Texas*, published in 1903 and subtitled "A Contest of Civilizations," and proceeds to set the stage for revolution by describing the opposing sides:

> On the one side was the Anglo-American immigrant, blunt, independent, efficient, a rebel against authority, a supreme individualist. On the other side was the Latin American master of the soil, sensitive, secretive, subtle and indirect in his ways, by training and temperament

[33] Claude Elliott, History 35 Notes (1929), The Elliott Collection, Southwest Texas State College Library (hereafter referred to as Elliott's Notes).

[34] Eugene C. Barker, *Mexico and Texas, 1821–1835*, iii.

a worshiper of tradition and a creature of authority. With the political ascendancy of the two elements reversed the situation would have held no threatening aspects, but with the Mexicans in the political saddle conflict was certain.[35]

To give added weight to the contrast in the political experience of the two groups of people, Barker points to the heritage of the English colonists as they entered America and returns to the significance of the frontier in American history with a statement to the effect that,

Generation after generation of thrusting their way through the American wilderness renewed and strengthened the self-reliance and efficiency of the English colonists. On every successive frontier adventurous pioneers re-enacted, with the necessary adaptations of time and circumstances, the experiences of and the expedients of the original immigrants. Daniel Boone's colonists at Boonesborough were not less dependent upon their own resources than were Captain John Smith's Englishmen at Jamestown. The Watagua Association repeated in the wooded valleys of eastern Tennessee a century and a half later the Mayflower Compact of the Pilgrims landing on the bleak, wintry shore of Massachusetts Bay.[36]

After reviewing the rapid advance of the American frontier, the distrust in which the Spaniards held the United States and its people, the immigration-colonization policies of Mexico, the reasons for colonization of Texas by the Americans, and the forms of government under which these pioneers lived in Texas, Dr. Barker summarizes his findings:

This study has sought to analyze and trace the history of four major colonial grievances—the denial by Mexico of religious toleration; the effort of the government to abolish slavery in Texas, or at least to prevent the continued introduction of slaves by incoming immigrants; the attempt to put an end to further immigration from the United States; and the want of an effective judicial system.

The first two grievances, denial of religious toleration and the restrictions on slavery, were a source of serious and continued annoyance,

---

[35] Barker, *Mexico and Texas*, 1 ff.
[36] Ibid., 3.

but the irritation caused by them was not acute enough to cause revolution. Much more exasperating were the last two grievances, the prohibition of immigration from the United States and the crying deficiencies of the judiciary system, and the way was prepared for the removal of both these grievances by the legislation of 1834. Removal of the abuses would not, of course, undo their injurious effects; scars would remain; but the Law of April 6, 1830, and the clumsy judicial system held no threat for the future. What was it, then, which precipitated the Texas revolution?[37]

In answer to the question, Barker emphasized that "The Law of April 6, 1830, was the turning point in the relations between the colonists and the government." After tracing the troubles between the Texans and Mexicans in 1832 and remarking that the untimely death of Manuel Mier y Terán removed from the scene one of the two men "who understood the affairs of Texas," and drove the other, Stephen F. Austin, "from his well-tried policy of holding Texas aloof from Mexican party wars," Barker answered the vital question:

The causes of popular movements are rarely concrete and simple; on the contrary, they are diffuse and complex. It was so in the Texas revolution. In the end, it was the development of national politics, I think, which precipitated the Texas revolution. Not to mention local and state insurrections and isolated "plans" and pronunciamentoes touching national affairs, there were four major revolutions during the six years from 1829 to 1835. . . . The really ominous fact, however, was that each successive change seemed to bring Texas more completely within the blighting sphere of the federal government's attention. Guerrero issued the emancipation decree of 1829; Bustamante approved the fateful Law of April 6, 1830, which, had it been enforced with its original design, would have paralyzed the development of Texas for many years. . . .

There are indications . . . that Santa Anna's about-face from Liberalism to Centralism was the last unbearable straw upon the proverbial camel's back.[38]

The student of Texas history might well ask the question: What was the role of the land speculator in the background of the

[37] Ibid., 99–100.
[38] Ibid., 145–146.

revolution? While Barker investigated this question along with the others, he never seemed to come up with a satisfactory answer. In 1911, and again in 1928 in *Mexico and Texas*, he reported that "it is certain that land speculation, of which there was unquestionably a great deal, tended rather to retard than to hasten the outbreak." This conclusion was apparently reached after a study of land speculation as a cause of the Texas revolution which Professor Barker completed in 1906 and published in the *Quarterly*. In a statement of his findings, Barker wrote,

As to the part played by the speculators in the beginning of the Texas revolution, contemporary opinion differs. By one we are told that the speculators for interested reasons prevented him from stirring the people up to their own defense. From another we have the contrary, that the speculators stirred up all the agitation in Texas, in order to shield themselves and save their grants. The truth seems to be that the speculators, who had spent some time in Mexico, had a keener sense of danger from Santa Anna's plan of Centralism than their neighbors who stayed at home. When, therefore, upon their return, they lost no time in sounding the alarm, their motives were easily misunderstood. And the indifference manifested by many Texans throughout the revolution was due, it seems probable, to this misunderstanding. It played some part, as we have already seen, in the cool reception of Governor Viesca's appeal for assistance in May; it probably delayed the calling of the general consultation, which began to be agitated in the latter part of June; and finally it caused many to hesitate in their support of Texan volunteers in the fall of 1835. They believed that it was a speculators war.[39]

In Barker's *Life of Austin*, the land frauds growing out of the infamous Monclova legislature of 1835 are largely omitted except for brief mention of their nature and their role as a contributing factor to Austin's defeat in the Texas presidential campaign of 1836. On the other hand, the activities of the Galveston Bay and Texas Land Company are introduced to the reader but not dis-

---

[39] Barker, "Land Speculation as a Cause of the Texas Revolution," *The Quarterly of the Texas State Historical Association*, X (July, 1906), 76–95. Apparently Barker never fully understood the role of Valentín Gómez Farías, Augustín Viesca, and the Mexican Federalists in the origins of the Texas Revolution.

cussed. Professor Barker turns from the subject, in his own words, because "the further history of the company need not be followed here," and "the internal history of the company can probably never be written" since the papers of General John T. Mason, a key figure in the enterprise, were destroyed in 1922. The critical historian cannot escape the conclusion that the real story of land speculation as a factor among the causes of the Texas revolution has never been told.[40]

Down through the years, Dr. Barker exhibited no patience at all with the typical, provincial Texan point of view that prevailed around the turn of the century to the effect that in the Texas question from 1821 to 1848 all of the fault was on the side of the Mexican government and its statesmen. In fact, his firm belief in dual responsibility for the events of the time was the underlying theme of his *Mexico and Texas* and the theme of all of his class-room teaching. True to his basic philosophy, Barker approached his investigations without prejudice; he collected all the evidence available; and he formed his deductions and conclusions with a critical mind. He tried to be impartial and objective in learning the truth as nearly as it could be learned and in relating this small segment of truth to the whole fabric of American history. In all of his teaching and writing centering about the theme of Mexico and Texas, he was intellectually honest and tolerant on matters and concerns where Texans often find objectivity rather difficult.

Dr. Barker's tolerance and understanding of this problem is best exemplified by his introduction to Ohland Morton's *Terán and Texas: A Chapter in Texas-Mexican Relations.* In this brief preface to an excellent work by one of his students, Barker wrote,

[40] For Barker's treatment of land speculation in his *Life of Austin,* see pages 321–324, 470–472, and 514–515. Elgin Williams in *The Animating Pursuits of Speculation: Land Traffic in the Annexation of Texas* (New York, 1949) contributes nothing to an understanding of the problem on the eve of the revolution. A note in the Barker History Center copy of Williams' book reads: "Reviewed by me in *American Historical Review,* October, 1949. Fundamentally, the author didn't want to tell the truth. Reviewed by Barnes F. Lathrop in *Journal of Southern History,* November, 1949; by Binkley in *Quarterly* of Mississippi Valley Association, November, 1950—both excellent. E. C. Barker."

The attitude of Texans toward Mexico and Mexicans, and of many other Americans, is influenced in the abstract by tragic and unnecessarily cruel incidents of the Texas revolution. Though the average citizen may know little or nothing of the facts, he has absorbed the impression that the colonists of Texas were the victims of persecution, tyranny, and calculated barbarism directed by the Mexican government and approved by all Mexicans. The truth is quite the contrary. Every important Mexican in San Antonio, whether official or citizen, was solicitous for the success and prosperity of the new settlers. Selfish interest alone would have made them so, but they were truly friendly. The same is true of most of the state officials who had any knowledge of Texas and of national figures connected with its administration. History, like Providence, works slowly and in mysterious ways its wonders to perform, but one of the essentials to improve understanding and mutual respect of Anglo-Americans and Latin-Americans today is a sound knowledge of the Mexicans who had a hand in the administration of Texas prior to 1836, and of the conditions under which they worked.[41]

The statement above, written in 1948, represents a personal opinion that was neither sudden nor impulsive on the part of Dr. Barker. The same reasoning, more simply stated, was set forth in a school history of Texas written in collaboration with Charles Shirley Potts and Charles W. Ramsdell in 1911. Designed for young Texans, Barker's contribution could just as well have been written for older Texans when it explained the fundamental cause of the revolution in the fact that the Texans and the Mexicans "never really got acquainted and learned to trust each other." Pointing out that the Mexicans soon observed the close connection between the American colonists and the United States and "began to suspect that the colonists would some day try to take Texas away from them," Barker emphasized that this was the beginning of the misunderstanding which prompted the Mexicans to do "exactly what you would do if you believed that somebody was going to try to snatch something from you—they took measures to prevent the success of such an attempt." After a survey of the traditional general causes of the revolt, he reminded his young

[41] Ohland Morton, *Terán and Texas: A Chapter in Texas-Mexican Relations* (Austin, 1948), introduction by Eugene C. Barker, v.

readers, "but we must not judge the Mexicans too harshly. Remember that Texas belonged to them and they honestly believed that they were in danger of losing it. They were merely trying desperately in the only way that they knew to save it."[42]

On another occasion in the year 1911, in a faculty address at the celebration of Texas Independence Day by the students of the University, Barker was completely objective as he told his audience that neither the traditional American historical approach to the effect that Texas independence was nothing more than a "wicked plot" on the part of southern slaveholders nor the explanation of Texas historians that independence was "the logical reply to unbearable oppression" was the true cause of the rebellion. Returning to his familiar theme of racial differences, Dr. Barker expressed the belief that the revolution was due less to actual oppression than "to ineradicable racial qualities" and warned, "our glory is not to be augmented by emphasizing the faults of the Mexicans, and historical justice demands that we measure their actions in the light of their racial experience."[43] The blame must be shared by the people of an age "more than a century before the first permanent white settlement was established in Texas," when "English radicals, discontented with one of the most liberal governments that then existed, were crossing the Atlantic to seek freer conditions in America. Here the formation along the coast of an aristocratic feudal society in the South and of a wealthy and conservative merchant class in the North drove the extremists into the Western interior."[44] Dr. Barker followed his prescribed formula of objectivity and balance in the lengthy investigation that preceded the publication of *The Life of Austin*, and the biography of Austin is replete with examples of Mexican tolerance and friendliness toward the American settlers in Texas; as Barker later phrased it, "it is hard to be concrete; one sees them [the Mexicans] weaving in and out of the picture; one feels a very

[42] Eugene C. Barker, Charles Shirley Potts, and Charles W. Ramsdell, *A School History of Texas* (Austin, 1911), 83–97.
[43] Eugene C. Barker, "Some Causes of the Texan Declaration of Independence," *The University of Texas Record*, X, no. 4, pp. 336–341.
[44] Ibid., 336–337.

definite friendliness. Specific facts are not wanting, but they are too fragmentary to lend themselves to an orderly narrative."[45]

Concerning the events of the revolution proper, Dr. Barker completed monographic studies on the finances of the Texas revolution, the Texas Revolutionary Army, and the San Jacinto campaign.[46] His major interest, however, was directed toward the role of the United States in the revolution, and his two studies, "President Jackson and the Texas Revolution," and "The United States and Mexico, 1835–1837" are classic explanations of the topic.

In his "President Jackson and the Texas Revolution," written in 1907, Professor Barker submits evidence for the defense of Andrew Jackson against the accusations of Machiavellian intrigues which have sometimes been ascribed to him "through a consideration of (1) the efforts of President Jackson to purchase Texas, (2) his connections with Sam Houston's alleged plot to revolutionize the country, and (3) the charges made against the government of breach of neutrality during the Texas revolution, (a) in contributing men, money, and supplies to the rebels, and (b) in the occupation of Nacogdoches by General Gaines."[47] Following a detailed survey of the efforts of Jackson to purchase Texas through the efforts of Joel R. Poinsett and Anthony Butler, Barker turns to the relation of Sam Houston to the Texas revolution with the following statement:

---

[45] Eugene C. Barker, "Native Latin-American Contribution to the Independence of Texas," *Southwestern Historical Quarterly*, XLVI (April, 1943); *Essays*, 162.

[46] Eugene C. Barker, "The San Jacinto Campaign," *The Quarterly of the Texas State Historical Association*, IV (April, 1901), 237–345; "The Texas Revolutionary Army," ibid., IX (April, 1906), 227–261; "The Finances of the Texas Revolution," *Political Science Quarterly*, XIX (December, 1904), 612–635. Other special studies of the revolutionary period include "The Organization of the Texas Revolution," *Publications of the Southern History Association*, V (November, 1901), 451–476; "The Tampico Expedition," *The Quarterly of the Texas State Historical Association*, VI (January, 1903), 169–186; "The Battle of Velasco," ibid., VII (April, 1904), 326–328; and "Proceedings of the Permanent Council," ibid., IX (April, 1906), 287–288.

[47] Eugene C. Barker, "President Jackson and the Texas Revolution," *American Historical Review*, XII (July, 1907), 788–809; see also *Essays*, 163.

He may have been nursing some Burr-like project in his active brain when he made his first visit to Texas. He did attend the Convention of April, 1833, and the constitution there adopted for the proposed state of Texas—which, be it remembered, was to remain a member of the Mexican confederation—was largely his work. But his life is a blank history for the next two years, and it is not till past the middle of 1835, when the revolution was well under way, that we find him at Nacogdoches, speaking at a public meeting. The revolution was principally developed in the so-called Department of the Brazos, which covered most of the territory between the Trinity and Guadalupe Rivers and did not include Nacogdoches. The writer has examined hundreds of letters and public documents, both Texan and Mexican, on the development of the revolution, has collected with few exceptions the proceedings of all the public meetings and revolutionary committees, and has found nowhere a single reference to General Houston. In August, 1835, the Mexican authorities made a demand for the principal leaders of the war party, but Houston's name was not on the list. This, of course, is negative evidence, but is strong, and ought to justify the conclusion that Houston was not even secretly active in instigating the revolution.[48]

Continuing his study, Dr. Barker presented evidence to show that "the Texan rebels had expected help from the United States, and they received it. They would unquestionably have received a great deal more, if the revolution had lasted longer." Making a point of the fact that the Mexican chargé d'affaires made repeated protests—to no avail—that neutrality laws were not being enforced by the Jackson administration, Barker notes that,

Another question of neutrality arose over the occupation of Nacogdoches by Major-General E. P. Gaines, after the revolution was practically over. He was ordered to the southwestern frontier, January 23, 1836, to enforce neutrality and keep the Indians quiet. By the thirty-third article of the treaty of April 5, 1831, the United States and Mexico had mutually pledged themselves to restrain the Indians under their respective jurisdictions from hostilities and incursions, and now it was feared that conditions in Texas might encourage the Mexican Indians to commit depredations which the Mexican government was in no condition to punish, and that this disorder would in turn extend itself to

[48] Barker, "Jackson and the Texas Revolution," 802–803.

the United States side of the border. In such an event our government held that it would be its duty to cross the frontier and check the hostilities. On a hypothetical statement of the case the Mexican minister, Gorostiza, agreed with [John] Forsyth in this view, September 23, 1836, but he was careful to add that he was sure no such measures were required on the Texas frontier.[49]

On June 28, 1836, General Gaines crossed the Sabine, occupied Nacogdoches, and held the town for several months. "To admit," wrote Barker, "that Gaines was over-credulous and extremely pro-Texan in sympathy is still far from showing that Jackson wished him to be so." In conclusion, it seemed to Dr. Barker that "throughout his administration General Jackson displayed a desire to maintain unsullied the dignity and honor of the United States in regard to the Texas question."[50]

Several years later Dr. Barker completed a similar study for publication in the first number of the *Mississippi Valley Historical Review*. This second investigation, entitled, "The United States and Mexico, 1835–1837," covered practically the same ground as had been covered by the prior work (with the deletion of Jackson's efforts to buy Texas and with greater detail concerning actual pro-Texas activities within the United States). A new element was added to the account of General Gaines and the occupation of Nacogdoches: Barker wrote,

It seems beyond dispute that General Gaines was over-credulous and that he exaggerated the danger of an Indian uprising. General Alexander Macomb wrote from New Orleans, April 25, 1836, that Governor White of Louisiana believed that Gaines was deceived by persons interested in Texan speculations; and the fact that General John T. Mason was one of those who urged him to occupy Nacogdoches lends color to this suspicion. Lieutenant Colonel Whistler, who commanded at Nacogdoches, wrote the war department on September 4 that there had never been any disposition on the part of adjacent tribes to attack our frontier, and that whatever intention they may have had to attack

---

[49] Ibid., 806.
[50] Ibid., 807–808.

the Texans had been removed by the presence of the United States forces.[51]

At the end of his article, Barker concluded: "My own opinion is that, despite President Jackson's desire to acquire Texas . . . the administration tried in a lukewarm manner to meet the spirit as well as the letter of its neutral obligations."[52]

In 1929 Dr. Barker edited *Readings in Texas History for High Schools and Colleges* in response to demands from teachers in search of a satisfactory textbook in Texas history for advanced study. Then as now there was no adequate text covering the whole field of Texas history. As a result, Barker designed the *Readings* to meet "the evident need for a handy compilation of significant studies and documents." The selections were "chosen and arranged to make a reasonably continuous narrative of the history of Texas." An important contribution to local history, the book gives a thorough coverage to the development of the Texas revolution; the provisional and constitutional governments of Texas during the rebellion; and such significant military events as the campaign of 1835, the siege and fall of the Alamo, the Goliad tragedy, and the San Jacinto campaign.[53]

About the year 1935 (in the words of Barker), the social science departments of the University were asked to recommend projects which could be used as a basis for application for a grant from the Laura Spellman Rockefeller foundation to promote research and publication in the social sciences. Among other projects, the History Department suggested the compilation and publication of the writings of Sam Houston. A grant was obtained and work on the project—a beginning had been made by A. J. Stephens, who had submitted a list of Houston writings in various libraries and collections as his M.A. thesis, and by the WPA copyists—was continued under the over-all direction of Dr. Barker and Amelia

[51] Eugene C. Barker, "The United States and Mexico, 1835–1837," *Mississippi Valley Historical Review*, I (June, 1914), 24–25.

[52] Ibid., 29.

[53] Eugene C. Barker (ed.), *Readings in Texas History for High Schools and Colleges* (Dallas, 1929), v–vi.

W. Williams. The principal repositories of Houston writings were searched; no known source was overlooked. The writings were arranged and edited by Amelia W. Williams and Dr. Barker and were published by the University of Texas Press as *The Writings of Sam Houston, 1813–1863*. The first volume of the eight-volume set came off the press in 1938; the last volume was finished in 1943.

On April 1, 1943, Dr. Barker addressed the Town and Gown Club of Austin on the subject, "Impressions suggested by the Writings of Sam Houston." After a review of the history of the project, Barker pointed out that to him (1) the collection was disappointing because while it added detail to the general knowledge of Houston it did not perceptibly enlarge the scope of this general knowledge, and (2) the collection gave no answer to the perennial questions of why Houston left his first wife, of why he came to Texas, and finally, what his attitude was toward the annexation of Texas. Pointing out that Houston's speeches and public papers ranged in quality from "mischievous trifling through distortion, vituperation, and vindictiveness to high statesmanship," Barker remarked that "at their worst they merit the epithet that Andrew Jackson bestowed on John Quincy Adams—utterance of 'that malicious old man.' At their best they yield to none in expressing patriotic veneration of state and nation and integrity of public service."[54] To Barker, it seemed that the most significant characteristics of Houston were his dullness in debate, his tendency to abuse personal and political enemies on the floor of the United States Senate, his sardonic sense of humor, and his defense of the American Indian. In addition,

On one subject—the greatest in his career—he was neither theatrical nor equivocal. He loved the Union and hated sectional animosities that threatened its stability. Here he stood above partisanship and personalities and expressed himself courageously, consistently, and honestly. (a) He disapproved the "squatter sovereignty" provision of the Compromise of 1850 because he saw that it would aggravate rather than allay controversy over the spread of slavery, but he supported the

[54] Barker Papers, unpublished speeches.

Compromise as a whole. (b) He vigorously opposed the Kansas-Nebraska Act of 1854, though southern partisans hailed it as a great victory for the South. (c) As governor of Texas he pleaded with all the eloquence of logic and prophecy for maintenance of the Union; and if secession must come, he favored tentatively, at least, the return of Texas to the status of single independence.[55]

Barker believed that the *Writings* justified the cost in money and labor expended upon them because they represent in one compilation Houston's portrait painted by his own words and, secondly, "this collection must hereafter be the starting point for any study of Houston that a biographer may choose to undertake."[56]

In many areas of Texas history where limitations imposed by time and energy prevented extensive investigations by Dr. Barker, the professor would send his graduate students in search of answers to historical problems. The result over the years has been many interesting explorations into previously unknown reaches of libraries and archival collections; explorations that have produced, among other things, such comprehensive works as Walter Prescott Webb's *Texas Rangers*; Rudolph L. Biesele's *German Settlements in Texas*; Raymond Estep's *Lorenzo de Zavala*; John Nathan Craven's *James Harper Starr*; William R. Hogan's *The Texas Republic: A Social and Economic History*; Herbert P. Gambrell's *Mirabeau B. Lamar* and *Anson Jones*; Asa Kyrus Christian's "Mirabeau Bonaparte Lamar"; William C. Holden's *Alkali Trails*; Rupert N. Richardson's pioneer study of the Comanche Indians as a barrier to the settlement of West Texas; Amelia Williams' "Critical Study of the Siege of the Alamo and the Personnel of its Defenders"; Annie Middleton's study of the annexation of Texas; Ruby Mixon's "William Barrett Travis"; Ruby Cumby Smith's "James W. Fannin, Jr."; Llerena Friend's *Sam Houston: The Great Designer*; and Ohland Morton's *Terán and Texas*. In addition to the published works, the thesis collection of the University of Texas Library contains scores of other contributions by Barker's students.

[55] Ibid.
[56] Ibid.

This appraisal of Eugene C. Barker's work thus far contains no reference to his contribution as a historical critic. During his long career as a teacher and scholar, Dr. Barker reviewed many books written by fellow historians. Many of his reviews dealt with topics related solely to the history of Texas and were published in the *Quarterly* of the Texas State Historical Association. The more significant reviews appeared in the *Mississippi Valley Historical Review* and the *American Historical Review*. It is in these concise reviews that the student of southwestern history finds a reflection of Barker's own opinions concerning the era of western expansion centering around James K. Polk's administration and the Mexican War.

In 1907 Jesse S. Reeves gave the Albert Shaw lectures on diplomatic history at Johns Hopkins and subsequently published his research under the title *American Diplomacy under Tyler and Polk*. In a review of the Reeves book Barker pointed out that while the author was "too confident of his conclusions as to Polk's motives" he does not accept the partisan contemporary view—too common still—that Polk made himself the wicked agent of the slave-holding interest to extend the area of slavery." It seemed to Barker that Reeves pictured Polk as "simply the intriguing and unscrupulous expansionist, who deliberately planned and accomplished the seizure of California at the cost of an unnecessary and bloody war against a power that was too weak to make any effectual resistance." Barker was of the opinion that Reeves' treatment of the annexation of Texas and the Mexican War was somewhat misleading because the author described it as dealing principally with the questions of boundary and concluded that the southwestern boundary question was "settled by conquest." Neither could Barker agree with the Reeves view that "Polk entered upon the presidency with the determination to use the unsettled question of the boundary of Texas as an excuse to take California; and that though this was not mentioned in [Polk's] message, it was the real reason for recommending a declaration of war." Barker described this view as a groundless contention disproved by "Polk's declaration to Bancroft" and the letter exchange between Slidell and Buchanan in November, 1845. It seemed to Barker that

Reeves should go further with his study and accord Polk "the justice that most historians have denied him."[57] Thus, very early in his career, Eugene C. Barker emerges as a staunch defender of President James K. Polk and the course of American diplomacy during the mid-1840's.

Three years later Dr. Barker dealt with a related subject in a review of E. D. Adams, *British Interests and Activities in Texas, 1836–1846.* Commenting that Professor Adams' book leaves "our previous conclusions upon the subject essentially unchanged," Barker pointed out that two questions come to the minds of historians. First, to what extent was the belief justified that the United States had to take Texas in order to prevent England from getting it? And, second, to what extent was there ground for the southern fear that England wanted Texas and would use her position there to "direct a campaign of abolition against the Southern states?" Although Adams held no thesis and offered no categorical answers, Barker believed that the book would probably set the above questions at rest by establishing proof that (1) England desired an independent Texas and at one time Aberdeen was ready, jointly with France, to prevent annexation by war, if need be; but, at the same time "the idea of incorporating the territory into the British Empire was never seriously entertained by either Palmerston or Aberdeen," and (2) England "was deeply interested in the abolition of slavery throughout the world, and Aberdeen did resolve in his mind tentative plans for effecting abolition in Texas; but in this procedure he was perfectly frank, and nothing is added to the exposition of his motives as presented in that portion of the Calhoun-Pakenham correspondence published in 1844." Then Barker added as an afterthought: "This is not to say, however, that there was no ground for American suspicion of British policy."[58]

The following year Barker reviewed Justin H. Smith's *The Annexation of Texas.* In his introductory paragraph he pointed out

[57] *Quarterly of the Texas State Historical Association,* XII (October, 1908), 161 ff.

[58] *Quarterly of the Texas State Historical Association,* XIV (April, 1911), 338.

that "exceptional opportunities and laborious industry have enabled Dr. Smith to give us a solid and comprehensive history of the annexation of Texas, based on a minute study of practically all the sources." As seen through Barker's eyes, Smith's most important conclusions were these: (1) the Texas revolution was "a legitimate measure of self-defense" against the despotism of Santa Anna; (2) the rebels were aided by the people of the United States, and there "were no doubt substantial violations of the neutrality law," but these "cannot be shown to have been the fault of our national authorities"; (3) very good reasons existed for the recognition of Texas in March, 1837, and Jackson "did well to follow the implied advice of Congress to recognize the new republic; (4) sectional influences caused the rejection of the Texan overtures for annexation in 1837, but by 1844 annexation sentiment was largely non-partisan"; (5) the British interest in Texas was very great, and though Aberdeen's government seems not to have entertained the idea of annexing Texas, in 1844 it calmly contemplated war to prevent its annexation by the United States; (6) Tyler's desire to affect annexation, therefore, though partly due to personal and political ambition, was backed by patriotism and sound statesmanship; (7) the annexation treaty violated no principle of international law and "real opposition to the acceptance of Texas makes a very small showing in the rejection of the treaty, domestic policies being mainly responsible for its failure"; (8) there was "no clear-cut issue between annexation and anti-annexation" in the election of 1844, and Polk's victory was not an endorsement of immediate annexation; nevertheless, "a majority of the people were in favor of accepting Texas at an early date"; and (9) the fear of injuring Clay's chances in the presidential campaign, and thereby furthering annexation, deterred France and England from a joint protest against annexation in 1844, but the subsequent withdrawal of France compelled England to work indirectly by inducing Mexico "to recognize Texas on condition that it should remain independent."[59]

Barker's next venture into the field of criticism came two years

[59] *Southwestern Historical Quarterly*, XV (April, 1912), 357–358.

later, in 1914, when he reviewed George L. Rives, *The United States and Mexico, 1821–1848*, for both the *Southwestern Historical Quarterly* and the *Mississippi Valley Review*. Barker found that "these dignified volumes" could be considered under four topics: (1) the political history of Mexico from 1821 to 1848; (2) the revolution and subsequent annexation of Texas; (3) the diplomatic history of the period; and (4) the political and military history of the Mexican War. Barker was of the opinion that with regard to the first and fourth topics—the political history of Mexico and the political and military history of the Mexican War—Mr. Rives had "added little that is new." It seemed to the reviewer that the treatment of the revolution and annexation of Texas and the account of the diplomatic history of the period comprised the "much better half" of Rives' work.[60]

When Justin H. Smith published his two-volume work entitled *The War with Mexico* in 1919, Dr. Barker was again called on for a review by the *American Historical Review*. Writing on a subject of intense interest, Barker had a few remarks of his own on the question:

No event in our history has been so distorted by ignorance, prejudice, misinterpretation, and downright misrepresentation as the Mexican War. Passions inflamed by the slavery question and the angry political struggles preceding and following the war created an emotional atmosphere in which vituperation took the place of sober reasoning and slanderous assertion too often supplanted proved fact. Probably not since the ratification of the Constitution has there been less national *esprit* and team-work than during the four years of Polk's administration. The multitude of presidential aspirants in and out of the [Mexican] army, each of whom believed his own success dependent upon the destruction of his rivals' claim[s] to honor and intelligence, the irritating jibes and innuendoes of the British press, and the natural bitterness of Mexican writers have left a fog of confusion which American historians until recently have shown little disposition to dispel.[61]

---

[60] E. C. Barker, a review of George L. Rives, *The United States and Mexico, 1821–1848* (2 volumes), in the *Mississippi Valley Historical Review* (June, 1914), and the *Southwestern Historical Quarterly*, XVIII (July, 1914), 109–110.

[61] E. C. Barker, review of Justin H. Smith, *The War with Mexico*, 2 vol-

It seemed to Barker that an historian laboring in the vineyard of the Mexican War would be confronted by a dual problem: on the one hand, a controversy at every step involving national and personal reputation and character in which a fine sifting of all the material would be essential to give the work permanent worth; and, on the other hand, the refutation (and to a less degree, confirmation) of traditional historical verdicts in plain language with emphasis enough to carry the point and abundant citations to sustain the position taken. To what degree did Smith meet these issues in *The War with Mexico?* Barker's answer follows:

Of the fruit of his labor—the success with which he attacked the second set of difficulties—there will perhaps be divergent opinions. In the main, the reviewer agrees with his conclusions concerning every important question affecting our national honor, and believes that they will become substantially the verdict of history. These are: the honest intent of our government to maintain neutrality during the Texas revolution; our own forbearance and Mexico's inexcusable shifting concerning the settlement of our claims; our right to annex Texas without just offense to Mexico; the sincerity of Polk's desire to avoid war by the Slidell mission; the necessity for and essential justification of the war; and the refutation of the charge that Polk provoked war to seize California. Knowing the scope of the author's investigation, it was to be hoped that his findings would be so clearly stated and so firmly buttressed as to carry conviction to every reasonable reader; but it is to be doubted whether they will have that effect.[62]

During the last twenty-five years of his life, Eugene C. Barker's primary interest in American history turned from the southwestern frontier to an investigation and re-evaluation of the doctrine of an economic interpretation of the Constitution of the United States as established by Charles A. Beard in 1913. Therefore, Barker became the pioneer of one of the major topics in the mainstream of current American historiography. Barker believed that the fundamental unsoundness of the Beard thesis could be explained

umes (New York, 1919), in the *American Historical Review*, XXV (July, 1920), 729 ff.
    [62] *Ibid.*, 730.

by "demonstrating the essential falsity of conclusions drawn from a partial statement of selected facts essentially true in themselves but deplorably incomplete."[63]

Many of Barker's colleagues on the University campus attributed his bitter denunciation of the economic interpretation to his equally bitter opposition to the New Deal policies of the Roosevelt administration. While Dr. Barker's well-known and outspoken criticism of the Roosevelt administration undoubtedly contributed to the development of his attack on the Beard doctrine, the source materials indicate that Barker's objections to the unsound and misleading conclusions reached by Beard originated long before the days of the New Deal. For example, in the spring semester of 1929 Barker told his students that Beard's *Economic Interpretation* was published in 1913 in the midst of "a wave of criticism against the American government" and that the book stated simply that the Constitution benefited the well-to-do class, that it was fundamentally an economic document, and that "the framers wanted the document to help them make money." "This entire theory," Barker pointed out, "is completely false." He then established that (1) "the Constitution was made by a few men, some opposing the document, (2) 160,000 participated—*suppose there was no property line?* (3) the Constitution protects all people the same regardless of the makers."[64] These sketchy notes from a student notebook reveal that Barker's days as a critic of the Beard hypothesis date before 1929.

After several public attacks on Beard's *An Economic Interpretation* during the late 1930's,[65] Barker consolidated his argument in a speech before the Town and Gown Club of Austin. He asked,

[63] Eugene C. Barker, "An Economic Interpretation of the Constitution," *Texas Law Review* (June, 1944), 21; Barker *Essays*, 259.

[64] Claude Elliott, notes in history 25, spring semester, 1929, in the Claude Elliott collection, Southwest Texas State College.

[65] At San Antonio, Texas, in November, 1937, in a speech to the Colonial Dames Society, Barker talked on "The Constitution and the Motives of Its Makers." At the dedication of the San Jacinto Museum of History in April, 1939, Barker read an address titled "Three Types of Historical Interpretation." In both of these speeches, he was highly critical of the Beard interpretation.

Were the men who framed the Constitution moved chiefly by their own selfish property interests? Did they manipulate elections to the Federal Convention? Did they injure the poor by taking from the state legislative powers to emit paper money and impair the obligation of contracts? Economic interpretation of the Constitution leaves the impression—whether intentionally or not—that the answer is *yes*. Is the doctrine of economic interpretation of the Constitution spreading in public schools and colleges? Is it as taught, based on sound historical foundations? My answer is that it is spreading, and that, as taught, its foundations are unsound.[66]

Barker pointed out that "the thesis of the so-called economic interpretation of the Constitution of the United States is that the Constitution was written and launched by a group of rich men seeking selfish property advantages against the interests of men of little or no property; that they were animated primarily, if not solely, by the hope of immediate personal gain; that representation of small farmers and debtors was deliberately excluded from the Federal Convention and as far as possible from the state conventions that ratified the Constitution; and that substantially all of the opposition to ratification came from debtors and small property owners."[67] It seemed to Professor Barker that Beard "established the plausibility of his thesis by ignoring much of the political, social, and economic history of the American people prior to 1786." Commenting that "it is only against that background" that a fair study of the Constitution can be made, Barker listed the pertinent facts that must be stated "before considering Beard's specifications." He placed special significance on the facts: (1) that the ideal of universal suffrage had not then entered the intellectual horizon, (2) that the revolutionary constitutions of 1776–1778 continued the traditional restrictions on manhood suffrage, (3) that the spirit of permanent union was hardly then conceived, and (4) that the "particularistic inheritance of the

[66] Barker Papers; Barker, "An Economic Interpretation of the Constitution," *Texas Law Review* (June, 1944), 21; Barker, *Essays*, 246; the above questions and answers appear in an introduction to a mimeographed copy of the Barker essay prepared for distribution to the American history classes at the University.

[67] Barker, "An Economic Interpretation," in *Essays*, 246.

states and the resultant weakness of the federal government" are either subordinated or ignored by advocates of the economic interpretation.[68]

It seemed to Barker that "the summary just concluded is the true perspective for studying the formation of the Constitution and the aims of its makers."[69] He then proceeded to evaluate Beard's *Economic Interpretation* chapter by chapter and finished his brief work with a remark to the effect that "indisputably, the members of the Convention owned public securities and other forms of property, and the government which they created paid their claims at par; but the conclusion that immediate selfish interest was the mainspring of their actions is tragically untrue."[70]

The following year, the school term of 1945 and 1946, Professor Barker originated a graduate seminar built around the period of the Confederation and Constitution and designed to test the Beard hypothesis by applying Beard's criteria—the economic biography approach—to the ratifying conventions in the several states. During each semester of the academic years immediately following the close of World War II, graduate students would gather in small numbers to hear Dr. Barker explain the fundamental weaknesses of the Beard thesis. Then, with Beard's statement in mind that his own pioneer work was "frankly fragmentary" and designed primarily to "illustrate the problem and furnish a guide to research and generalization,"[71] Barker's students were instructed to make a detailed application of the Beard methodology to the local area of their choice. As a matter of fact, the Barker students applied the Beard criteria to a study of the economic background of delegates to state ratifying conventions in an effort to isolate the economic and political interests of the Federalists and Antifederalists; to divide these political groups into (1) the land barons and planters, (2) money lenders, (3) investors in public securities, (4) speculators in western lands, and (5) the so-called

[68] Ibid., 246–248.
[69] Ibid., 249.
[70] Ibid., 259.
[71] Charles A. Beard, *An Economic Interpretation of the Constitution of the United States*, xix, 16.

small farmer and debtor groups; and to determine, in conclusion, whether these various classes in early American society were influenced in their vote for or against the Constitution by their immediate and personal economic interests. The results of Barker's seminar form a substantial contribution to the recent re-evaluation and criticism of Charles A. Beard's pioneer work.

Forrest McDonald was one of several graduate students to sit in Barker's seminar in the late 1940's. Gaining his inspiration and early guidance from the Barker seminar, McDonald completed his master's thesis for Barker in August, 1949, entitled, "An Economic Interpretation of the Constitution of the United States." In brief, McDonald concluded,

1. The immediate causes of the movement for the Constitution of the United States were (a) a nearly complete breakdown of commerce and trade relations and (b) the ousting from political power of the aristocracy that once ruled the states. The movement was carried through by a small group of men who were willing to sacrifice their fortunes.
2. The members of the Philadelphia Convention which drafted the Constitution represented a nearly perfect cross-section of the economic and political interests and factions of the country: creditors, debtors, merchants, mechanics, farmers, bankers, planters, manufacturers, public security holders; and radicals, moderates, conservatives, and reactionaries.
3. The Constitution established primarily because of existing economic and political conditions, provided an answer to the immediate ills of the country.
4. . . . It must be concluded that the fundamental motivating force in the movement for and against ratification had its source in the facts of life remote from occupational or economic elements.[72]

For McDonald, this initial survey was only the beginning. Building on the original foundation established with the aid of Barker, McDonald continued his study of the economic origins of the Constitution under Professor Fulmer Mood. Following an attack on the Beard thesis by Professor R. E. Brown, McDonald published the results of his investigation in 1958 in a remarkable

[72] Forrest McDonald, "An Economic Interpretation of the Constitution of the United States," master's thesis (1949), University of Texas library.

volume entitled, *We the People: The Economic Origins of the Constitution*.[73] According to McDonald, the "first objective of the present work is thus to subject Beard's thesis to the most careful scrutiny, to fill in the details, on his own terms, in the framework of his own assumptions, methodology, and questions—in short, to discover whether the details are compatible with the broad outlines he sketched." Then, if the Beard thesis proved to be inadequate beyond repair, McDonald proposed to investigate alternate hypotheses of the relation between economic motivation and the contest over the Constitution. Many pages later, at the close of a great multitude of facts based on extensive and intensive research, McDonald concluded:

> From a thorough reconsideration of the Philadelphia Convention, however, the following facts emerge. Fully a fourth of the delegates in the convention had voted in their state legislatures for paper money and/or debtor relief laws. These were the very kinds of laws, which, according to the Beard thesis, the delegates had convened to prevent. Another fourth of the delegates had important economic interests that were adversely affected, directly and immediately, by the Constitution they helped write. The most common and by far the most important property holdings of the delegates were not, as Beard has asserted, mercantile, manufacturing, and public security investment, but agricultural property. Finally, it is abundantly evident that the delegates, once inside the convention, behaved as anything but a consolidated economic group.
>
> In the light of these and other facts presented in the foregoing chapters, it is impossible to justify Beard's interpretation of the Constitution as an "economic document" drawn by a "consolidated economic group whose property interests were immediately at stake."[74]

Interpreting his vast amount of evidence, McDonald further concluded that in the state ratifying conventions in Delaware, New Jersey, and Georgia (where Beard assumed that ratification had been pushed through by personalty interest groups before the opposition could organize) agrarian interests dominated the con-

---

[73] Forrest McDonald, *We the People: The Economic Origins of the Constitution* (Chicago, 1958), 16; R. E. Brown, *Charles Beard and the Constitution*.
[74] McDonald, *We the People*, 349–350.

ventions; that in the states of Virginia and North Carolina "the great majority of delegates on both sides of the question were farmers"; and that Beard's assumption that ratification in Connecticut, Maryland, New Hampshire, and South Carolina was the "outcome of class struggles between commercial and other personalty groups (Federalists) on the one hand and farmers and the advocates of paper money (anti-Federalists) on the other represents nothing more than a groundless generalization." As a final result it was apparent to McDonald that "Beard's thesis—that the line of cleavage as regards the Constitution was between substantial personalty interests on the one hand and small farming and debtor interests on the other—is entirely incompatible with the facts."[75]

In the forty-five year interval between the publication of Beard's *Economic Interpretation* and Forrest McDonald's *We the People* it is apparent that a further generation of additional research had made it rather clear that the Beard doctrine cannot be sustained in its entirety. During the greater part of this period Eugene C. Barker stood as one of the most severe critics of the Beard thesis. When the infirmities of old age forced Barker to drop his active investigation of the fallacies of the Beard doctrine, he found an ambitious student who was willing to take up the task and continue the investigation to a definitive conclusion. Forrest McDonald has made a significant contribution to American constitutional history—but the original theme was Barker's.

[75] Ibid., 351, 355.

The Late Years

It is altogether possible that conservatism was an innate characteristic of the scholarly mind of Eugene C. Barker. On the other
hand, perhaps his conservative nature was the product of the difficult early years at Riverside and Palestine. At any rate, as the
years passed, Dr. Barker's conservative nature grew and deepened.
As the great depression of 1929–1930 swept over the land, bringing calamity to the nation and a crisis to the old order, Barker remained steadfast in his unqualified support of the log-cabin
individualism, thrift, self-reliance, and free enterprise that formed
the traditional concept vaguely known as "the American way." His
reluctance to abandon these principles, his bitter denunciation of
Franklin D. Roosevelt, the policies of the New Deal, and the ram-
ifications of the welfare state became tradition on the campus of
the University of Texas during the depression decade from 1930
through 1940.

In writing of Dr. Barker's conservatism and opposition to the
New Deal, Professor Walter P. Webb recalls that he never heard
Barker "discuss the New Deal in a quiet philosophical manner.
He felt deeply on the subject and had for it nothing but condem-
nation and abuse." According to Webb, Barker's opposition to the
Roosevelt revolution was based on two factors:

1. He grew up toward the end of the 19th and the beginning of the
20th century in the age of rampant individualism, at a time when
everyone did everything for himself. He worked very hard . . . and
what he had he made himself. The idea of the government taking any-

thing away from him was repugnant, and he resented it bitterly. His resentment became something of an obsession which grew as he grew older, and in my opinion made him pretty miserable in his later years when he had many reasons to be happy.

2. The second factor has to do with his lack of understanding of economic forces. Figures were always a mystery to him, and . . . he never met the mathematics requirement for his degree. The University waived the requirements in his case and granted him the degree. This fact was brought home to me once in a staff meeting when he remarked that he did not see how anyone could spend more than three class periods on the Industrial Revolution, the force that has upset the modern world. He was a political historian, and dealt mainly with documents, preferably official documents.[1]

Dr. Webb then pointed to the fact that the remarkable thing about Dr. Barker was "the divergence between his attitude toward individual persons and his attitude toward the government." As noted in an earlier chapter, Webb gives emphasis to the unselfish nature of Barker concerning individuals and the great divergence from this characteristic with regard to public aid:

For the unfortunate individual he [Barker] had unlimited compassion, and to such his purse was always open. I doubt that any individual in distress ever went to him for help who did not get it. He took upon himself the task of alleviating human suffering in every way he could, and I could cite numerous examples. Any student in trouble could get money from him, provided he got his nerve up to going into his office and asking for help. He told me once that so far as he knew all this money came back, some of it twenty years later. He was one of the most considerate men that I have ever known.

Now as to the divergence. If mankind was suffering in mass, that was their own business. Though he would do everything as an individual that he could for another individual, he would not tolerate the government performing the same function for a group of individuals.[2]

Thus, in the late years of his life, Barker found himself confronted by a cruel dilemma; as a scholar he had tried constantly to be unbiased, impartial, and objective; now, he frankly admitted

---

[1] Walter P. Webb to W. C. P., July 22, 1960.
[2] Ibid.

that he could not be objective about the presidential administration of the New Deal Democrats. Milton R. Gutsch described Barker's political and economic views:

Although at the top of his profession he has been inclined in recent years to question its method, its truth, and its value as a guide to life and a teacher of lessons. For have not the same pitfalls ensnared us? Have not the concepts which up to the present have withstood the test of time—thrift, frugality, industry, self-help, the balanced budget, honoring of a debt—been repudiated by an irrational world and given away to such ideas as "spending the nation into prosperity," "abundance by scarcity," "industrial freedom by the closed shop," "liberty by regimentation," and "unlimited benefits from an unlimited debt." The mind has been befuddled by the babble and prattle of the modern economist and the silken phrases of the suave and sometimes unctuous politician. The readiness with which the masses have accepted these doctrines has engendered an attitude of futility and despair among those who still believe in the old fashioned but proven virtues of thrift, self-help, and individual freedom. And Dr. Barker is one of these.[3]

Although primary evidence concerning Dr. Barker's political philosophy is fragmentary and incomplete, he did outline his anti-New Deal point of view on several widely separated occasions during the early 1940's. For example, in the summer of 1940 he wrote: "I am a Democrat sixty-five years old. I voted for Hoover in 1932 because I honestly thought that he was doing a good job —if we only exercised a little more patience—and I voted against Roosevelt in 1936 because I believed he was actually transforming our government (by indirect bribery) into a dictatorship. Now it's off my chest."[4]

A few months earlier Barker had attacked the domestic policy of the Roosevelt administration in a speech to the Phi Beta Kappa chapter of The Rice Institute. Speaking of what he called distorted history, he said:

[3] Milton R. Gutsch, March 26, 1942, Barker Papers, "Portraits of a Historian."

[4] Barker to Mr. Lawrence, July 18, 1940.

We can learn rapidly enough how the AAA and successive agencies of the Department of Agriculture raised the price of cotton by paying the farmers first to plow under ten million acres of the growing crop and later to let their land stand idle for "soil conservation." But it is very difficult to find in a school or college textbook that a million black and white tenants were driven by this policy from self-subsistence on southern farms to the relief rolls of southern towns; or that the normal annual exports sank from eight million bales of cotton before 1933 to a bare three and a half million bales in 1938. These peoples and thousands of families on the drouth-stricken lands of the western plains were actually driven by the government from the economic frontier.[5]

He also announced the belief that when historians implied that the desperate economic plight of the country during the great depression could be attributed to the disappearance of the frontier they were failing to tell the whole story. It seemed to Barker that such a distorted view of history was not deliberate deceit but represented and illustrated "chiefly the historian's unwillingness to think." He hastened to add that he was criticizing New Deal policies but that he was criticizing "historians who write only of their real or fancied benefits and wholly conceal their equally real and potential evils."[6]

The Rice address marked the second occasion where Barker used the frontier thesis to strike at nonobjective interpretations of the New Deal. In April, 1939, at the dedication of the San Jacinto Museum of History, he remarked that "we must all have heard during the past few years that the evils which we suffer were brought upon us by the 'disappearance of the frontier.'" To Barker,

The explanation of the potent influence of the frontier, when expressed runs like this: Prior to the disappearance of the frontier, it is claimed, the discontented inhabitants of the industrializing East could go West, obtain free land, and maintain independence and self-respect on a small ranch or farm; after the frontier vanished, free land no longer existed and they remained to swell the teeming population of the cities and to become the victims of the industrial revolution. Briefly, in other

[5] Barker, *Essays*, 285.
[6] Ibid., 286.

words, mobility of population was retarded—the bold statement implies that it was stopped; urbanization increased; private industry became unable to provide jobs for all; hence the necessity for the WPA and other forms of government relief.[7]

Barker then made the point that "the explanation is too simple." He continued his rebuke of the frontier historians by pointing out that their explanation ignored the fact "that there remained in the hands of the government in 1890 more than a hundred million acres of land subject to homestead settlement; that the transcontinental railroads owned vast areas that they offered at a moderate price; that much land is still available on conditions that the average pioneer would have thought alluring if not irresistible."[8] At the same time Barker pointed out that those who blamed the evils of the depression on the disappearance of the frontier ignored the fact that "the policy of our present government favors reduction rather than expansion of tilled acres; that it prefers idleness and relief to subsistence farming, which is the sort of farming that the 'disappearance of the frontier' might have affected." He expressed the opinion that such an interpretation was a careless attempt by the historian (indulged in by the best of historians) to explain "complex social and economic conditions by unsound generalizations."[9]

It should be noted, however, that Professor Barker's condemnation of the domestic program of the Roosevelt administration was mild in comparison to his denunciation of New Deal foreign policy. Governed by an abiding fear of German military might and fearing that the United States would be drawn into World War II, Barker wrote an urgent letter to Senators Morris Sheppard and Tom Connally in the summer of 1940 to explain that "the most effective thing Congress can now do to avoid war is to remain in session." Explaining that in his opinion a great many people in the United States were anxious to push the country into a war with Germany, Barker remarked,

[7] Ibid., 239–240.
[8] Ibid., 240.
[9] Ibid.

I know very well, and I think you will admit, that a President can maneuver foreign relations into a situation in which it is almost impossible for Congress to avoid a declaration of war. I am not going into the controversial field of the reasons for my distrust of the President. They are profound and deliberate. I believe that it would be fatal to leave him unchecked by the presence of Congress for six months. I hope that you will ponder the matter thoughtfully and patriotically, not politically, before voting to adjourn.

Fearing that his motives might be misunderstood by the Texas senators, Barker continued,

Now, lest you classify me as a pro-German or as a professional pacifist, which I emphatically am not, let me add that I regard Germany's victory as utterly horrible and devastating to all the finer elements of our civilization. I am bewildered and heartsick when I try to picture our world stripped of the stabilizing influence of England. Yet with all that, I think that this is no time for us to thrust ourselves into this war. Unprepared as we were, we might have had some useful influence if we had whole-heartedly assisted the Allies with supplies at the beginning. But the Johnsons and Borahs and pacifists and politicians would not permit that. Now in a state of unpreparedness and with France crushed and England almost beaten to her knees it would be imbecile folly to allow this country to be drawn in.

But I could write eternally on this theme. *Don't give Roosevelt six months of unchecked freedom to involve us.* It is the duty of Congress to remain in intermittent session.[10]

Among the papers of Eugene C. Barker is a newspaper clipping bearing the dateline Washington, June 19, and carrying a statement by Senator Tom Connally to the effect that he had changed his mind concerning a previous announcement that he favored the immediate adjournment of Congress; the Texas senator remarked that developments of the previous few days were responsible for the reversal of opinion. Dr. Barker has scribbled in the margin: "I hope my letter helped reinforce him. I sent it by air mail."[11]

As the dreary days of the summer and fall of 1940—days when Hitler made a determined effort to destroy Britain from the air

[10] Barker to Morris Sheppard and Tom Connally, June 17, 1940.
[11] Barker Papers.

by sending his mighty armada of Messerschmitts, Dorniers, and
Heinkels across the channel—gave way to the early months of
1941, Franklin D. Roosevelt asked Congress to lend greater support to those people everywhere who were fighting for the "four
freedoms." A few days later, he submitted a program designed to
circumvent the current neutrality legislation and make American
war materials available to the fighting democracies; it was in this
manner that the Lend Lease Bill, soon to be enacted into law,
became an American household word. None of these developments pleased Dr. Barker; in April, 1941, he recorded his opinions
for Professor Timm of the University Government Department:

> I realize that I am sort of a mug-wump: (a) I do not favor convoy;
> (b) I do not favor transfer of the navy to Britain; (c) I do not favor
> investing the President with power (or authority) to do as he pleases.
> I think the wise thing for this govt to do is to use such influence as it
> may still have to bring about a negotiation for peace. Short of a miracle,
> I don't think the U.S. and England together can conquer a peace. I
> believe that the longer the war is now prolonged the worse the final
> terms will be for the U.S. and England. I shudder with horror to think
> of the collapse of the British empire, but do not believe that we can
> aid Britain or the world by inviting our own collapse and the break-
> down of republican govt. I favor continuing aid in food and material
> while working for negotiation.[12]

If Dr. Barker's morale was low on the eve of Pearl Harbor, it
had good reason to sink lower during the days and weeks that
followed the Japanese attack on Hawaii and the Philippines. On
February 16, 1942, he penned a letter to his friend and fellow
historian Henry Steele Commager to express apprehensions about
the eventual outcome of the war. Barker wrote,

> As I think you know, I have regarded the British empire as the very
> foundation of law and order and sanity in the world. Its peril has wrung
> my sympathy and shaken my faith in any guiding principle in the
> universe except brute force. My sense of judgement is outraged by its
> peril. Nevertheless, I have thought that we ought to stay out of this
> war. I have thought that peaceful negotiation at the beginning was
> preferable to swash-buckling bluster, and that it offered far more to

[12] Barker to Timm, April 21, 1942.

England and all the rest of the world than universal war, no matter which side might win. I don't think I am either an appeaser or an isolationist—certainly not an isolationist. And this has been my conviction in spite of a realistic understanding of the utter untrustworthiness of Hitler and all his crew. . . .

As to our conduct of war operations, it is certainly humiliating. I catch myself saying sub-consciously, "when we win the war"; but I consciously feel very doubtful about our winning the war even to the extent of participating very actively in the writing of the peace terms. It seems to me that our government (meaning really Mr. Roosevelt) has been incredibly stupid, and ignorant and arrogant. Not to know even a little about the Japanese preparations and intentions; not to have warned our military and naval outposts effiectively; not to have made reasonably adequate plans for defense on the off-chance that Japan might decide to commit suicide, as we were assured it could never do—such outrageous recklessness is beyond condonement. I suppose you are inclined to blame it all on the Republicans and isolationists; but I think it rests with the 14-year old diety in the White House and the sycophants who inflate his self-importance. He had it all planned: "When one is attacked by two enemies, one first whips one and then the other." As simple as that! Last August there appeared a few times a trial balloon in the papers designed to float his reputation as one of the greatest naval strategists of all time. The gas was defective and the balloon fell flat, but the strategist continued to weave his strategy, and see where we are. One hopes for better things when the billions begin their bombardment. I have had a cartoon in mind for a good many years. A bland gentleman sits in his office waving his long cigarette holder in carefree nonchalance. Messengers of Job struggle for his attention, reporting calamity and catastrophe. To each he answers with a graceful wave of the magic cigarette holder: "Spend a billion! "Spend ten billion!!" "Spend a hundred billion!!" Billions will win the war. I wish I wholly believed it.[13]

A self-styled "short range pessimist and a long range optimist," an often-repeated remark attributed to Dean H. Y. Benedict, Dr. Barker's disposition improved only slightly as the war progressed. On March 14, 1944, he wrote Raymond Estep to repeat, "I have never been convinced that we had to get into this war to save civilization and I don't believe the gods who frequent the White

[13] Barker to H. S. Commager, February 16, 1942.

House had any conception of the job they loaded onto this country; but being in we simply have to fight our way out. In the end we will certainly be much worse off than when we began."[14] Barker remarked again that his comments would not be taken as a confession of isolationism but that he was simply "convinced our government never wanted peace by peaceful methods and didn't honestly try to prevent or avoid war."[15] And finally, on the day of victory, August 15, 1945, Professor Barker wrote John A. Lomax to the effect: "Well, we have lived to see peace again (relatively). Thank God Roosevelt will have nothing to do with reconstruction and that Truman shows signs of intelligence and honesty."[16] In retrospect it seems that Dr. Barker's downcast state of mind during the war years was based primarily, if not solely, upon his bitter dislike of Franklin D. Roosevelt in both the foreign and the domestic field. As a consequence, Barker's bitterness over affairs of state brought great unhappiness to the aging professor. To make his life more unhappy, a real "bear fight" known in academic circles as the Rainey controversy was about to break over the University community.

The morning mail of October 17, 1944, brought Dr. Barker a letter from Dudley K. Woodward, Jr., of Dallas. The opening sentences read, "Newspaper reports leave no doubt that the University has again come upon seriously troubled days. The difficulties of the Ferguson era would appear small by comparison, if I appraise correctly the issues underlying the present controversy."[17] Mr. Woodward, of course, had reference to the fact that while the battles of World War II raged along a global battlefront the faculty of the University, the President, and the Board of Regents approached an armageddon of their own in a bitter and emotional academic crisis known simply as the Rainey controversy. This is neither the time nor the place for a definitive presentation of the underlying issues of the Rainey dispute, but since Dr. Barker was

---

[14] Barker to Raymond Estep, March 14, 1944.
[15] Ibid.
[16] Barker to John A. Lomax, August 15, 1945.
[17] D. K. Woodward, Jr., to Barker, October 16, 1944.

directly involved and has been frequently and severely criticized for his role in certain aspects of the story, it is essential to review the more significant developments between 1939 and 1946. The storm clouds that were to shake the University to its foundations began to gather many months before the Woodward letter of October, 1944. It is safe to assume that when Homer Price Rainey accepted the presidency of the University of Texas in 1939 he little realized that he would soon be the center of a prolonged academic controversy.

Homer P. Rainey, late of Bucknell University and the American Youth Administration, took office as president of the University of Texas in June, 1939. It appears that within a few months of his inauguration friction began between the president and his Board of Regents. Briefly, the significant events of the early stages of the controversy were as follows:

(1) In the summer of 1939 Regent H. H. Weinert asked Dr. Rainey to remove Dr. J. C. Dolley from his position as chairman of the athletic council because Dolley was personally unsatisfactory to Weinert. Rainey gave due consideration to the peculiar request and refused to comply with Weinert's wishes. According to J. Evetts Haley's interpretation, ex-Regent J. R. Parten implied that if Dolley would resign as faculty chairman of the athletic council, Weinert would support the majority of the Board in other matters—specifically, the Medical School issue.[18]

(2) The next incident to be brought before the public took place in June, 1940, when former Regent H. J. Lutcher Stark requested the dismissal of Dean Shelby, Roy Bedichek, and Mr. J. Rodney Kidd from the Division of Extension because they were leaders in the attempt to institute an eight-semester limit upon the participation of high school students in interscholastic athletics. The Board of Regents refused to act on this ridiculous motion, but at the same meeting Fred Branson moved to strike from the budget the position and salary of Dr. Robert H. Montgomery, professor of economics. The Board refused to consider the equal-

---

[18] Henry Nash Smith, *The Controversy at the University of Texas, 1939–1945: A Documentary History*, 6.

ly ridiculous Branson request, but these antics of the governing board were disturbing to the General Faculty of the University.

(3) On July 8, 1941, the Board of Regents, including new Regents Orville Bullington of Wichita Falls and Dan Harrison of Houston, announced that it would not re-employ Dr. John W. Spies as dean of the Medical School. A few weeks later the decision was reversed, but the Medical School tangle continued unabated. After hearings were held in Galveston in May and June, 1942, Dr. Spies was dismissed from his position on August 2, 1942; Dr. Chauncey Leake was named as the new dean, and the Board of Regents apparently instructed President Rainey that he was not to interfere in the administration of the Medical School.

(4) March of 1942 brought the much-discussed case of the three economic instructors. On March 17, 1942, the Dallas *Morning News* carried an advertisement announcing a mass meeting to be held on Sunday, March 22, to discuss the implications of the Fair Labor Standards Act; citizens of Texas were invited to express their opinions and sentiments concerning the controversial law. On the day of the meeting, Wendell Gordon, W. N. Peach, and Fagg Foster, all instructors in the Economics Department of the University, accompanied by Dr. Valdemar Carlson, a visiting assistant professor from Antioch College, went to Dallas to attend the meeting. After their arrival and prior to the opening of the meeting, they asked Karl Hoblitzelle, the chairman, that one of their number be allowed to speak for two minutes in order that widespread misunderstanding concerning the provisions of the Fair Labor Standards Act might be corrected—namely, they wished to explain that the Act simply required payment of overtime wages for hours of work in excess of forty hours per week. Hoblitzelle denied this request. The four faculty members attended the meeting but made no attempt to speak from the floor. Before leaving Dallas, however, they called by the offices of the Dallas *Morning News* and left a written statement to the effect that (1) the Sunday mass meeting was not spontaneous as advertised but, to the contrary, was well organized and controlled, (2) volunteer speakers were refused permission to address the crowd, (3) the speakers invited to address the meeting had been

carefully selected well in advance (Reverend Humphrey Lee, Reverend George W. Truett, and Karl Hoblitzelle were the main speakers), and (4) organized labor was the object of prolonged condemnation by the speakers at the meeting. The statement was published in the *News* on the following day. A few days later Judge T. Whitfield Davidson wrote letters of complaint to members of the Board of Regents. At a meeting on June 27–28, 1942, the Board of Regents refused to renew the contracts of Gordon, Foster, and Peach in spite of objections from the budget council of the Department of Economics, the dean of the College of Arts and Sciences, and President Homer P. Rainey.

In the meanwhile Dr. Barker had been sitting quietly on the sidelines watching the development of the Rainey controversy with little or no visible emotion. He considered Dr. Rainey to be his friend and the two frequently played golf together. Knowing something of the nature of the contest between the president and his governing board, Dr. Barker was instrumental in the presentation of a faculty resolution of appreciation to Dr. Rainey. This expression of gratitude read,

> We have it on higher than earthly authority, according to the Gospel by St. Luke, that "the laborer is worthy of his hire." We interpret this to justify not merely the laborer's right to expect material wages stipulated in his contract, but also the spiritual satisfaction of knowing that his work is appreciated. You have now completed three years as President of the University of Texas, and we, the undersigned members of the General Faculty, all of whom have been employed by the University for more than twenty years, wish to assure you of our esteem and appreciation.[19]

Besides the name of Dr. Barker, the long list of signatures included the names of Milton R. Gutsch, Thad W. Riker, Charles W. Hackett, and Frederic Duncalf of the Department of History.

When the complicated Medical School tangle arose to plague administrative tranquility in the spring and summer of 1942, Dr. Barker expressed the following opinion:

---

[19] Barker Papers, Report of the Meeting of the General Faculty, November 10, 1942.

I always thought Rainey went too far in defending Spies. As a matter of fact, I wrote him a long letter one time, just before the meeting of the Board at which Spies was finally discharged, urging him not to continue his defense of Spies. My opinion of Spies was based on the fact that he had created or had allowed to develop an utterly impossible situation. I never supposed that he was wholly to blame. I felt sure that a number of the faculty members at Galveston were just as nasty as Spies was, but just as a practical matter, the Regents could not discharge a large number of teachers and replace them immediately without a great loss to the institution. Spies, as an administrator, was largely to blame, I thought, and in any case, must be dispensed with in order to straighten the situation out. I confess that I actually knew very little about the history of the relations of Spies to the Board, and I have not perhaps learned a great deal since. My understanding, however, is something like this, that some pressure was brought on Rainey not to recommend Spies for reappointment. Rainey yielded and made no such recommendation and the Board discharged Spies. Then pressure was brought to bear on the Regents ostensibly by the Texas Medical Association, and they re-employed Spies. Subsequently they decided again that Spies ought to be discharged and they wanted Rainey to take the initiative. I think that this statement is substantially correct and, if so, it does, in a measure, explain Rainey's reluctance to throw Spies overboard the second time. The fact still remains, however, that Spies was inefficient and had to be removed, and, in my judgement, Rainey ought to have taken the initiative, or at least ought to have fallen in with the action of the Board with no more than formal reluctance.[20]

Concerning the unhappy situation of Gordon, Peach, and Foster, Dr. Barker wrote Raymond Estep to remark, "as you see by the papers, some young gentlemen in the Economics Department have been advertising themselves. Personally, I think they had no business trying to capture the Dallas Mass Meeting. Why not start a mass meeting of their own?"[21] On another occasion he expressed the belief that "the young economists were wholly out of bounds and had no justification whatever for being in that mass

[20] Barker to Harbert Davenport, September 7, 1943.
[21] Barker to Raymond Estep, July 3, 1942, in private possession of Raymond Estep, Montgomery, Alabama.

meeting and demanding the right to speak. Personally, I think they got exactly what they deserved and had been begging for. I think, in the main, they were reaching out for publicity and were there for the purpose of getting it."[22] But Dr. Barker could not remain aloof from the Rainey controversy for many more days; the fall semester, 1942, brought on the dispute over John Dos Passos' *The Big Money*, and this phase of the battle involved Dr. Barker directly.

John Dos Passos' *The Big Money*, the third novel in a trilogy entitled *U. S. A.*, was placed on the reading list in English 312Q, a three-semester-hour sophomore course offered for the first time in the summer session of 1942. In the fall semester of the same year young David Barker registered for the course. When David carried his books home, Dr. Barker discovered and read *The Big Money*. He found it obscene and wholly objectionable, and he was "perfectly certain that somebody would complain to the regents."[23] He was also certain that "the regents would order the book dropped from the course when they learned the nature of the book."[24] Believing that it was unfortunate when the Regents have to settle a problem "that the teachers ought to handle themselves," Dr. Barker decided that he would try to get the book dropped before the Regents learned about its use. Therefore, he called the attention of Vice President J. Alton Burdine to the shortcomings of *The Big Money*. Barker made no effort to clothe his action and his opinion in secrecy; in fact, members of the English faculty who were responsible for selecting the book voiced their disagreement with Barker's position as well as their disapproval of his meddling in the affairs of their department. In defense of the use of Dos Passos' work, Ralph B. Long, of the English staff, wrote Dr. Barker to say,

I happen to be chairman of the committee directing English 312Q, the three-hour sophomore course that came into existence last summer. I have been hearing that our use of Dos Passos' *The Big Money* is under

[22] Barker to Harbert Davenport, September 7, 1943.
[23] Barker to Nettie Barker Arledge, February 18, 1943.
[24] Ibid.

fire and that some of the fire comes from you. I hope that this letter will not sound belligerent, for I have always had great respect for you and your judgements; but I should like to express what I take to be the feeling of the committee. . . .

We are not greatly impressed by the objections raised against the book. Most of these seem to be concerned with the sexual immorality of characters in it. The classics of every language abound in such things as this, and every good teacher of literature knows how to handle the problem which is posed. One or two people have raised the question of the economic philosophy of the author. We should hate to draw our lines on this basis, either in contemporary literature or in the literature of the past. On the whole, we are inclined to think that teaching Dos Passos would be about like teaching Shelley, or Whitman, or Swift, or any of the other rebels of the literature of the past. We do not like to regard our sophomores as children, to be given expurgated editions or empty romance.[25]

In conclusion Long remarked that "changes are quite possible," and that he was of the opinion that the Dos Passos book would be dropped at the end of the semester.

In his reply to the Long letter, Barker made it clear that he was no specialist in literature and that his judgment about the merit of a book would have little standing "in a court of specialists"; Barker continued,

At the same time, I have an ignorant notion that literature should obtain an element of permanency, and I don't think there is anything in this book that anybody ought to remember. Like most filth, unfortunately, some of it will stick in the mind. I could elaborate my opinion that for the sane non-specialist this book has few qualities associated with literature, but such elaboration would probably not impress you.

My chief reason for calling the book to Burdine's attention is that it simply begs for very embarrassing intervention by the Regents in the internal administration of the University. There is a lot of nonsense talked about academic freedom. Freedom involves responsibility and a sense of reciprocal obligation to use freedom with discretion—even with good taste.

I have read a few things in my course through life, even pornographic, and I think my judgement of this book is probably more tol-

25 Ralph B. Long to Barker, December 4, 1942.

erant than would be the reaction of at least two million other adults in Texas, if the book should unfortunately come to their attention. Why, then, invite disaster?[26]

The decision of the committee in charge of the course to drop *The Big Money* came too late to avoid an investigation. Within a few weeks after Barker's letter to Professor Long, the attention of the Board of Regents was called to the use of John Dos Passos' book. As Dr. Barker had predicted, a very embarrassing investigation by the Regents into the internal affairs of the University resulted. The Board of Regents, with Judge John H. Bickett as temporary chairman, met on the campus of the University on January 8–9, 1943. During the course of the meeting, various members of the committee in charge of English 312Q were called before the Board in an examination which lasted for two hours. Judge D. F. Strickland led the investigation to determine the responsibility for the use of *The Big Money* and apparently remarked repeatedly that "he wanted to fire someone." It was in this manner, therefore, that *The Big Money* became an inseparable part of the larger Rainey controversy. As the result of the January meeting of the Regents, the announcement was made that *The Big Money* had been "dropped from the required reading list in English 312Q."[27] As hundreds of students hitherto uninterested in either John Dos Passos or his book stormed the library and bookstores to secure copies of the forbidden work, the embarrassed members of the English Department searched for a scapegoat; it was only natural that their suspicions would fall upon the broad shoulders of the history professor who first questioned the book within the faculty.

Although Dr. Barker had consulted Dr. Robert A. Law, professor of English, before sending his complaint to Vice President Burdine, certain members of the English Department were angered by Barker's interference in the internal affairs of their department. When the investigation by the Board of Regents fol-

---

[26] Barker to Ralph B. Long, December 5, 1942.

[27] *Daily Texan*, January 10, 1943; January 13, 1943; Smith, *The Controversy at the University of Texas*, 12 ff.

lowed in January, these misinformed individuals thought that Dr. Barker had been the informer. In a letter to the editor of the *Daily Texan*, published on January 15, 1943, Barker admitted that he had called Burdine's attention to the undesirable aspects of the Dos Passos book and that he did so "to try to prevent intervention by the Board of Regents."[28] As Barker remembered the story,

> Before any action was taken [by the English Department] some parent did complain to the Regents. Some of the regents examined the book and ordered the English teachers to drop it. Since I had complained of the book to the vice president, some of them [the English faculty] believed that I had also complained to the regents. As a result, somebody wrote me a rather dirty anonymous letter and sent a copy to the *Texan* and to various officers of the University. I permitted the *Texan* to print the letter, partly to show just what sort of skunks we sometimes unfortunately get in University faculties.[29]

The anonymous letter mentioned by Barker was published by the *Daily Texan* on January 15, 1943, and motivated an instant reaction from two of Barker's friends. Orville Bullington wrote that "the entire Board of Regents was outraged because of the publication of the criminally libelous communication referring to Dr. Barker." Furthermore, Bullington revealed that "the Board instructed the president to take whatever steps were necessary to find out who was the author of this anonymous communication."[30] Dr. Robert A. Law, professor of English, was quick to inform the editor of the *Texan* that he was the professor of English whom Eugene C. Barker consulted for an opinion of *U. S.A.* before the attention of Vice President Burdine was called to the nature of the book. Law also remarked that he had never "in the history of the University, known the *Daily Texan* to carry on such a scurrilous campaign"—a campaign designed to bring harm to the University and "a personal affront to Dr. Barker."[31] Less than a

28 *Daily Texan*, January 15, 1943.

29 Barker to Nettie Barker Arledge, February 18, 1943.

30 Orville Bullington to John A. Lomax, February 5, 1943 (forwarded to Barker by Lomax).

31 *Daily Texan*, January 15, 1943; January 16, 1943.

month later the level-headed Barker remarked, "It's all settled now, and almost forgotten." But as a factor in the so-called Rainey controversy, the John Dos Passos episode would not be forgotten by the Board of Regents.

Henry Nash Smith remembered, "So far as I know, the next important incident in this chronology [of the Rainey controversy] occurred at the meeting of the Board on January 8, 1943."[32] At this meeting it appears that Judge D. F. Strickland introduced "a resolution requiring all members of the faculty and staff to fill out a questionnaire which he had prepared so that the regents might ascertain whether any members of the University community cherished unpatriotic or subversive attitudes."[33] Strickland later said that his concern was to uncover communists on the University faculty. The Strickland resolution was not adopted by the Board. At the same meeting, however, Judge Strickland introduced what has been described as "a resolution to strike from the rules of the Regents the paragraph setting forth the conditions of faculty tenure and providing for a hearing of charges against any professor or associate professor by a faculty committee, before he might be dismissed by the Board."[34] At Dr. Rainey's request no action was taken on this proposal at the time, and the President was allowed to appoint a faculty committee to work with members of the Board of Regents to draw up a revised tenure rule. Rainey named Eugene C. Barker, John W. Calhoun, and Robert W. Stayton to work with Regents D. F. Strickland, John H. Bickett, Jr., and H. H. Weinert.

On March 22, 1943, Calhoun, Stayton, and Barker framed a letter to Judge John Bickett and asked for a conference with a committee of Regents. Chairman Bickett granted the request of the unofficial committee representing the University faculty and informed the professors that Bickett, Strickland, and Weinert would represent the Regents. In summarizing the discussions Dr.

[32] Smith, *The Controversy at the University of Texas,* 11.
[33] Ibid.
[34] Ibid., 12.

Barker remembered, "We had difficulty, however, in arranging a meeting with the committee of the Regents. Judge Bickett found it inconvenient to come to Austin or to arrange a meeting at Dallas. Ultimately, we had one meeting with Mr. Strickland . . . and two meetings with Mr. Strickland and Judge Bickett together. Mr. Weinert was never able to attend a meeting."[35] In the several meetings that followed the general purpose was to re-phrase the rule of tenure as published in the *Rules and Regulations of the Board of Regents* in the edition of 1936. According to Barker's statement to the faculty, the purpose of the faculty committee here was to meet "the scruples of Mr. Strickland with as little material change in the rules as possible."[36]

The final revised rule was adopted by the Board on June 25, 1943. The new rule differed from the old one in that no contractual or legal obligations were to be construed from the wording of the tenure rule, the Board was given emergency powers to hear and determine a tenure matter and to "take such action as it may deem proper," fact-finding faculty committees were not to be entitled to the procedure previously set up only for professors and associate professors, and in case of dissatisfaction with the findings of the faculty committee by the accused teacher or by a member of the Board, a second trial was provided for *de novo* before the Board; there the decision was to be final.[37]

At the close of the discussion of the final draft of the new tenure rule, Barker expressed the opinion that the new rule was a better statement of principle than that proposed in the old *Rules and Regulations*; that it safeguarded the rights of the faculty even more strongly than did the wording of the old rule. At the same time Barker stated that in his judgment the mere change of the wording of the old rules would result in uneasiness and dissatisfaction among members of the faculty. Calhoun and Stayton agreed with Barker. Bickett and Strickland expressed the belief

[35] Minutes of the Meeting of the General Faculty, The University of Texas, November 3, 1944, p. 2829, Barker Papers.

[36] Ibid., 2830.

[37] Ibid., 2821.

that "publicity from the University" would prejudice the reception of the new rule and would report it "as in some way an infringement of faculty rights and freedom."[38]

On July 13, 1943, Dr. Barker received a letter from President Homer P. Rainey expressing his approval of the work of the committee and saying that he thought the matter had been adjusted satisfactorily and that it preserved "the fundamental principle in our tenure system." In the months to come, however, Rainey was outspoken in his criticism of the new tenure rule. The University president explained that at the time of the letter to Barker he felt gratified that the Strickland resolution had been averted and that some sort of tenure rule had been preserved. Nevertheless, it appeared that Rainey considered the new rule a compromise and inferior to the old in that it omitted nonteaching members of the staff from its provisions and because it contained an emergency clause allowing the Regents to dispense with the recommended procedures concerning hearings from members of the faculty. And a considerable portion of the faculty agreed with President Rainey.[39]

As a result of the series of conferences with the Regents concerning the new tenure rules, Eugene C. Barker became better informed than ever before with regard to the serious nature of the Rainey controversy. Armed with knowledge of the situation, Barker reviewed the University trouble for Judge Harbert Davenport and suggested a solution to the problem. After discussing the Medical School tangle and the case of the three economics instructors, Barker expressed the following view:

Now here is what I want to put before you for your consideration. I believe that Rainey is a thoroughly honest man. I think he has good intelligence, and that he earnestly desires to promote the welfare of the University. He has the unqualified confidence of a large number of the faculty, and those who are not enthusiastic in his support are, I believe, convinced that the welfare of the University would be promoted by an amicable understanding between Rainey and members of the Board. On the other side, as to members of the Board of Regents, I

[38] Ibid., 2832.
[39] Ibid.; Smith, *The Controversy at the University of Texas*, 12.

have recently had occasion to confer with a committee of the Board
concerning the revision of our tenure rule. Calhoun and Robert Stayton were the other members of the faculty committee, and we met
several times with Strickland and Bickett. We adjusted our problem
in a very satisfactory way, and I confess that the conferences which
rambled over a very considerable field gave me a large measure of confidence in the good will of Bickett and Strickland particularly. I have
no doubt that they desire the welfare of the University and that they
have devoted and will continue to devote a great deal of time and
thought toward looking after the interests of the University. So far as
their attitude toward the faculty is concerned, I have never had much
apprehension and now have practically none. In other words, I think
that Bickett and Strickland, and I feel sure Bullington of the new ap-
pointees, desire nothing but the best interest of the University and the
State. I do not mean to say that other members of the Board do not
equally desire the welfare of the University and the State, but I simply
have not been in contact with them.

At the same time, our conferences with members of the Board and
necessary conferences with Rainey make it perfectly clear that there is
an almost total lack of mutual confidence between the Board and the
President. Now, is there any way to straighten that difficulty out? I do
not think that it will straighten itself out by simply drifting. I believe
there is a fair possibility that a frank conference between Rainey and
two or three strong members of the Board might lead to a basis of cooperation if not of complete confidence. If that is true—and it is just
a guess on my part—the next point to bring about is that conference.
I think I could suggest to Rainey that he ask members of the Board to
sit down to such a conference. At any rate, I would have no hesitancy
in presenting the matter to him, urging on him all the arguments that
occur to me; but if Rainey took the initiative and asked for a conference
and members of the Board declined to meet him, then his situation
would be much more uncomfortable than it now is. It seems to me,
therefore, that the initiative should be taken by members of the Board,
and what I want to know from you is whether you are in a situation to
present that idea to members of the Board and bring about the conference.[40]

The significance of Barker's attempt to resolve the Rainey controversy lies in the fact that "the Chief," subsequently much

[40] Barker to Harbert Davenport, September 7, 1943.

maligned by fellow faculty members for his anti-Rainey role, was using every means known to him to aid the embattled University president. There can be no doubt, therefore, that Barker supported the Rainey administration at this time.

In the twelve-month interval between the autumn of 1943 and the autumn of 1944—as the gulf between President Rainey and his Board of Regents widened and deepened—Eugene Barker remained loyal to his president despite efforts by John A. Lomax and Dudley K. Woodward, Jr., to undermine this sense of loyalty. As early as the spring of 1943, Lomax told Barker that Rainey's ability as a University administrator was open to question because "while he was still president of Bucknell University I [Lomax] visited that institution and found that many members of the faculty were outraged at the presence of two 'peedoggies' from the University of Chicago who were then on the campus making a 'study' (for a big fee) of the courses, methods of teaching, etc., etc., at the invitation of the President and eventually against the will of the members of the faculty."[41] Again in the fall of 1944 on the eve of Rainey's dismissal, Lomax wrote Barker to say, "I've known 'em all—some more intimately; other less intimately —from Waggener-Winston on down to the present holder of the University presidency. Some I admired and respected, some I pitied and despised, personally and institutionally. In my judgment you have reached the all-time low in Dr. Homer Rainey. When he indicts the Board of Regents in appealing to the *students*, I quit him."[42] All indications point to the fact that Barker was not disturbed by the Lomax point of view. According to Barker, he never attached "much importance to Lomax's opinion because I think his judgments are not always well-balanced."[43] In a letter written in late October, 1944, Dudley K. Woodward, Jr., agreed with the Lomax opinion of Rainey and spoke of the dangers of communism on the University campus when he remarked that he thought "the vulnerability of the whole fabric of higher education in the United States seems to rest on the general

[41] Lomax to Barker, May 29, 1943.
[42] Lomax to Barker, October 28, 1944.
[43] Barker to Harbert Davenport, September 7, 1943.

belief, outside University circles, that teachers have not been content to stop with the discovery and exposition of facts, but have to a pernicious degree made themselves active propagandists . . . of the various theories of government and procedure which they have come upon in their studies."[44] Implying that Rainey was "generally believed to be far more interested in propaganda than in facts," Woodward revealed the true basis of his distrust of the University president:

Statements of his which have come to my notice incline me to the belief that these criticisms are not without foundation. If they are true and he is really undertaking to commit the University and its staff to what may for the want of a better term be called radical or new deal propaganda, then he has started a fight which will not be ended until the freedom which the University, if properly conducted, should enjoy has been greatly restricted.[45]

Writing at a time when Dr. Rainey neared the end of his administration, Woodward was of the opinion that "it may be doubted whether there remains any further field of usefulness for Dr. Rainey in his present capacity." The majority of the members of the Board of Regents agreed with Woodward's position. A few days later, on November 15, 1944, Dudley K. Woodward, Jr., was appointed to the Board of Regents. Woodward would have been willing, if he considered limitations necessary, to restrict academic freedom at the University.

During the summer of 1944 the crisis between Rainey and the Board continued to grow. The climax came in late October. On October 12 Dr. Rainey called a meeting of the General Faculty and read to them a public statement containing sixteen instances of what he termed improper behavior on the part of either individual regents or the Board as a group. The University president divided these so-called violations into two classes: violations or attempted violations of freedom of thought and expression, and interference or attempted interference in the details of University administration. On October 27 a hostile Board of Regents as-

[44] Dudley K. Woodward, Jr., to Barker, October 27, 1944.
[45] Ibid.

sembled at Houston and, following a stormy session, adjourned
on the evening of November 1 with the terse announcement that
Homer Price Rainey had been dismissed as president of the University of Texas. The Board based its decision on the issuance of
the "sixteen points"—a statement "which reflected upon the motives and good faith of the Board in exercising its official duties,"
and the failure of Dr. Rainey to abide by the orders, regulations,
and policies of the Board.[46]

During the tense time preceding Rainey's dismissal, Professor
Barker, who thought that Governor Coke Stevenson displayed
weakness in refusing to use his office to bring about a settlement
of the differences, made a courageous effort to save Dr. Rainey
for the University. In a letter to Rainey, Barker reminded the
University president that governing boards change with time and
that a more moderate, conciliatory attitude toward the Regents
might result in the eventual realization of a considerable part of
his administrative program. After Rainey failed to heed his advice, Barker, as late as October 29, 1944, made a desperate effort
to prevent Rainey's dismissal. Acting on suggestions from the
members of a General Faculty Committee consisting of Theophilus S. Painter, Frederic Duncalf, and Robert Stayton, Barker
appealed to Judge Joseph Hutcheson:

> This will lead up to a request for your consideration and, if you
> judge it advisable, intervention with the Board to secure a *modus vi-
> vendi* between Board and President.
>
> The faculty committee is agreed that, regardless of cause, the mutual
> distrust of Rainey and the Board cannot be easily settled. The com-
> mittee thinks (and I think) that dismissal of Rainey now might be
> particularly harmful: (1) It would be difficult to get an outside aca-
> demic man to succeed him; (2) the appointment of a non-academic
> man would raise the cry of politics. If some arrangement could be

---

[46] Minutes of the Meeting of the General Faculty, November 3, 1944;
"Reasons of Dudley K. Woodward, Jr., Chairman of the Board of Regents of
the University of Texas, for voting against the Election of Dr. Homer P.
Rainey as President of the University of Texas, January, 1945," in the Barker
Papers.

made to ease the situation temporarily the University might be the gainer.[47]

Barker also expressed the opinion that "too much public bickering, too much dirty laundry" had already been run in the newspapers of Texas, that this was "a bad policy within itself," and that a possible solution to the crisis might lie in the creation of a "special faculty council to advise with Rainey on policies and particularly on the matter of controversial publicity." It was Barker's opinion that such a committee, chosen by the Regents, would be "an unpleasant expedient for Rainey, but if the Regents are willing to try it, it would probably be better for the University than continuance of the present disharmony or the dismissal of Rainey."[48] Despite Barker's efforts toward appeasement the Regents dismissed Rainey, and disharmony in the University community mounted with each passing day and week.

Two days after Rainey's dismissal an angry and bewildered General Faculty assembled in the Geology Building on the campus of the University under the leadership of Dr. Theophilus S. Painter as acting president. In the meanwhile the students of the University had demonstrated their anger and disapproval of the Regents' action by parades through downtown Austin and a general strike from all classes. Tension filled the air as the Faculty meeting was called to order to hear a report from its committee —Painter, Stayton, and Duncalf. After listening to Duncalf and Stayton report on their experiences at Houston, the group passed resolutions to the effect (1) that the Governor be requested, in making new appointments to the Board, to continue to consult with representatives of the Ex-Students' Association and of the Faculty with a view toward selecting persons qualified by ability, variety of interests and occupations, and a knowledge of University problems, (2) that the Board of Regents, when the membership is completed, be informed of "our considered desire that as soon as practicable, Dr. Rainey, who continues to enjoy our

[47] Barker to Hutcheson, October 29, 1945.
[48] Ibid.

confidence and loyalty, be returned to the position of President of the University of Texas," and (3) that Dr. T. S. Painter "be requested to accept, even at a personal sacrifice, the post of Acting-President for the interim, to the end that the university work be interrupted as little as possible."[49]

During the debate on the resolution requesting the reinstatement of Dr. Rainey, Eugene C. Barker remarked that the wording of the resolution "seems to ask the Regents to accept our decision and judgment without consideration." Barker pointed out that if he were a member of the Board he would resent "the form of the resolution" because it implied that the Faculty "wanted to be the judge, jury, and sole witness in the case." He then offered a substitute resolution to the effect that "the Board of Regents, when membership is completed, be informed of our earnest desire that the members give thoughtful consideration to the re-appointment of Dr. Rainey, who still enjoys our confidence and loyalty." The Barker amendment, after a brief discussion was voted down with 99 votes for and 158 against the resolution. The Faculty then proceeded to adopt the original resolution.[50]

When the Faculty came to consider the third resolution, requesting Dr. Painter to accept the position of acting president of the University, a difference of opinion and some confusion arose regarding the exact nature of the resolution. Not realizing that the decision of the Board would ultimately prove final, some members of the Faculty expressed the fear that an affirmative vote for Painter might possibly compromise Rainey's position before the Board of Regents. Therefore, they seemed reluctant to give Painter a vote of confidence. In asking for a record vote, by signed or unsigned ballot, Dr. Barker stated his opinion with honesty and frankness; he said,

I deplore the dismissal of Dr. Rainey. I think it created a situation which makes it impossible for us to get a satisfactory academic man for president at this juncture outside our own faculty; and the selection of

[49] Minutes of the Meeting of the General Faculty, November 3, 1944, 2836–2837.
[50] Ibid., 2837.

a non-academic man would be disastrous. I think we are extremely fortunate in the selection of Professor Painter for Acting President. I love him too well, however, to expose him to the hell that will surely be his if the overwhelming majority of this faculty is unwilling to support him wholeheartedly and loyally. His acceptance of this thankless job would be no disloyalty to Dr. Rainey, but a great personal sacrifice to the welfare of the University to which we are devoted. I think that Dr. Painter is entitled to a record vote of the members of the faculty here present.

He concluded: "I don't know how you are going to vote. There are, of course, some of you that are convinced that Painter ought not to accept. If he did not get at least 85% of the votes, I think his life would be hell."[51] Again the Barker motion (for a record vote) was defeated as a motion to table carried. Barker said no more during the course of the faculty meeting. As far as Barker's position is concerned, it is significant that as late as November 3, 1944, he was still on Rainey's side; this would not be the case a few short weeks later.

In the short interval of time between November 4 and November 14, 1944, Eugene C. Barker ceased to be a member of the pro-Rainey faction of the Faculty of the University. Apparently, Barker was angered by the emotional display on the part of the General Faculty and the bitterness of the organized campaign to discredit the Regents and compel the re-employment of Dr. Rainey. At a meeting of the General Faculty on November 14, Barker arose to challenge the position of the so-called Committee of Eleven, a Faculty group established to promote the Rainey cause. Beginning with a remark to the effect that "if this agitation is to continue in the faculty, it furnishes an appropriate opportunity for me to say several things that I think ought to be said for the record," he then called attention to the fact that "Personally, I think it wholly out of place for the faculty to continue to request resignation of the Regents who removed Dr. Rainey from the presidency," and he gave a reasonable defense of his position. Barker, in effect, followed his earlier analysis of the Spies case as he voiced the opinion that Dr. Rainey had created or had allowed

[51] Ibid., 2840–2841.

to develop an utterly impossible situation; the Regents, therefore, were completely justified in removing him from the presidency.[52]

A few days before Christmas, Barker wrote Raymond Estep to bring Estep up to date on the "terrible plight" of the University; the letter read, in part:

Opinion is not nearly as unanimous as propaganda would have you believe. Much of the defense of Rainey (and that is the active element) is far from objective. Certainly the Regents have done some imprudent things; but certainly also Rainey has never tried to cooperate with them and lead them. His self-confessed program for administration is to tell the Regents what to do and assure them that he will take the case to the public if they disagree with him. The *Texan* publishes letters from all the continents telling exactly what must be done—restore Rainey. They know nothing except what they read, and to my knowledge a lot of that is untrue in essence. I am possessing my soul with as much resignation as possible, and am helpless wherever I look. So you see I am about as cheerful as usual.[53]

Accepting the *fait accompli* with ease and influenced by a series of events rather than by a single factor, Barker had abandoned Rainey completely by the early weeks of 1945. When the General Faculty assembled on January 11, 1945, to discuss and vote on a resolution calling for the re-election of Dr. Rainey, Barker rose to voice his opposition to "this resolution, demanding, *in the name of the faculty*, the reinstatement of Dr. Rainey in the presidency of the University, and I hope that it may not pass." In a clear, concise speech he pointed out that he did not believe that academic freedom had been threatened by recent actions of the Board of Regents, that he agreed with "the judgment of the Regents that the 'interest of the University does [did] require the removal of Dr. Homer Price Rainey from his office as President,'" and that he did not believe that Dr. Rainey's return to the presidency would benefit the University.[54]

[52] Barker Papers, 1944, undated speech in meeting of the General Faculty.
[53] Barker to Raymond Estep, December 21, 1944 (in private possession of Raymond Estep, Montgomery, Alabama).
[54] Minutes of the Meeting of the General Faculty of the University of Texas, January 11, 1945, p. 2926.

After long debate the resolution favoring the re-election of Dr. Rainey was put to a vote and carried 203 to 18, and a Faculty committee was appointed to carry the resolution to the next meeting of the Board of Regents. Only a few Faculty members joined Dr. Barker in the minority; the list of those voting "nay" included, besides Barker, Professors E. W. Bailey, E. C. H. Bantel, W. J. Battle, J. W. Calhoun, Frederick Eby, H. J. Ettlinger, H. L. Lochte, R. C. Lubben, Stuart A. McCorkle, R. L. Moore, C. P. Patterson, and O. H. Radkey. The Faculty committee[55] then prepared its case for presentation to the Board.

When the Board of Regents assembled in Austin on January 26, 1945, the Faculty committee, an ex-student group, and a student committee were ready to present and defend their respective requests for the reinstatement of Dr. Rainey. After listening patiently to all protesting groups, the Regents voted six to one not to re-employ President Rainey. The remainder of the day was spent listening to Chairman Dudley K. Woodward, Jr., read his prepared statement explaining the reasons for his vote. As far as the governing board was concerned the Rainey matter was officially closed. A large percentage of the Faculty, however, thought differently.

Two days after the meeting of the Regents and two days before the Faculty meeting of January 30, 1945, Dr. Barker wrote Walter Prescott Webb a letter urging him to use his influence to stop agitation among the dominant majority of the University Faculty:

Only our mutual interest in and love for the University enable me to write what follows:

The situation in which the University finds itself is the worst in its history. I don't particularize. The situation is due, I think, to errors of regents, president, and faculty. As to the faculty, I think it has been hysterical over an assumed threat to freedom and tenure that did not exist. Granting that the danger existed (I don't believe it did), I believe that the Board could have been instructed and set right by an honest president and calm action of the faculty. I am perfectly certain that freedom and tenure are no longer in danger, if they ever were.

I do not believe that it would benefit any phase of University inter-

[55] Henze, Umstattd, Penick, Weeks, H. N. Smith, Duncalf, and Stocking.

est to re-elect Rainey. As I see it, a "sit down" strike and a pledge not to cooperate with any other president would be the final and fatal blow that the faculty could strike the University in the present deplorable situation. The welfare of the University—spiritual and material—can best be served by a return to calmness. . . .

I do not believe that you and numerous other members of the dominant majority in the faculty do actually believe that Rainey's re-election would solve the difficulties now existing. Some others, no doubt, think re-election the only solution. It is hard for me to believe that their interest in the University is uppermost. But no need to discuss that. Can't something be done to establish a working basis for the present and future welfare of the University without regard to persons?[56]

When the General Faculty assembled on January 30 to receive a report from the Committee of Seven on Dr. Rainey's reinstatement and to consider a resolution from the Committee of Eleven pertaining to the Rainey controversy, several other members of the faculty agreed with Barker's point of view. James Anderson Fitzgerald reported that in the determination of a future course of action he would "disagree completely with any person who may now endeavor to bring censure upon the University of Texas"; Dean B. F. Pittinger remarked, "I felt first that the faculty had the right of petition and the Board of Regents has the responsibility of receiving and hearing petitions from the faculty. . . . the resolution . . . adopted by this faculty as a petition to the Board of Regents and which was presented . . . was wholly appropriate. . . . I think that in this matter [the Rainey question] we have exercised the right of petition"; and Frederick J. Eby and Caleb Perry Patterson joined in expressing their displeasure at a course of action calculated to bring censure on the University. Speaking before a heckling audience and expressing opposition to a resolution pledging continued defiance of the Board of Regents, Eugene C. Barker said,

Mr. President, I have very strong feelings about the purpose of this resolution and about the method of procedure followed since November 3 in promoting the re-election of Dr. Rainey. In the only statement that I have made to the faculty previously, I have studiously tried to

[56] Barker to Walter P. Webb, January 28, 1945.

avoid personalities, except, of course, in expressing my convictions that Dr. Rainey is no longer suitable for the presidency of the University. I try to follow the same course here. I would be untrue to the University and to myself, however, not to express my disapproval of this resolution.

Barker continued by saying that he thought the resolution was "deliberately calculated" to keep up agitation, that he believed the time had come to adopt "a constructive attitude for the welfare of the University," and that it seemed to him that the majority of the Faculty was "on the wrong track" in their desire "for the Southern Association to suspend the University."[57] He concluded with a reminder of his long record of honest, intelligent, and courageous service to the University of Texas and remarked that he would yield to no member of this Faculty in the sincerity of his veneration for "the principle of academic freedom" or in his appreciation of the "importance of the policy of tenure." He then begged the faculty to "put itself in an attitude of helpful cooperation with the Regents and work for the welfare of the University by abandoning the program of agitation."[58] Barker's subsequent motion to table the pro-Rainey resolution lost by a vote of 156 to 22; a motion to adopt the resolution as amended was then put to a voice vote and carried. The Faculty had decided, in effect, to continue the Rainey battle.

While agitation continued through the months of 1945, the Rainey controversy lost some of its sting. On May 30, 1945, a statement was issued by 132 members of the University Faculty asserting that "in our judgment faculty tenure and academic freedom are secure at the University of Texas. We invite with confidence a comparison of its record for the past twenty years with the records of universities of the highest standing on freedom and tenure." The statement went on to say that "on the basis of information that we know to be far from complete some organizations have been considering disciplinary pronouncements against

[57] Minutes of the Meeting of the General Faculty of the University of Texas, January 30, 1945, Barker Papers.
[58] Ibid.

the University of Texas. There is no reasonable ground for such action." This statement was the result of the work of a small group of University professors under the leadership of J. W. Calhoun, W. J. Battle, M. R. Gutsch, and Eugene C. Barker. The final draft was a combined pronouncement taken from preliminary drafts written by several members of the group. In a concise draft statement that was subsequently withdrawn, Dr. Barker re-affirmed his controversial stand on the Rainey matter:

President Rainey was not dismissed because he stood for academic freedom and secure tenure for the faculty. The Regents in all sincerity granted these principles.

President Rainey's public declaration of October 12, 1944, his "Sixteen Points," was, in effect, a statement of "no confidence" in the Regents; and the action of the Regents on November 1, 1944, was an expression of "no confidence" in the president. For a long time prior to his statement of October 12, 1944, President Rainey had made no secret of his distrust of the Regents; both publicly and privately he declared that, in effect, they were political tools and agents of a conspiracy that aimed to control education in Texas and suppress "liberal" teaching. The Regents, on the other hand, found grounds for suspecting the good faith and integrity of President Rainey. The Regents said little about their distrust of Dr. Rainey and their reasons for distrusting him; he said a great deal about his distrust of them. By a process of assumption, inference, and interpretation both sides to the controversy could make out a plausible case against the other . . .[59]

Since Eugene C. Barker usually said what he meant and meant what he said, it is apparent that his actions after November 1, 1944, were motivated by the fact that Dr. Rainey allowed a situation to develop that destroyed his effectiveness as president of the University. In general it may be said with regard to Barker's role in the Rainey controversy that two facts are clearly visible: (1) prior to Dr. Rainey's dismissal both the President and the Regents were at fault in allowing an impossible administrative situation to develop through mutual suspicion and distrust, but

[59] "History of Statement of May 30, 1945, on Tenure and Academic Freedom Signed by One Hundred Thirty-Two Members of the Faculty" (prepared by Milton R. Gutsch), 8–9, in ibid.

Barker supported his president at all times and tried to help him; and (2) when Rainey took his case to the public on October 12, 1944, and was subsequently dismissed from his office by an angry Board of Regents, Barker turned against both Rainey and the Rainey majority on the University Faculty because of his concern for the welfare of the University and his desire to avoid the unfavorable publicity that was sure to follow continued agitation for Dr. Rainey's re-employment.

Years before, Dr. Barker had confided to a friend: "I've fought many fights, but they wear you out." Tired of the ceaseless bickering, "the Chief" withdrew from the main stream of the Rainey episode after the early months of 1945; except for a rebuttal to Bernard De Voto's article in the August, 1945, issue of *Harper's*, Barker had nothing more to say of the unfortunate matter. Two years later he wrote Edward Carey Crane that "time in the end will obscure if not obliterate the controversy, and I am afraid that time is the only effective remedy."[60]

Although the Rainey controversy dominated the University scene during the year of 1945, other events took place on the campus. The Board of Regents directed that all books, archives, letters, and documents relating to Texas and Southwestern history be housed in the Old Library Building; the collection was to be designated as the Eugene C. Barker History Center. Five years later, as noted in the first chapter of this narrative, the Barker History Center was dedicated. At the dedication exercises Dr. Herbert Gambrell had the following to say about Dr. Barker:

Through more than half a century, without striving for it, he has been achieving immortality. Both because of what he has written and because of the disciples who have been attracted to him and who have caught the spirit of his integrity and patient and honest work, Eugene C. Barker will probably live longer than any contemporary historian of this region. This is not what he set out to do; not even what he thought he was doing. It has come about because he is a symbol of something that transcends himself. And it is "that something" that he symbolizes that will be perpetuated in this Eugene C. Barker Texas

[60] Barker to Edward C. Crane, May 11, 1947.

History Center, a living monument whose usefulness will increase with the years and become literally the lengthening shadow not merely of a man but of a man's integrity and character and work.[61]

Almost two decades later, forever unfinished, the Barker collection consists of the books, pamphlets, manuscripts, maps, microfilms, pictures, and other materials which pertain to all phases of the history of Texas and adjacent regions. In summary, the collection includes (1) archival and manuscript holdings comprising more than 2,500 collections ranging in size from a few pages to several thousand pages, (2) the Charles W. Ramsdell Microfilm Collection, and (3) 50,000 printed volumes.

In the meanwhile, old age decimated the ranks of the "old" Department of History—the department that had been built by Barker in the early years of the century. Death claimed Frank Burr Marsh in 1940, Charles W. Ramsdell in 1942, Charles W. Hackett in 1951, and Thad Weed Riker in 1952. The retirement of Dr. Barker, Milton R. Gutsch, and Frederic Duncalf in 1950–1951 made the late Walter P. Webb and Rudolph L. Biesele the only survivors of the "old guard." The vacancies thus created by death and retirement were difficult to fill in the midst of the competition that characterizes the contemporary academic scene.

When Eugene Campbell Barker became professor emeritus of history in 1950, he had six years of life remaining. He was rather philosophical about old age and death. As early as 1942, in a letter to Hally Bryan Perry, Professor Barker commented on the approaching end of life:

The only impression of immortality that I have ever understood is the assurance of having transmitted some service more or less identifiable to others. It is diluted with time and successive generations, but the strain is there. So I see you and your influence touching worlds you cannot know.

I have reached the age and state of despondency about our own country and the world that reconciles me more or less to death. One wants to fulfill his obligations, and yet has no rational basis for plan-

[61] Herbert Gambrell, "The Eugene C. Barker Texas History Center," *Southwestern Historical Quarterly*, LIV (July, 1950), 4–5.

ning the future of loved ones. Death at least is the end of personal frustration and in that sense I suppose our friends who have gone before are lucky. Don't imagine, however, that I go around sighing for death; I just shan't worry much when I see it coming.[62]

Like an old general home from the wars, Dr. Barker, following his retirement from the classroom, took an office across the hall from the Texas State Historical Association in the Barker History Center. There he could remain close to the work of a lifetime. It was at his desk in the research center that bore his name that he spent considerable time during the years 1952 and 1953 selecting the articles, some published previously and some unpublished, that were to comprise the content of his *Speeches, Responses, and Essays, Critical and Historical.* This book was published in 1954 under the joint auspices of the James Harper Starr Fund for Texas History and the Hally Bryan Perry Fund for the Collection, Preservation, and Dissemination of Archival Material for the Eugene C. Barker Texas History Center. Dr. Barker worked closely with Miss Winnie Allen, archivist at the Center, in the various stages involved in the preparation of what was to be his last publication. It is also significant that during these months, the Barker letters, notes, and speeches, many of them still in the firm longhand of "The Chief," were transferred from the Barker home to the archives of the Barker History Center. As a result it may be said that one of Dr. Barker's greatest contributions to Texas history came when he made his personal papers available to the student of history.

But the sand in the hour glass was running low. As the months passed the various ills of old age slowly took their toll on the rugged frame of Dr. Barker. He was never really ill; he merely played out. In the autumn of 1956 he was moved from his home to nearby Seton Hospital. It was there that the end came shortly after dusk on the evening of October 22, 1956—counting the years spent as a student, a sixty-one year association with the University of Texas had come to an end. At the time of his death Dr. Barker was eighty-two years of age.

[62] Barker to Hally Bryan Perry, August 11, 1942, Perry Papers.

On the morning of October 24, the *Daily Texan* carried an editorial written by Walter Prescott Webb. Although brief mention of Webb's remarks has been made in prior chapters, the full text of his memorial—addressed "to the Chief"—read,

Dr. Eugene C. Barker's work as a historian is everywhere recognized. His greatest contributions were in the field of Texas history. His biography of Stephen F. Austin is designated in many bibliographies as a classic. He did more than any other historian to show the influence that Texas exerted in shaping the destiny of the nation.

On the University campus Dr. Barker's reputation as a scholar was surpassed only by his reputation for character. He was a tower of strength among his colleagues. His clear-headedness, integrity, and unflinching courage made him a powerful advocate and a respected adversary.

A few of his closest associates knew of his great heart and his deep sympathy for all those who needed it. His generosity knew no bounds where the human being was concerned. All this kindness was covered with an austerity that made familiarity impossible, even with his intimates. He was a master of brevity, rarely used a surplus word, and because of his taciturnity he inspired awe.

Because of his bold features and aquiline nose he conveyed the impression of power. Had he been a military man, he would have been a general and looked like one; had he been an Indian he would have been a Chief, and he looked like one. More than thirty years ago, A. C. Krey, then a young instructor in the Department of History, noted these features and gave him the title of Chief.

To the end he was the Chief.[63]

As he wrote the above paragraphs, Dr. Webb expressed the thoughts of everyone who had known Eugene C. Barker as a scholar and teacher.

Later in the afternoon of the same day the final rites were held for Dr. Barker with the Reverend Edmund Heinsohn of the University Methodist Church officiating. There were those present that afternoon who realized—as the Barker Memorial Committee of the General Faculty realized—that Barker's passing "marked the end of an era in the department of history, and it marked the

[63] *Daily Texan*, October 24, 1956.

passage of an era in the University." Led by Barker and his contemporaries, the Faculty followed policies that determined the affairs of the University for more than a quarter of a century. These leaders were "all men of character and integrity; they differed in personality, but they were held together by their devotion to the University. They did not lay the foundation, but they built a university on the foundations put down by their predecessors. They made the University what it is today."[64]

[64] "Report of the Special Eugene Campbell Barker Memorial Resolution Committee" (prepared by Walter P. Webb, Joe B. Frantz, and Robert A. Law), in Barker Papers.

BIBLIOGRAPHIC NOTE

Aside from the scholarly writings of Eugene C. Barker, the great bulk of information used in this work came from the Eugene C. Barker Papers, found in the Archives of the Library of the University of Texas at Austin. To be more specific, these included twenty-six volumes of letters, speeches, and notes covering the years 1899–1951. In addition to the Barker Papers, the following source materials (all in the Archive Collections of the University of Texas, Austin) were useful: the Lester Gladstone Bugbee Papers, the Orville Bullington Papers, the George Pierce Garrison Papers, the John A. Lomax Papers, the Hally Bryan Perry Papers, and the R. E. Vinson Papers. Letters to the author from Mrs. Edgar Arledge, Hal B. Armstrong, Roy Bedichek, Judge Joseph C. Hutcheson, and Walter P. Webb contained valuable information. Use was also made of the Claude Elliott Collection, Southwest Texas State College Library, San Marcos.

In addition to the manuscript sources listed above, the following items were used extensively: J. Evetts Haley, "The Eugene C. Barker Portrait: Presentation, Acceptance, and Acknowledgement Addresses," *Southwestern Historical Quarterly,* XLVI (April, 1943); *The Catalogue of the University of Texas* (Austin, 1910–1945), all issues; *The Cactus* (Austin, 1895–1900), all issues; John A. Lomax, *Will Hogg, Texan* (Austin, 1956); W. P. Webb, *An Honest Preface and Other Essays* (Boston, 1959); *The Alcalde* (Austin, 1913–1935), all issues; J. Evetts Haley, *George Littlefield, Texan* (Norman, Oklahoma, 1943); Paul W. Schroeder, "The Littlefield Fund for Southern History," *The Library Chronicle of the University of Texas,* VI (Spring, 1957); H. Bailey Carroll, "A Half-Century of the Texas State Historical Association," *Southwestern Historical Quarterly* (extra number, February 1, 1947); *The Quarterly of the Texas State Historical Association* and the *Southwestern Historical Quarterly* (Austin, 1898–1960), all issues; Ralph Steen, "Ferguson's War on the University of Texas," *Southwestern Social Science Quarterly,* XXXV (March, 1955); and Henry Nash Smith, *The Controversy at the University of Texas, 1939–1945: A Documentary History* (Austin, 1945).

Also useful were *Will C. Hogg, An Interview* (Austin, 1917); Herbert P. Gambrell, "The Eugene C. Barker Texas History Center," *Southwestern Historical Quarterly*, LIV (July, 1950); H. Y. Benedict (compiler), *A Source Book Relating to the History of the University of Texas: Legislative, Legal, Bibliographical, and Statistical*, University of Texas Bulletin No. 1757 (Austin, 1917); W. J. Battle, "A Concise History of the University of Texas, 1883–1950," *Southwestern Historical Quarterly*, LIV (April, 1951); Milton W. Humphreys, "The Genesis of the University of Texas," *The Alcalde*, I (April, 1913); J. W. Mallet, "Recollections of the First Year of the University of Texas," *The Alcalde*, I (April, 1913); Maude Houston Ross, "The Education of John Lomax," *Southwestern Historical Quarterly*, XL (October, 1956); *The Daily Texan* (Austin, 1917–1958), all issues; Dallas *News* (Dallas, 1917–1918, 1944–1945), all issues; Austin *American* (Austin, 1917–1918, 1944–1945), all issues; and Tom Bowman Brewer, "A History of the History Department of the University of Texas," unpublished master's thesis, University of Texas, 1957.

Among the many works of Eugene C. Barker, this study relied heavily on *A School History of Texas* (with Charles S. Potts and Charles Ramsdell; Evanston, Illinois, 1912); *The Life of Stephen F. Austin, Founder of Texas, 1793–1836* (Dallas, 1925); *Readings in Texas History for High Schools and Colleges* (Dallas, 1929); *The Story of Our Nation* (with William E. Dodd and Walter P. Webb; Evanston, Illinois, 1929); *The Growth of a Nation: The United States of America* (with Walter P. Webb and William E. Dodd; Evanston, Illinois, 1934); *The Father of Texas* (New York, 1935); *The Austin Papers* (3 vols.; Washington and Austin, 1924, 1927); *The Writings of Sam Houston* (with Amelia W. Williams; 8 vols.; Austin, 1938–1943); and the countless articles that he wrote and edited for the many historical publications of the nation.

The following general works were also consulted: Frederic L. Paxson, *History of the American Frontier* (New York, 1924); Ray Billington, *The Far Western Frontier* (New York, 1956), and *Westward Expansion: A History of the American Frontier* (New York, 1949); Le Roy Hafen and C. C. Rister, *Western America* (Englewood Cliffs, New Jersey, 1957); Charles E. Beard, *An Economic Interpretation of the Constitution of the United States* (New York, 1913); Robert E. Brown, *Charles Beard and the Constitution* (Princeton, New Jersey, 1956); and Forrest McDonald, *We the People: The Economic Origins of the Constitution* (Chicago, 1958).

INDEX

academic freedom: Barker's speech on, 131–134; and dispute over *The Big Money*, 192–196; and Rainey controversy, 201, 209–210

A. C. Baldwin Company: publishes anti-Ferguson pamphlet, 70 n., 84

Adams, E. D.: and American Historical Association controversy, 67; Barker reviews book by, 169; mentioned, 66

Allen, W. P.: 79

Allen, Winnie: on Barker's temper, 99–100; and UT Archives, 122; works with Barker, 213

Alvord, C. W.: 67

American, Austin: 50

American Historical Association: Barker on Executive Council of, 66; controversy within, 66–68; and the value of history, 112; publishes Austin papers, 148–149; mentioned, 48, 51

American Historical Review: controversy over, 66; mentioned, 32

American Nation series: 104

American Revolution: Barker teaches about, 104–105

Ames, Herman: advises Barker, 43; and Ferguson-UT conflict, 81

Anahuac, Texas: customs house at, 33

Andrews, Charles M.: 34

Annexation of Texas, The, by J. H. Smith: Barker reviews, 169

Archives, Bexar: acquired by UT, 32

——, State. SEE Texas State Library

——, UT: Bexar Archives in, 32; supported by Barker, 122–124; Austin papers given to, 145–146; Barker papers given to, 213

Armstrong, Hal: as Barker's friend, 105, 106; on Barker's personality, 109

Asbury, Samuel E.: 64

Austin, Moses: Barker's account of, 143; papers of, 145–146

Austin, Stephen F.: character of, 145, 148–149, 150–151; papers of, 145–146; political policies of, 157. SEE ALSO *Life of Stephen F. Austin, The*

Austin *American*: 50

Austin papers: history of: 32–33, 145–146, 148; publication of 147, 148–149

Austin Papers, The: publication of, 147, 148–149

Babcock, K. C.: 126

Bailey, E. W.: 207

Baker, Burke: 125

Baker, R. H.: 125

Baker, R. S.: 29, 30

Baker, W. P.: 29

Baldwin Company, A. C. SEE A. C. Baldwin Company

Bantel, E. C. H.: 207

Barker, Alita Humble: 17

Barker, Altha: 17

Barker, Amanda: 17

Barker, Charles: 17

Barker, Cicero: 17

Barker, David (Barker's son): and dispute over *The Big Money*, 192; mentioned, 97, 111

Barker, Eugene C.: birth of, 16; character of, 16, 50, 53–55, 90–102, 113–115; and Town and Gown Club, 16, 109–110, 166, 173; youth of, 17–21, 27–28; as UT undergraduate, 22, 24–32; and Lester

30; and Ferguson-UT conflict, 77, 79, 83; and UT archives, 123; on Rainey controversy, 200; mentioned, 29, 187
Long, Ralph B.: 192–193
Lubben, R. C.: 207

McCleary, Robert E.: 60
McCorkle, Stuart A.: 207
McDonald, Forrest: on economic interpretation of the Constitution, 176–178
McDonald, William: book by, 104–105
McFarland, Bates: and UT, 21; recalls Barker's undergraduate days, 28–29; and Phi Delta Theta, 29; fishes with Barker, 106
McLaughlin, A. C.: book by, 104; mentioned, 51
McMaster, John Bach: book by, 41, 104; influence of, on Barker, 41–42, 142; philosophy of, 42
McReynolds, G. S.: 69
Main Building, Old. SEE Old Main Building
Making of Roumania, The, by T. W. Riker: 49
Making of the Constitution, The, by C. Warren: 104
Manning, William R.: and UT History Department, 46, 53, 118–119
Marsh, Frank Burr: and UT History Department, 46, 53 n., 118; career and publications of, 47–48; on Splawn, 128; death of, 212
Marshall, John: and judicial review, 104
Marshall, Thomas Maitland: and Southwestern Historical Quarterly, 64; mentioned, 73
Mather, W. T.: and Ferguson-UT conflict, 77, 83
Mathis, J. M.: 79
Matthews, W. H.: 30
Mayes, W. H.: 83
Merriman, Roger: 42
Mexico: UT Archival materials purchased in, 122–124

Mexico and Texas, 1821–1835, by Barker: 155–157, 159
Meyer, P. N.: 21
Meyers, A. C.: 41
Mezes, Sidney Edward: as UT teacher, 24; and Barker, 44, 56; as UT president, 44, 69
Middleton, Annie: 167
Miller, W. T.: 30
Mississippi Valley Historical Association: Barker as president of, 66; and American Historical Association controversy, 66, 68; mentioned, 51
Mississippi Valley Historical Review: Ramsdell on editorial board of, 47; Barker on editorial board of, 66; Barker publishes in, 164
Mixon, Ruby: describes Barker as a teacher, 98–99; mentioned, 167
Monroe Doctrine: 104
Montgomery, Robert H: 188
Mood: Fulmer: 176
Moore, John Bassett: 26
Moore, R. L.: 207
Morning News, Dallas: and Rainey controversy, 189
Morton, Ohland: book by, 159, 167
Munro, D. C.: recommends Gutsch for UT History Department, 49; and Ferguson-UT conflict, 80–81

Neff, Pat M.: as candidate for UT presidency, 120, 125, 128
New Deal: Barker's opposition to, 93, 103, 138, 173, 179–183, 185. SEE ALSO depression, the; Roosevelt, Franklin D.
Nixon, P. I.: 15
Norlin, George: 126

Oberholtzer, E. P.: 41
Old Library Building: Barker Texas History Center in, 15, 211–212
Old Main Building: description of, 23; mentioned, 32, 98, 119
Osgood, Herbert E.: 26
Outlines of General History, by P. N. Meyer: as influence on Barker, 21

DATE DUE